$$30$$
$$\times 20$$
$$\overline{600}$$

# Charles A. Lindbergh and the Battle Against American Intervention in World War II

Also by Wayne S. Cole

America First:
The Battle Against Intervention,
1940–1941

Senator Gerald P. Nye
and American Foreign Relations

An Interpretive History
of American Foreign Relations

Wayne S. Cole

# Charles A. Lindbergh and the Battle Against American Intervention in World War II

Harcourt Brace Jovanovich

New York and London

Excerpts from *The Wartime Journals of Charles A. Lindbergh* are reprinted by permission of Harcourt Brace Jovanovich, Inc.; copyright © 1970 by Charles A. Lindbergh.

Library of Congress Cataloging in Publication Data
Cole, Wayne S
Charles A. Lindbergh and the battle against American intervention in World War II.
Bibliography: p.
1. World War, 1939–1945—United States. 2. United States—Neutrality.
3. Lindbergh, Charles Augustus, 1902–    I. Title.
D753.C593    940.53′12 [B]    73–22247
ISBN 0–15–118168–3

First edition

B   C   D   E

*To my son*
Tom

# Preface

On December 7, 1941, the Japanese attack on Pearl Harbor brought the United States into the most destructive and bloody war in human history. That attack also ended America's so-called "isolationism." The United States played a massive role in helping to defeat the Axis Powers in World War II. Since that war the United States has been involved continually in military, diplomatic, and economic matters all over the world. It never returned to its earlier policies of "no entangling alliances" and nonintervention in European political and military affairs—to what Charles A. Lindbergh had called "an independent destiny for America." In that sense Pearl Harbor was a watershed in the history of American foreign affairs. There was no turning back.

Before Pearl Harbor, however, the American people and their leaders had earnestly debated alternative courses for the United States in world affairs. That "Great Debate" was a part of the democratic process in shaping American foreign policy. Few debates have had such important long-term consequences for the United States and the world. The debate grew increasingly heated, but Americans conducted it without resort to domestic violence. It provided them with opportunities to consider, argue, and advocate alternative foreign policies during those alarming times in world affairs. That debate raged from the highest decision-making levels in Washington, D.C., to the grass roots all over the United States. Countless Americans in and out of the government played active roles.

# Preface

Easily the most popular and controversial "isolationist," or "noninterventionist," leader was the famed aviator Colonel Charles A. Lindbergh. From September, 1939, when he began speaking out against American entry into World War II, until he was silenced by the Japanese attack more than two years later, Lindbergh was the most praised, the most criticized, and the most maligned noninterventionist in the United States. No one played a more prominent role in opposing the foreign policies of the Franklin D. Roosevelt administration. A study of Lindbergh's battle against American entry into World War II goes to the heart of that noninterventionist effort. His defeat was the defeat of American isolationism.

Though Lindbergh's battle against intervention ended with Pearl Harbor, many of his ideas looked ahead to issues of more recent times. His emphasis on the importance and limits of power in international affairs was consistent with the "realist" approach so popular after World War II. His contention that the United States could not and should not remake the world in its own image has a decidedly contemporary ring to it. His warnings against excessive presidential power, secrecy, and deception in foreign affairs have striking parallels with American concerns a generation later. The abuse he suffered at the hands of his opponents, moreover, illustrated the heavy toll that can be exacted from those who exercise their democratic rights and responsibilities by opposing administration foreign policies that they believe to be unwise.

This study is based on unrestricted research access to Charles A. Lindbergh's personal letters and papers relating to his noninterventionist effort. Lindbergh's massive manuscript collection in the Sterling Memorial Library, Yale University, is one of the most valuable sets of materials in existence relating to the opposition to American entry into World War II. Also, drawing on his unusual memory for factual detail, General Lindbergh spent many hours patiently and candidly answering my many questions. He did not evade any of my questions, no matter how probing, sensitive, or controversial they were.

In addition to the essential Lindbergh papers, I have also

researched dozens of other manuscript collections (both non-interventionist and interventionist) relating to Lindbergh's battle against intervention. Of particular importance were the America First Committee papers, at the Hoover Library on War, Revolution and Peace, Stanford, California, and President Roosevelt's papers, in the Franklin D. Roosevelt Library, Hyde Park, New York. Over the years I have also interviewed many of the leading figures who shared with Lindbergh in the battle against intervention.

This volume is, in effect, the third in a series of books I have written on the opposition to American entry into World War II. The first, published in 1953 and reissued in 1971, was a history of the America First Committee, the leading noninterventionist pressure group before Pearl Harbor. The second, published in 1962, was an interpretive study of the role of Senator Gerald P. Nye of North Dakota in American foreign relations. Each of these three volumes has been based on unrestricted research access to previously unused manuscript collections. Each entailed interviews in depth with the principals. And in preparing each of the three I earnestly tried to be as accurate and balanced as possible. My object has been neither to vindicate nor to indict, but, rather, to describe and explain.

It has been my custom in each of the three volumes not to ask any of the principals to read the manuscripts in advance of publication. Thus General Lindbergh did not read the manuscript of this book. The publisher, however, did ask him to read the galley proofs. The General prepared comments on the galleys, and the publisher sent them to me. As a result, I made minor factual corrections in seven instances, but I made no changes in analysis or interpretation. I am extremely grateful to General Lindbergh for his essential help with this project but it is important to make plain that this book is not an "authorized" account. The analyses and interpretations are mine. Any errors of fact, emphasis, or interpretation are my responsibility alone.

I am indebted to scores of librarians and archivists, whose knowledge of their materials and whose willingness to help have

# Preface

made my research both possible and pleasant. Most essential was the aid I received from Miss Judith A. Schiff, Chief Research Archivist, Manuscripts and Archives, Yale University Library. Without her help this book could not have been written. Thomas D. Flynn gave me permission to use the papers of his father, John T. Flynn, and Dr. Martin Schmitt at the University of Oregon Library made key items from that collection available to me. Dr. Milton O. Gustafson and Leslie C. Waffen of the National Archives, Dr. Paul T. Heffron of the Library of Congress, William J. Stewart of the Franklin D. Roosevelt Library, and their staffs all provided special help for my research.

I owe a unique debt to the University of Maryland. No scholar could have had better opportunities for research and writing in the history of American foreign relations than the University of Maryland provided. Its location just outside Washington, D.C., made it easy for me to do research in the Library of Congress and the National Archives. It has allowed me to teach exclusively in the field of American diplomatic history, and it has provided stimulating students to test and challenge my ideas. A sabbatical leave facilitated my research. The University's scheduling policies allowed me full days free for research and writing, and even enabled me to make repeated flights to New Haven to use the Lindbergh papers there. A summer grant from its General Research Board furthered my writing. Dean David S. Sparks and Professors Walter Rundell, Jr., Francis Haber, and Horace S. Merrill provided essential help and encouragement. Richard P. Hallion generously shared his knowledge of aviation technology with me. I am deeply indebted to them and to the University of Maryland. I am also grateful for help from Professor Ross B. Talbot of Iowa State University.

A Fellowship at the Woodrow Wilson International Center for Scholars in Washington, D.C., gave me released time and a delightful setting in which to complete the research and write this book. W. R. Smyser, Raimi Ojikutu, Choon-ho Park, W. Taylor Reveley, and Eugene Trani, Fellows at the Center, helped make my stay there both pleasant and intellectually

# Preface

stimulating. Staff members who provided welcome aid and encouragement included William M. Dunn, Gaenor Willson, Edythe Holbrook, Frances Hunter, Mernie Weathers, and Waltraud Larson.

My wife, Virginia Rae Cole, shared my interest and provided quiet encouragement. Only our son, Thomas Roy Cole, benefits so much as I do from her devotion. And to him I proudly dedicate this book.

WAYNE S. COLE

*University of Maryland*
*January, 1974*

# Contents

# Contents

# III

## The Battle of the Committees

# IV

## "War Agitators" and American Democracy

# V

## Aftermath

# Contents

# Illustrations

# Charles A. Lindbergh and the Battle Against American Intervention in World War II

.

# 1/The Great Debate

I T was a clear, beautiful summer evening in Southern California, before smog had spoiled those lovely skies. Men and
women began to arrive early at the Hollywood Bowl. The more
than 20,000 seats filled rapidly. People stood in the aisles. And
still they came. As dusk settled and the sun dipped below the
horizon, thousands covered the hills on three sides looking
down on the Bowl far below. They backed up a quarter of a
mile on nearby streets. Estimates of the crowd that evening
ranged up to 60,000 or 70,000; the actual figure may have been
closer to 40,000, with some 23,000 in the regular seats and
thousands more patiently adjusting in the overflow. Officials at
the time said it was the largest attendance ever at the Hollywood Bowl. Sweeping lights under the stars revealed an orderly,
serious, concerned audience; most were couples under the age
of forty or over sixty. As one newspaper reported, it was "the
type of audience that would be found in the Bowl at the Easter
morning service."[1]

But it was no religious service. And those thousands were not
turning out to witness an athletic competition, listen to a rock
concert, or ogle Hollywood movie stars. They were not attending a political rally to elect a President or a Governor. Those
thousands that Friday evening of June 20, 1941, were nevertheless a significant part of democracy in action. The America First
Committee rally they were attending was billed as a "Peace and

1. The notes are on pages 243–275.

3

Preparedness Mass Meeting." It was a dramatic episode in America's "Great Debate" on foreign affairs before the United States entered World War II. That orderly, nonviolent foreign policy debate between so-called "isolationists" and "interventionists" extended from America's greatest cities to every small town and main street in the land, from every bar and barbershop to the halls of Congress in the nation's capital and to top-level Cabinet meetings presided over by President Franklin D. Roosevelt in the White House.

Millions of Americans in the period 1939–1941 believed that the outcome of that debate could shape the future of the United States and possibly the world. If citizens and their government followed mistaken policies, the consequences conceivably could destroy national security and end American democracy and freedom. The results could determine the future of the United States and of Western civilization. Those earnest people worried whether their sons would get to live out their lives peacefully or would die on foreign battlefields. And if they must die, those concerned Americans wondered whether their deaths would or would not make for a better world and for a more secure, prosperous, and free America.

On matters of such importance, those thousands in Southern California were not turning out to hear the President of the United States, his Secretary of State, or any other top government or military official. Of the four main speakers that evening, only one held public office and he (Democrat D. Worth Clark of Idaho) was a first-term United States Senator and not a major power in the Congress. Two of the speakers were women: a grey-haired novelist, Kathleen Norris, and a talented middle-aged actress, Lillian Gish. They spoke ably and movingly that evening, as they had at earlier America First rallies and as they would again at later meetings.[2]

But the man those thousands most eagerly waited to see and hear was a tall, slender, thirty-nine-year-old aviator, Colonel Charles A. Lindbergh. Since he had first burst upon the front pages of the world's newspapers nearly fifteen years before with his unprecedented solo flight from New York to Paris in 1927, he had been cheered by crowds larger than this one. He had welcomed those earlier plaudits for their help in building public support for America's fledgling aviation industry. This time he welcomed the cheers as he earnestly urged his audience to oppose American entry into World War II, then raging in Europe and Asia.

And well they might ponder America's course carefully, for that was already a terrifyingly destructive war—and the worst was yet to come. In Asia, Japan's modern military forces had occupied Manchuria between the years of 1931 and 1933. In July, 1937, Japan had thrown its land, air, and sea power against China's vast area and teeming millions in an undeclared war that was to last for eight long years. By the time Lindbergh addressed his audience that evening, Japanese troops controlled the coastal areas and major cities of China, had moved into northern Indochina, and were soon to take over the rest of that French colony in Southeast Asia. Few felt certain of the limits of Japanese military ambitions and capacities. The war in Asia would have been alarming enough by itself. But it also linked with comparable developments in Europe. Japan had concluded an Anti-Comintern Pact with Germany in 1936. In September, 1940, Japan had joined with Adolf Hitler's Nazi Germany and Benito Mussolini's Fascist Italy in a Tripartite Pact. Those three Axis Powers appeared to threaten freedom, democracy, peace, and security all over the world.

Mussolini and his Fascists had come to power in Italy in 1922, in the aftermath of economic dislocation and political disorder that followed World War I. In the years 1935–1936, Mussolini's Italy had triumphed over the primitive warriors of Emperor Haile Selassie's Ethiopia, in East Africa. In 1936, it had joined in a pact with Nazi Germany setting up the Rome-Berlin Axis. From 1936 to 1939, those two dictatorships had sent guns, planes, and men to help fascism under Generalissimo Francisco Franco triumph in Spain's bloody Civil War. In April, 1939, Italy had seized Albania. Mussolini's forces fared badly in Greece and North Africa, but in combination with the other two Axis Powers they were not to be ignored.

5

But it was Adolf Hitler's Nazi Germany that seemed most completely evil and most militarily invincible by the time Lindbergh rose to speak that summer evening. In January, 1933, Hitler had become Chancellor of Germany's Weimar Republic. He quickly and ruthlessly converted the government into a Nazi dictatorship, eliminating opposition parties and suppressing dissenters. Blaming Germany's woes on the Versailles Treaty and the Jews, he insisted that his National Socialist regime provided the only alternative to a Communist take-over. He promised economic prosperity as he repudiated the Versailles Treaty, rebuilt Germany's military power, and set out to restore Germany to glory and greatness in Europe and the world.

In 1936, German troops remilitarized the Rhineland in violation of existing agreements. In the *Anschluss* of March, 1938, Hitler's forces seized Austria and incorporated it into Greater Germany. He used Spain's Civil War as a testing ground for his rapidly growing military forces. In October, 1938, Britain's Neville Chamberlain and France's Edouard Daladier had tried to appease Hitler in the Munich Pact by yielding the Sudetenland of Czechoslovakia to Nazi Germany. In November, the Nazis abruptly stepped up their violent oppression of German Jews. Violating his promises at Munich, Hitler seized the rest of Czechoslovakia in March, 1939. He pressured Poland for the Corridor that separated Germany from East Prussia. Finally convinced that Hitler's ambitions were insatiable, Britain and France decided to yield no further. But they would have insurmountable military difficulties against Germany in eastern Europe unless the Soviet Union helped defend Poland. That possibility dramatically disappeared with the conclusion of the Nazi-Soviet Non-Aggression Pact on August 23, 1939. That agreement opened the way for Hitler's conquest of Poland beginning on the morning of September 1, 1939. Britain and France promptly declared war, but they were helpless to prevent Germany's blitzkrieg from crushing Poland's antiquated forces.

Though Poland fell quickly, there was little fighting on the western front. The lull during the winter of 1939–40, the "sitzkrieg," or "phony war," encouraged some to hope that World

War II might not be the horribly destructive nightmare so many had feared. Headlines that winter went, instead, to the Russo-Finnish War as the Finns fought bravely, before finally succumbing to Soviet power in the early spring of 1940.

The winter lull in the west did not last long. In April, 1940, Hitler once again unleashed his mechanized panzer divisions and his Luftwaffe. His blitzkrieg quickly overran Denmark, Norway, the Netherlands, Luxembourg, and Belgium. Nazi forces sliced between British and French armies and pinned Britain's troops against the sea at Dunkirk. Britain miraculously evacuated most of its men, but they left their equipment behind on the beaches. The French had no island redoubt to flee to, and no channel to protect them. Torn by internal cleavages, weakened by shattered morale, and harried by Mussolini's decision to attack in the south, France under Marshal Henri Pétain surrendered to Hitler's might on June 22, 1940.

Hitler then turned his Luftwaffe and submarines against Great Britain. Under Prime Minister Winston Churchill, the British braced for the attack. Despite heavy damage inflicted by German bombers, however, the Royal Air Force denied the Germans control of the air in the Battle of Britain. And despite heavy shipping losses, the Royal Navy retained its command of the seas. For the first time Nazi Germany's mighty forces were checked. But whether Britain could survive the long pull remained to be seen, and whether the British could defeat Hitler's armies on the European continent seemed very much in doubt.

Pending the final outcome of that contest, Hitler turned his forces east toward the Balkans. And at the very moment that Charles A. Lindbergh began his speech to his vast audience in California, German generals were positioning their armies in preparation for the massive assault their Fuehrer had secretly ordered against the Soviet Union in eastern Europe. That Russo-German War began early on June 22, 1941, just two days after Lindbergh's America First rally in the Hollywood Bowl. Most experts expected Nazi Germany to crush Soviet military resistance quickly, just as it had overrun every other country it had attacked on the European mainland. In that event, an even

7

stronger Germany might then turn again on the British Isles, with greater chances for success.

If Nazi Germany and Fascist Italy triumphed in Europe and Africa, and if militarist Japan overran Asia, those emboldened aggressors might then turn on the Western Hemisphere. In that event many doubted America's capacity to defend itself successfully, despite the protection of the Atlantic and Pacific oceans. Even if the Axis Powers should never invade the United States, many worried whether American democracy, freedom, and prosperity could survive in a world dominated by the fascist dictators. Little wonder that the American people that warm summer evening were troubled and torn as they deliberated on various alternatives for the United States in world affairs.

In the face of the alarming developments abroad, the Americans and their leaders felt conflicting emotions and desires. With near unanimity, they abhorred Hitler's Nazi Germany and hoped for a British victory. Increasingly the majority followed President Roosevelt's leadership in favoring aid short of war for the victims of Axis aggression. After the fall of France in June, 1940, the majority of Americans believed it was more important to assure a British victory over the Axis than it was for the United States to stay out of the European war. At the same time, however, Americans and their elected representatives in both houses of Congress overwhelmingly opposed a declaration of war by the United States against the Axis. Until the Japanese attack on Pearl Harbor in December, 1941, public opinion polls consistently showed that approximately 80 per cent of the American people opposed a declaration of war by the United States. Opposition to Hitler's Germany, sympathy for Britain and China, support for aid short of war, and opposition to a declaration of war—those were the American views. But they left ample room for debate.[3]

The "interventionists" believed it more important to assure a British victory over the Axis than to keep out of the war. Following the President's lead, many of them hoped aid short of war would be sufficient; a growing minority, however, believed the United States must enter the war as a full belligerent. The "isolationists," or "noninterventionists," believed it was more important for the United States to stay out of the European war than it was to assure a British victory over the Axis. They were convinced that the United States could defend itself successfully in the Western Hemisphere if it properly prepared and maintained its own military forces. Charles A. Lindbergh was the most popular and controversial spokesman for that noninterventionist view.[4]

Under the stars that evening in the Hollywood Bowl, Lindbergh criticized interventionist attempts to involve the United States in the war "by subterfuge and propaganda." He attacked two interventionist "fallacies." First, he discounted the claim "that the developments of modern warfare make this country more vulnerable to foreign invasion than before." Then he took issue with the contention "that the best way to defend America is by defending England." In opposition to those views, Lindbergh maintained that modern warfare developments, particularly air power, made the United States "less vulnerable to invasion than we have ever been in the past." And, speaking in 1941, he insisted that "the surest way for us to lose a war is by trying to defend England or any other part of Europe." Drawing on his long experience and observation of air power in America, Europe, and, to a lesser extent, Asia, he said that "Aviation, if we use it intelligently, will make American shores impregnable to attack."

Lindbergh pointed out that the interventionists and the British in urging "the defense of England" really meant "the defeat of Germany." He dramatically described the formidable difficulties facing the United States in any attempt to defeat the Axis states on the European and Asian continents. Preparation to accomplish that task would, in Lindbergh's opinion, require turning the United States "into a military nation that exceeds Germany in regimentation." He feared that "Life as we know it today would be a thing of the past," and he worried that the military operations "would probably mean the loss of millions of American lives." He insisted that "No foreign power can invade us today, and with reasonable preparation on our part, no combination of foreign powers will ever be able to invade us." He voiced confidence in the "American ability to hold its own" in trade with Axis states.

Even if the United States were able to defeat Germany after a long and bloody war, Lindbergh feared that the resulting chaos and devastation would result in "the downfall of all European civilization, and the establishment of conditions in our own country far worse even than those in Germany today." He thought no one would be winners of such a war "except Russia and Japan." After that analysis, Lindbergh urged a negotiated settlement in Europe. In his opinion, "The alternative to a negotiated peace is either a Hitler victory or a prostrate Europe, and possibly a prostrate America as well." He insisted that "the only way our American life and ideals can be preserved is by staying out of this war," and that "the only way European civilization can be saved is by ending [the war] quickly." He reminded his California audience that in a democracy they had both the right and the duty "to decide the direction your country takes—to peace or to war."[5]

Lindbergh spoke earnestly and directly, without oratorical flourishes or bombast. As his clear voice filtered through the loud-speakers to his listeners seated above him, the thousands listened with rapt attention. Not all agreed with what he said, but they took his analysis seriously. And they reflected on his views and on their own as the meeting ended, the huge crowd dispersed, and they wended their separate ways homeward that night.

Though the "Great Debate" was impressively orderly and nonviolent, emotions mounted as concerned Americans earnestly jousted verbally on what were literally life-or-death issues. Passions grew, and so did intolerance of conflicting foreign policy views. Increasingly, many on each side saw their adversaries in the debate as not merely wrong, but evil and perhaps subversive as well. It was then only a short step from such emotions to justifying methods against opponents that were not really "fair play." Isolationists charged interventionists with being "warmongers" and "Anglophiles," who were more dedicated to foreign causes than to the lives and freedom of Americans. Interventionists charged that isolationists were "appeasers" and "defeatists," and were serving the cause of Hitler's Nazis. As the most prominent and frank of the leading noninterventionists, Lindbergh came under particularly severe attack. Millions of Americans then and later saw him as little better than a Nazi. His image has never fully recovered from the stereotypes fostered by his interventionist assailants from the White House on down.

The hostility and discrimination that he and other noninterventionists encountered extended into circumstances surrounding America First rallies he addressed. For example, ten weeks after the meeting in the Hollywood Bowl, Lindbergh spoke near Oklahoma City. The Democratic South was the most fervently interventionist section of the country; isolationists found little support and suffered much abuse there. The America First Committee had met with little success in its efforts to organize local chapters in the South. The rally in Oklahoma City was a major attempt by the Committee, using its star attraction, to penetrate that hostile territory.[6]

Scheduled for Friday evening, August 29, the planned meeting encountered all sorts of difficulties. Three days before the rally the city council of Oklahoma City voted unanimously to cancel permission to use the Municipal Auditorium. Some 250 people attended the council meeting, most of them strongly opposing Lindbergh. Among his adversaries were spokesmen for two local American Legion posts. The commander of one of them said flatly that "the time for freedom of speech is past." Newspapers were hostile.[7]

As news of the city council action broke, other cities in Oklahoma invited America First to hold the rally in their communities. A friend of Lindbergh in Texas offered money to help—though he did not agree with the aviator's views. Senator Burton K. Wheeler, Democrat from Montana, volunteered to speak on the same platform with him. Governor Leon C. Phillips of Oklahoma criticized the city council and even offered use of the Capitol steps. The America First organizer believed that if the Committee "changed cities and postponed even one hour, all opportunity to break into the South was gone and a defeat at Oklahoma City meant opposition to our speaking in every other city where sentiment was not strongly organized to our viewpoint." With his help and encouragement, the state chairman of America First in Oklahoma, Herbert K. Hyde, said Lindbergh would make his scheduled address "even if we have to use a street corner or a pasture."[8]

The rally went off on schedule. The free speech issue attracted more attention than the meeting would have won without the controversy. But the atmosphere was tense, with alarming threats of violence. Local thugs pressured owners not to permit use of their property for the rally, so the Committee did not announce the location until the day before. It arranged to use a park a mile west of Oklahoma City that belonged to amateur baseball teams. The field representative, hearing of plans to demolish the seating facilities, did not have the seats built until the day of the meeting. Special police guarded highline poles approaching the park. Batteries for emergency lighting and broadcasting were provided in case the lines were cut. Flashlights were even available by which to read the speeches if the power were cut.

When Lindbergh arrived in Oklahoma City the day before the meeting, armed motorcycle police escorted him to his hotel for his own protection. People drove in from all over the state and adjoining states to attend the meeting. Former Governor "Alfalfa Bill" Murray, a crusty old isolationist in his own right, came in from his home in Broken Bow to introduce Lindbergh at the meeting. By the time the police escorted Lindbergh, Wheeler, Murray, and their platform party to the ball park at 7:45 that Friday evening, some 8,000 people were already there, with cars backed up for miles on approaching roads. The ushers hired for the evening had reneged at the last moment, but people managed to find seats on the planks laid on bundles of shingles for that purpose. There was no applause when the speakers arrived, but there was no violence, either. Microphones were placed carefully to muffle any heckling from the crowd. After organized singing, Hyde spoke (and challenged a heckler to come up to the platform—which he did). At nine o'clock, by the time Murray finished introducing Lindbergh, there were perhaps 15,000 people in the park.[9]

Lindbergh spoke for half an hour on "Air Power." He began his address with a concise summary of the noninterventionist view he had advanced repeatedly during the preceding two years: "I have said that I did not believe it was within our power to control the wars, or to solve the problems that have existed in Europe since European history began. I have said that we were not prepared to wage war abroad successfully at this time, and that we would not be prepared to do so for months if not for years to come. I have said that our participation in this war would simply add to bloodshed and prostration in Europe, and bring confusion to our own country. I have said that the United States is strong enough and able enough to protect itself, and that we in America do not have to depend upon any foreign country for our security and welfare. To these statements, and beliefs, I hold as firmly today as I have at any time in the past."

Lindbergh then turned to his favorite subject, "air power, its capabilities, its limitations, and its consequences." Again drawing on his long and varied experience in aviation all over the world, he developed the theme that "while aviation greatly strengthened our position in America from the standpoint of defense, it greatly weakened our position from the standpoint of attacking Europe." He conceded that scientific and technological development could change circumstances for the future, but he contended that in 1941 and for the immediate future "the quickest way for Germany to lose a war would be to attack America, and the quickest way for America to lose a war would be to attack Germany." Maintaining that the United States had "the most perfect defensive position of any nation," he asked his audience if America should sell its "birthright for the mess of pottage that is offered us in Europe and Asia today; or shall we preserve for our children the free and independent heritage that our forefathers passed on to us?" And he closed with an

**13**

appeal for support for the America First Committee's noninterventionist efforts so "that freedom and independence, and representative government, may continue to live in this nation."[10] The warm applause he received at the close of his address indicated that he was not without supporters and respect in that Oklahoma audience.

Many people left when organizers of the meeting attempted a collection, but perhaps 10,000 stayed on to cheer Senator Wheeler's address. The feared disturbances did not materialize. Lindbergh never accepted a fee for any of his noninterventionist addresses, and he paid all his own expenses. But the special precautions necessary at Oklahoma City had increased expenses for the rally, and at the same time the collection had to be canceled. Consequently, America First national headquarters had to provide $3,000 to cover the local deficit on the meeting. The audience that left the ball park that night, however, was more sympathetic than the one that had gathered there three hours before. The speeches had been broadcast throughout the state and carried nationally over the Mutual network. Even local Legion officials and newspapers (while sharply disagreeing with the views expressed there) conceded afterward that the meeting had been conducted properly.[11]

Most who heard Charles A. Lindbergh that night concluded that he was, indeed, an impressive man. During the twenty-seven months between Hitler's invasion of Poland and the Japanese attack on Pearl Harbor, more than any other individual he personified the abortive but earnest battle against American intervention in World War II.

# I

## Preparation

# 2/The Making of a Hero

THE slender young man captured the popular imagination with his solo nonstop flight from New York to Paris in his single-engine *Spirit of St. Louis* on May 20–21, 1927. And, unlike most whose daring or skills brought momentary fame, Charles A. Lindbergh retained public attention and acclaim through his personal character, his continuing accomplishments, and what a later generation would have called his charisma. Quick, strong, and well co-ordinated, he was an exceptionally skilled aviator, with plenty of courage and a love of adventure. His flying career eventually was to extend from Jennys to jets. But young Lindbergh was no harebrained daredevil. Careful advance planning was standard *modus operandi* for him. Schools and organized churches had little appeal. But he was bright, and had wide-ranging interests, a talent for manipulating things mechanical, an experimental temperament, and a self-discipline, persistence, attention to detail, and capacity for sustained concentrated effort that enabled him to convert curiosity into action. He also had impressive qualities of character: integrity, independence, modesty, consideration for others, an even temper, and personal morality. His penchant for practical jokes only served to make him seem more appealingly human. And his qualities were consistent with his background.[1]

Born in Detroit, Michigan, on February 4, 1902, less than two years before the Wright brothers made their first powered flight, he grew up on a farm near the town of Little Falls,

Minnesota, in the upper Mississippi Valley. His father, Charles A. Lindbergh, Sr., had been born in Sweden, was reared in rural Minnesota, graduated from law school at the University of Michigan, and practiced law in Little Falls. Widowed in 1898, he then married Evangeline Lodge Land, the chemistry teacher in the local high school. She was of English, Scottish, and Irish descent, had a family background of dental science and medicine, and had graduated from the University of Michigan. Strong and independent people, both C. A., as he usually was called, and Evangeline were devoted to their only son. From his father the boy learned to love the out-of-doors and rural life. From his mother and her family he gained scientific and technical interests.

In 1906 his father won election as a progressive Republican to the United States House of Representatives, a position he filled for ten years. In Congress the elder Lindbergh was an agrarian radical and insurgent. Sharing values of the earlier Populists and of the later Non-Partisan League, he often followed the lead of Theodore Roosevelt, Robert M. LaFollette, and George W. Norris on public issues. Critical of the Money Trust and Wall Street, he blamed those "special interests" for many of America's ills at home and abroad. Those considerations led him to oppose American entry into World War I. In his book *Why Is Your Country at War,* he urged an independent foreign policy for the United States, and denounced business and financial interests for promoting war to serve their selfish economic ambitions. His opposition to preparedness and war hurt him politically, and he was subjected to abusive and unfair charges of disloyalty. Defeated in his bid for the Senate in 1916, he never again won election to public office. Though he supported the American government after Congress declared war, the former Congressman suffered politically for his noninterventionist opposition from 1914 to 1917.[2]

The elder Lindbergh spent as much time with his son as his law practice and political career permitted. He taught the boy how to shoot, including the skills, discipline, and responsibilities of handling a gun. Young Charles learned to drive their Model T Ford when he was only eleven years old, and thereafter drove

for his father on campaign trips. He distributed campaign literature and heard the political speeches. One might have supposed
that young Lindbergh was consciously following his father's
footsteps when he opposed American entry into World War II
more than two decades later.[3]

He insisted, however, that his father had no direct influence
on his own course in foreign affairs. He did not share his
father's agrarian radicalism or his hostility to the Money Trust.
He thought his father's economic views were too extreme and
oversimplified. As a boy he had had little interest in his father's
analysis and did not entirely understand it. He had learned early
to dislike politics. As an adult he had even married into the
Money Trust when, in 1929, he wed the daughter of a former
partner in the House of Morgan. Through his wife's family,
Lindbergh gained the valued friendship of J. P. Morgan, his
partners, and others on Wall Street. He liked and respected
them, and thought his father would have liked them, too, had he
known them. Senators William E. Borah of Idaho, Burton K.
Wheeler of Montana, Gerald P. Nye of North Dakota, and
others operated from agrarian radical frames of reference in
opposing American entry into World War II. Colonel Lindbergh did not. Many years later he contended that he had not
consciously followed his father's example when he battled
against intervention during the years 1939–1941.[4]

Nonetheless, young Lindbergh greatly admired and respected
his father. He shared his father's preference for rural values and
dislike of cities. He was affected by his interest in Darwin and
evolution.[5] He admired and shared his father's qualities of
character, including his independence, integrity, courage, and
sense of responsibility. He felt pride in his father for standing
firm for what he believed to be right, even in the face of abusive
and unfair attacks. In the years from 1939 to 1941, Colonel
Lindbergh was not an agrarian progressive as his Congressman
father had been in the like period of 1914 to 1917, but both
were courageously independent noninterventionists trying to
serve the interests of their country as they saw them. And both
paid the price those efforts exacted.

Charles had wanted to become a flyer in World War I, but

was too young. Fifteen when America entered the war and sixteen when it ended, he was old enough to help on the farm. He eagerly seized the opportunity when Little Falls high school permitted academic credit without attending classes for those who wished to work on farms producing food for the war effort. He operated his father's farm, sold milking machines on the side, and took time out only briefly to get his diploma in 1918. He enjoyed farming and felt mixed emotions when he turned the place over to a tenant in 1919. Lindbergh has never lost his love for the land, for the out-of-doors, and for values he associates with rural living.[6]

Encouraged by his parents, however, in 1920 he enrolled at the University of Wisconsin to study mechanical engineering. He was bright enough, but was less than enthusiastic about his studies. He found much greater interest in his motorcycle and in the rifle and pistol teams. In 1922, after only three semesters, he left the University to begin his career in aviation.[7]

On April 9, 1922, at the age of twenty, Lindbergh made his first airplane flight, as a passenger. The Nebraska Aircraft Corporation at Lincoln barely honored its agreement to teach him to fly, but he got his start there. Working as a parachute jumper, wing 'walker, and general handyman, he barnstormed with pilots through the West that summer and fall. With help from his father, he bought his first airplane in 1923. He paid $500 for that old Jenny, and in April made his first solo flight in it, at Souther Field in Georgia. During much of the next year he barnstormed through the South and Middle West, giving rides for hire and increasing his flying skills in the process. In 1924, he enlisted in the Army Air Service, and as an aviation cadet trained to be a military pilot at Brooks and Kelly fields in Texas. In 1925, he graduated at the top of his class as a pursuit pilot with a commission in the Reserve. The following year he became a Captain in the Missouri National Guard and chief pilot for the Robertson Aircraft Corporation, flying the mail between St. Louis and Chicago.[8]

While flying the mail, in a DH-4, he became fascinated by the idea of competing for the $25,000 prize offered by Raymond

## The Making of a Hero

Orteig for the first nonstop flight across the Atlantic between New York and Paris. He successfully interested several St. Louis businessmen in his project. They provided most of the money (along with $2,000 he had saved) for a single-engine monoplane to be specially constructed for him by the Ryan Company in San Diego. In California Lindbergh helped to design the plane, closely followed its construction, plotted his route across the Atlantic, and piloted the new plane through careful test flights. In a record-breaking flight, he flew the *Spirit of St. Louis* across the continent from San Diego to New York, with an overnight stop in St. Louis. Death was already taking its toll in the prize competition, and other pilots and planes faced delays caused by weather and other problems. On the morning of May 20, 1927, Charles A. Lindbergh took off from the rain-soaked Roosevelt Field, on Long Island, in his heavily loaded plane. Thirty-three hours and thirty minutes later, after flying through fog, rain, storms, and ice, and after desperately fighting against sleep (he had not slept the night before his departure), he landed at Le Bourget Aerodrome, near Paris. His flight won the Orteig prize. And it brought him fame and acclaim far beyond his wildest expectations—and beyond his personal preferences. Life would never be the same again for that middle-western farm boy and air mail pilot.[9]

Some 100,000 wildly cheering people enthusiastically greeted his arrival at Paris. Ambassador Myron T. Herrick made him his guest in the American Embassy. Honors showered upon the young man from all over the world. After rousing welcomes in Paris, Brussels, and London, Lindbergh and his airplane sailed back to the United States aboard the cruiser *Memphis,* which President Calvin Coolidge had provided for his return. He was promoted to the rank of Colonel in the Air Corps Reserve. Countless tens of thousands welcomed him in Washington. The President awarded him the Distinguished Flying Cross, and later the Congressional Medal of Honor. Four million people in New York City cheered him in a magnificent ticker-tape parade. And St. Louis would not be outdone in the enthusiasm of its welcome. Few people in human history have won such acclaim and honors as were showered upon that tall, slender, twenty-five-year-old aviator in 1927 and after.[10]

Through it all, Lindbergh kept his poise, his modesty, and his sense of proportion. He turned aside lavish offers of wealth and concentrated on promoting aviation in America and the world. During the summer and fall of 1927, the Daniel Guggenheim Fund for the Promotion of Aviation financed a tour in which Colonel Lindbergh, flying the *Spirit of St. Louis,* visited each of the forty-eight states to promote aviation. In December, he flew the *Spirit of St. Louis* to Mexico City, in response to an invitation arranged by America's Ambassador Dwight W. Morrow, as a gesture toward improving United States relations with its neighboring country. In response to other invitations, he flew on from Mexico to visit a number of Latin American countries, returning to the United States in February. On April 30, 1928, he made his last flight in the *Spirit of St. Louis,* piloting it from St. Louis to Washington, D.C., before turning the plane over to the Smithsonian Institution for permanent exhibition.[11]

On May 27, 1929, Charles married Anne Morrow, whom he had met on his trip to Mexico. Her father had been a partner in J. P. Morgan and Company before he became Ambassador to Mexico. Morrow later won election to the United States Senate as a Republican from New Jersey. Anne, a foot shorter than her six-foot-two-and-a-half husband, was slender, dark haired, blue eyed, and attractive. A graduate of Smith College, she was shy and seemed a bit timid. The marriage of the flying hero and the daughter of the financier-diplomat captured popular interest. Theirs was a successful marriage, in which each enriched the spirit and continued growth of the other. Encouraged by her husband's confidence in her, Anne blossomed into an unusually talented writer. The couple eventually had six children, four boys and two girls.

Anne shared her husband's love of flying. Under his instruction she earned licenses as an airplane and glider pilot, and also as a radio operator. She accompanied him on adventurous flights in the United States, Latin America, the Pacific, Asia, Europe, and Africa to explore air routes and help inaugurate airline services. For example, in the fall of 1929, they flew routes in South America in the service of Pan American Airways. In the summer of 1931, they piloted their low-wing Lockheed "Sirius" plane on a survey flight from New York to Japan and China by way of Canada, Alaska, and the Soviet Union.[12] Anne's book based on that flight, *North to the Orient,* became a best seller when it was published in 1935.[13] In 1933, they flew the plane, which they named *Tingmissartoq,* on an exploration of air routes across the Atlantic. Her description of their adventures in connection with the flight from Africa across the South Atlantic to Brazil became a best-selling book in 1938 as *Listen! the Wind.*[14]

But the romance and adventure were not entirely idyllic. Fame exacted its price and produced its own appalling tragedy. Publicity was not entirely unpleasant, and it opened certain opportunities. But when carried to extremes by newsmen and press photographers the nutrient of publicity became poisonous. Charles and Anne both treasured their privacy. They co-operated with the press in their public activities while trying at the same time to guard their private lives from the glare of publicity. But newsmen would not honor that distinction. As Anne wrote many years later, "the freedom of privacy was denied us." Nothing was sacred to reporters seeking stories. If they could not get facts (or if the facts were not sufficiently sensational), they relied on their imaginations. Newspapers carried so many inaccurate and false stories about them that the Lindberghs almost despaired of accuracy, restraint, and responsibility from the press. Colonel Lindbergh's own emphasis on factual precision made the press performance seem particularly abhorrent to him. When the couple's attempts to co-operate with reporters failed, they began to refuse all press interviews. The result was a feud with newsmen that led many reporters and photographers to be still more obnoxious in invading the privacy of the young couple. Even on their honeymoon, when news photographers discovered the cabin boat in which they were cruising, they pursued them in a speedboat and demanded that the couple come on deck for pictures and questions. When

Charles and Anne refused, the newsmen circled the Lindbergh boat for six hours, rocking it with waves from the wake of the speedboat, until the Colonel finally escaped them and headed out to the open sea.[15]

On June 22, 1930, their first baby was born, a son they named after his father. Lindbergh sought a home where he and his wife and son might live in peace and safety. He located a rural, wooded spot near Hopewell, New Jersey, and built a fine house for them there. They moved into their new home near the beginning of 1932. Despite its remote, rustic setting, however, they required fences, guards, and police help to protect them from newsmen, photographers, crackpots, and curiosity seekers. Despite all precautions, on the evening of March 1, 1932, their curly-headed eighteen-month-old son, Charles A. Lindbergh, Jr., was kidnapped from his crib in their new home and murdered.

Charles and Anne faced the tragedy with courage and dignity. They co-operated fully with law enforcement officers and sought the co-operation of the press in their futile efforts to recover the boy alive, and then to apprehend and convict the kidnapper. After locating the boy's body in a shallow grave a few miles from his home, the police finally captured the kidnapper. And in one of the most publicized trials in history Bruno Richard Hauptmann was tried and convicted.

Some newspapers co-operated and performed responsibly during the long ordeal, but others did not. People all over the world closely followed the sensational details of the crime and trial in their newspapers. Anne could not avoid the thought that "If it were not for the publicity that surrounds us we might still have him." Colonel Lindbergh never forgave press photographers for breaking into the morgue to photograph their son's corpse. The birth of their second son, Jon, on August 16, 1932, helped ease their earlier loss.[16] But by the time the state of New Jersey executed Hauptmann for the crime of murder on April 3, 1936, the Lindberghs had long since fled the United States to seek refuge abroad.

# 3/The English, the French, and the Russians

FOR Charles and Anne Lindbergh the Great American Dream had turned into a terrible nightmare. Hounded and harassed by newsmen, photographers, hero-worshippers, curiosity seekers, and crackpots, the Colonel and his lady had found a modicum of privacy and security only through strong fences and armed guards. Relaxed recreation and social activities taken for granted by others were impossible for them. The immediate future in America held little promise for anything approaching a normal and happy environment for the young couple and their son, Jon. Consequently, in December, 1935, they quietly slipped out of the country and sought temporary refuge in England. As Walter Lippmann wrote at the time, they were "refugees from the tyranny of yellow journalism" and had been denied "their inalienable right to privacy." In personal correspondence Lindbergh explained their move as an escape from corrupt New Jersey politics, from an irresponsible press, and from fanatics.[1]

Friends of Anne's family helped ease the move. Agents of J. P. Morgan and Company handled arrangements for their secret departure from the United States. They stayed a few weeks with the Morgan family in Cardiff, Wales (Aubrey Niel Morgan had married Anne's older sister, Elisabeth, who had died the year before; later he married her younger sister, Constance). Then the Lindberghs stayed for a time in London hotels. In March, they moved into Long Barn, an old country home that they leased from Harold Nicolson, Dwight Morrow's biographer.[2]

# Preparation

Long Barn, located some twenty-five miles south of London near the small town of Weald in Kent, provided a tranquility the Lindberghs had rarely known. Trees hid the nearest village cottages from view, and in other directions they saw peaceful fields and hedges. Townspeople honored their wish for privacy. Even newsmen let them alone for the most part. Fanatical and threatening letters, so numerous and disturbing in America, were no real problem in England. The Lindberghs arranged to have their Scottish terrier and giant German shepherd, Skean and Thor, brought from the United States. Anne and Charles found time to read, study, and write. Lindbergh continued the scientific work in collaboration with the French physician and scientist Dr. Alexis Carrel that he had begun in New York. He had a small single-engine airplane built in England. The couple enjoyed private dinners with hospitable friends and royalty. They could go about freely without being bothered (except by American tourists). They were grateful to their civilized English hosts, enjoyed their good manners, and benefited from "the best conditions of law and order of any country in the world." Their situation was not intended to be permanent, but it was a welcome respite after the ordeal in their native America.[3]

For all that, however, Lindbergh had growing reservations about certain English qualities, particularly in an air age, as the possibility of general war loomed ever more menacingly over Europe. His own quick, systematic, efficient style found the British slow, inefficient, and complacent. Confronted with delays and difficulties in the manufacture of technical equipment required for his scientific work, Lindbergh missed "the delicate lines of France, the detailed efficiency of Germany, and the balanced construction of America." He complained of the casual English driving habits and the consequent high accident rate on English roads. He found the British Imperial Airways with a reputation for often being late, for operating obsolete equipment, and for inadequate safety. He wondered whether the English were "simply attempting to make others believe that British is always best, or if they actually believed it themselves, as would seem from outward appearance. If the first is the fact,

26

then they have admirable ability. But if the latter is the case it is an alarming condition." He worried about the decadence and loss of spirit in England.[4]

It was in the matter of air power, however, that Lindbergh found British deficiencies particularly disturbing. In 1938, he wrote that it was "necessary to consider the character and traditions of the English people. Their concept of time is based on a world of ships, and not of aircraft. The speed and flexibility demanded by aviation are contrary to English temperament. Their genius lies in a slow and steady growth, protected from surprise by the British Navy, and the Channel." He feared Britain had "neither the spirit nor the ability needed for a modern war." Seeing "a combination of bluff and vanity in the English," Lindbergh concluded that "the assets in English character lie in confidence rather than ability; tenacity rather than strength; and determination rather than intelligence." He conceded, however, that "any conclusion one reaches in regard to the English is constantly shaken by the exceptions which arise."[5]

The Colonel felt very real affection and sympathy for the French. But his misgivings about French capacities to cope with the challenges of the 1930's were even greater than those he had about the English. His attitudes toward the French may have been affected by his high regard for Dr. Alexis Carrel, whose scientific accomplishments had been rewarded with a Nobel Prize in 1912. The aviator and the scientist first met in the latter's laboratories at the Rockefeller Institute in New York in 1930. Over a period of years, the tall, slender American and the small, alert Frenchman collaborated in scientific work that culminated with the publication in 1938 of their book, *The Culture of Organs,* on the organ-perfusion pump and procedures they had developed jointly.[6]

The contrasting appearances and backgrounds of the two men blurred important similarities. They shared practical scientific interests, experimental temperaments, obsessions for precision and accuracy in the laboratory, and wide-ranging and unfettered intellectual curiosities. Dr. Carrel had "the most stimulating mind" Lindbergh had ever encountered. Though meticulously careful in his scientific work, Carrel "liked to jump over the moon" while playing with ideas in discussions. Dr. Carrel's friend Boris Bakhmeteff once said: "If Alexis was right twenty percent of the time, it was enough." Lindbergh believed that Carrel "made himself vulnerable because he spoke so freely."[7] The two men, one an American and the other a Frenchman, also shared a devotion to their respective native lands, though both were later accused of disloyalty by many of their compatriots. The Lindberghs' respect and affection for Dr. Carrel also extended to Mme Carrel, a remarkable person in her own right. Through the Carrels, the Lindberghs in 1938 bought and lived for some months on the beautiful island of Illiec, off the north coast of Brittany, and near the island of Saint-Gildas, which the Carrels owned. Anne and Charles made frequent visits to France while they lived in England, and they made their home in Paris during the winter of 1938–39.[8]

On his sojourns in France from 1936 to 1939, Lindbergh was troubled by the difficulties, domestic and foreign, that he observed there. Political corruption, lack of strong leadership, an air of discouragement, and the loss of spirit there all worried him. In contrast to the English, however, the French, in Lindbergh's view, recognized their failings and deficiencies. They were simply unable to correct them satisfactorily.[9]

Early in 1941, nearly two years after he had left Europe and returned to America, Lindbergh wrote that before the European war started "France was alert to her danger but disorganized; while England was organized but only half awake. In France, internal conditions were so bad that I often wondered whether war or revolution would break upon the country first. In England, there was no danger of revolution, but the people of that nation had never adjusted themselves to the tempo of this modern era. Their minds were still attuned to the speed of sail rather than to that of aircraft." More than three decades later Lindbergh remembered the prewar British as lethargic and "rather blind." He remembered the French as "alive" to the threat "but not sufficiently organized to counter it."[10]

## The English, the French, and the Russians

Colonel Lindbergh formed an even less attractive view of the Soviet Union. He and his wife had visited eastern Russia on their flight to the Orient in 1931 and had first visited European Russia in 1933. They returned on a flying visit in August, 1938, shortly before the Munich Conference. The Russians entertained them lavishly. Officials and airmen proudly demonstrated their military aircraft and toured their guests through selected aircraft production facilities. Lindbergh found the Russians "an open, likable people." But he "left Russia with a very depressing picture of the conditions in that country." With the notable exceptions of the Russian ballet and the Moscow subway, he felt "almost always surrounded with mediocrity unparalleled in any other place." Though he considered Russian flyers to be skillful, courageous, and potentially dangerous adversaries, he did not believe them "in the class of the American, English, and German pilots." He took a dim view of the Soviet practice of including women among military pilots. "After all, there is a God-made difference between men and women that even the Soviet Union can't eradicate." Russian aviation seemed to depend largely on the copying of foreign aviation developments. "The only typically Russian development lies in the personnel and this is undoubtedly their greatest weakness." He thought that the Soviet Union had enough reasonably modern military airplanes to make its weight felt in war but was decidedly not in a leadership position in aviation. Lindbergh predicted "a collapse of the Russian system in the fairly near future"; it could come "at any moment or it might take several years but it is as much a certainty as anything of this type can be."[11]

After the Lindberghs had left the Soviet Union and returned to England, a badly garbled third-hand account of the Colonel's critical impressions was carried in an obscure mimeographed news sheet, *The Week,* in London. The account was then published sensationally in Russia and elsewhere. The episode infuriated the Russians, embarrassed Lindbergh, and complicated matters for America's Military Attaché in Moscow.[12]

Those images that Charles A. Lindbergh gradually formed in his European travels might have been of little significance in less troubled times. But in the midst of the crisis-plagued depression years of the 1930's, with the increasingly alarming storm clouds of a devastating general war looming on the horizon, his observations had disturbing connotations for the future. And between 1936 and 1939 Colonel Lindbergh obtained unique opportunities for firsthand study of the military air power that Nazi Germany under Adolf Hitler and Hermann Goering was to loose upon its European neighbors.

# 4/Air Power and Nazi Germany

COLONEL LINDBERGH became fascinated by Germany in general, and by German air power developments in particular. Despite his world-wide travels, he had never visited Germany before the summer of 1936. Neither he nor his wife spoke or read the German language. He never met Adolf Hitler, and he never embraced Hitler's National Socialism. He disapproved of much that occurred in Nazi Germany. At the same time, however, he admired the German efficiency, spirit, and scientific and technological accomplishments. To a degree he began to "understand" and sympathize with certain German attitudes and actions in the 1930's, even when he did not approve of them. He was tremendously impressed by the Germans' accomplishments in military aviation. He became persuaded that Germany was the natural air power of Europe and that Germany's growing supremacy in the air required major defense actions and diplomatic adjustments by other European countries—and by the United States. In his fascination, Lindbergh welcomed opportunities to learn more about developments in Germany.

The United States Military Attaché in Berlin arranged the invitations that brought Lindbergh to Germany in 1936, 1937, and again in 1938. He wanted Lindbergh to help him get information for the United States about military aviation developments in Nazi Germany. Major Truman Smith had become the Military Attaché in Berlin in August, 1935, and he served in that capacity until April, 1939. An Army infantry officer since World War I, he knew little about aviation. Though he had an Assistant Attaché for Air, Smith's responsibilities extended to both land and air developments in Germany. And he was not satisfied with the quality of the air intelligence he was obtaining and reporting to Washington.[1]

At the breakfast table one morning in May, 1936, Smith's wife brought to his attention a newspaper item reporting a visit by Colonel Lindbergh to a French aircraft factory. Smith had never met the aviator, but he began to speculate that such a Lindbergh visit in Germany could increase America's knowledge of German aviation developments. Without consulting Lindbergh, he explored the possibility of a visit with the German Air Ministry. The response was favorable, and a list of combat units, factories, and research installations to be shown Lindbergh if he came was worked out. It was also arranged that Major Smith or his Air Attaché would accompany Lindbergh in visiting those installations. In the absence of Ambassador William E. Dodd, who was on leave in the United States, Smith cleared the idea with Ferdinand Mayer of the American Embassy.[2]

On May 25, 1936, Major Smith wrote Colonel Lindbergh extending to him "in the name of General Goering and the German Air Ministry an invitation to visit Germany and inspect the new German civil and military air establishments." Smith reported that Goering promised "the strictest censorship would be imposed" with regard to the visit. Major Smith wrote that from "a purely American point of view" he would consider Lindbergh's visit "of high patriotic benefit." He expected the Germans to "go out of their way" to show Lindbergh more than they would show the Military Attaché or his assistant. Lindbergh welcomed the invitation, and was grateful for the assurances of protection from newsmen.[3]

On July 22, 1936, Colonel and Mrs. Lindbergh flew from England to Berlin. During their eleven-day stay in Germany they were house guests of the Smiths. In the course of their visit they had good opportunities to meet Goering, State Secretary for Air General Erhard Milch, Chief of the Technical Office of the Air Ministry Colonel Ernst Udet, the German Ambassador to the United States Hans Dieckhoff, and others.

At a luncheon in his honor on July 23, Lindbergh gave a short prepared speech. In it he emphasized the awesome destructive potential of air power in war. He contended that aviation had "abolished what we call defensive warfare." In his view, that terrible power imposed "heavy responsibility" on people in aviation. He hoped that the intelligence required for aviation could also be used for peace and civilization. "It is the responsibility of aviation to justify the combination of strength and intelligence."[4]

On that first visit to Germany, Lindbergh inspected an elite Luftwaffe fighter group, a major German air research institute, and Heinkel and Junkers aircraft factories. He piloted two German planes and inspected others—including the JU-87 Stuka dive bomber that was so terrifyingly effective in ground support operations early in the European war. He obtained data on the ME-109, which was to become Germany's workhorse fighter of World War II. On July 28, Goering gave an elaborate formal luncheon at his official residence on the Wilhelmstrasse in honor of Colonel Lindbergh. On August 1, Lindbergh attended the opening ceremonies of the Olympic games in Berlin as Goering's guest and got a distant glimpse of Hitler there.[5]

Colonel Lindbergh met regularly with Major Smith and the Assistant Attaché for Air, often with a shorthand stenographer on hand, to discuss the aviation developments they had seen. Lindbergh helped to educate the former infantry officer on aviation, and he compared the German planes with those of France, Britain, and the United States. According to Smith, Lindbergh's visit greatly helped his subsequent access to Luftwaffe personnel and developments and made possible vastly improved air intelligence reports to Washington. Just before the Lindberghs had left England on that first trip to Germany, Roger Straus, cochairman of the National Conference of Jews and Christians in the United States, had cabled Lindbergh a regret that he was going, believing that German propaganda would interpret the visit as approval of the Nazi regime. There were more social activities and reporters than Lindbergh would have preferred, but generally the press coverage in the United States was not critical.[6]

The visit was a major success for American air intelligence in Germany, and it was a fascinating experience for the American aviator. Lindbergh found Germany "in many ways the most interesting nation in the world today." Despite reservations, he left "with a feeling of great admiration for the German people." He was impressed with the German spirit, technical ability, and leadership. The aircraft designs he saw there in 1936 were inferior to those in America at the time, but he believed the United States had "nothing like the margin of leadership today which we have held in the past." He thought it would not "take very much more political bungling to remove the margin of leadership which we still hold in America."[7]

He found Hermann Goering, the Nazi head of the German Luftwaffe, to be "a unique combination of diplomacy and force (and possibly ruthlessness); of taste and vanity, of propaganda and fact." He formed a tentative impression of Hitler: "With all the things we criticize, he is undoubtedly a great man, and I believe he has done much for the German people. He is a fanatic in many ways, and anyone can see there is a certain amount of fanaticism in Germany today. It is less than I expected, but it is there. On the other hand, Hitler has accomplished results (good in addition to bad,) which could hardly have been accomplished without some fanaticism." The Colonel concluded "that when conditions became as chaotic as they were in Germany after the war, one must expect fanaticism to result, and hope that moderation comes later." Viewing the various European countries, he gained the impression that "moderation is possible only with an already established strength."[8]

On the basis of that first visit, Lindbergh was persuaded that the Germans were "especially anxious to maintain a friendly relationship with England." He thought Germany had no intention "of attacking France for many years to come, if at all."

Lindbergh was convinced, however, that the Germans considered war with the Soviet Union as "inevitable, and expect it to come in the fairly near future." When that war erupted "the German frontier may have to withstand a French attack."[9]

The fundamental impact that first visit to Nazi Germany made upon the American aviator is suggested by the introspective ruminating he included in a personal letter to a friend in the United States: "Modern Germany does not permit a superficial judgment. She challenges our most fundamental concepts. . . . What measures the rights of a man or of a nation? . . . Are we deluding ourselves when we attempt to run our governments by counting the number of heads, without a thought of what lies within them? Are our standards true? . . . Is it possible to perpetuate a government, or a League of Governments unless representation is clearly proportional to the strength which is available to support it? And how is strength to be measured? Not by counting people, or guns, or geographical areas, but by a combination of these material things with others, less tangible and unmeasurable by any system we have yet developed. Germany knows that she has more than her share of the elements which make strength and greatness among nations. She also knows that she has less than her share of peacetime representation, measured by the type of force which has so often changed history."[10] After World War II, "realists" in the United States were to use somewhat similar terms in analyzing international relations.

Lindbergh had "some very serious reservations" about developments in Nazi Germany, and he bemoaned "the instances of incredible stupidity which seem to arise constantly among their actions." But he thought accounts in England and the United States gave "a very distorted and incomplete picture." On balance, in 1936 he found developments in Germany to be "encouraging . . . rather than depressing," and he viewed Germany as "a stabilizing factor" in Europe at that time.[11]

After the German trip, Lindbergh continued his scientific collaboration with Dr. Carrel. Anne continued her writing. They made trips to France and elsewhere. From February to early April, 1937, the two of them enjoyed an interesting flight to India and back in their small plane. (The airman found that trip "almost too normal. We had no forced landings, and always stopped on regular flying fields.") Their third son, Land, was born in May. And in October, 1937, they returned for another visit to Germany.[12]

With Major Smith again playing a central role, the Lilienthal aeronautical society invited Colonel Lindbergh to its annual meeting in Munich, Germany. Charles and Anne landed their plane in Munich on October 11, 1937. After four or five days of meetings on technical aspects of aviation, they went on to Berlin. In the course of their two-week stay in Germany, Lindbergh visited an air testing station, Focke-Wulf and Henschel airplane factories, and the Daimler-Benz engine factory. He examined various aircraft, including the Dornier 17 twin-engine bomber and the Messerschmitt 109 single-engine fighter. He may have been the first American given the opportunity to examine the ME-109 closely, and he was highly impressed. Again Lindbergh reported his observations to Smith and to his Assistant Attaché for Air, who then reported the data to Washington. Newspapers in both Germany and the United States gave little attention to his visit, and it seems to have provoked little criticism.[13]

Before the Lindberghs left Germany on October 25, the Colonel spent three days helping Major Smith prepare a formal intelligence "General Estimate" of German air power as of November 1, 1937. The report was over Smith's name in his capacity as Military Attaché, but most of its data and ideas belonged to Lindbergh and they often were in Lindbergh's words. The four-page report contended that so far as military technology was concerned Germany had "outdistanced France in practically all fields" and was "on the whole superior to Great Britain in the quality of her planes, but is still slightly inferior to Great Britain in motors, but rapidly closing the gap." With regard to Germany and the United States, "if the present progress curves of these two nations should continue as they have in the past two years, Germany should obtain technical parity with the USA by 1941 or 1942." Any American blunder could bring German superiority sooner. The report concluded: "In November 1937 it appears that the development of German air power is a European phenomenon of the first diplomatic importance. The upward movement is still gaining momentum."[14]

Writing years later, after World War II had ended, Smith thought the conclusions of the report stood up "extremely well." He considered its "most significant omission" was its "failure to state that the Luftwaffe was not a long range air force, built around heavy bombers with the primary mission of destroying cities and factories far behind the enemy's lines, but rather an air force designed to operate in close support of Germany's ground armies." That is, the report did not make clear that Nazi Germany was building a powerful tactical ground-support air force well suited for Hitler's blitzkrieg operations on the European mainland, but was not building the strategic heavy bomber force needed if Hitler intended decisive operations against England—or against the United States. It also "failed to mention the inexperience and inefficiency of many Generals of the Luftwaffe." In Washington, the General Staff and War Department gave the report wide circulation.[15]

Early in 1938, America's newly appointed Ambassador to Great Britain, Joseph P. Kennedy, forwarded to President Roosevelt a four-page letter written by Lindbergh describing what he had observed on aviation developments in Germany. The President sent it on to Army Chief of Staff Malin Craig and to Chief of Naval Operations William D. Leahy. General Craig replied that the information checked "very closely" with what he already had "except as regards the number of men employed at the Junkers and Heinkel factories." Admiral Leahy wrote the President that the information was "confirmatory of our information received from other sources."[16]

The 1937 visit strengthened the general impressions that Lindbergh had obtained the year before. "The growth of German military aviation is, I believe, without parallel in history; and the policies in almost every instance seem laid out with great intelligence and foresight." He correctly foresaw German actions against Austria, Czechoslovakia, Poland, and Russia. He was persuaded that "the people in Germany are thoroughly behind Hitler." He disliked the Nazi fanaticism but felt "a sense of decency and value which in many ways is far ahead of our own." He felt so particularly when he walked "among the headlines of murder, rape, and divorce on the billboards of London." He considered Germany and Italy "the two most virile countries in Europe today."[17]

So far as Germany was concerned, Lindbergh believed that after World War I "there were two general policies which could be followed by the Allied powers. One, to permit her to eventually regain her strength as a first class power, with everything this implies. Two, to prevent her rearming by the exertion of force if necessary. The time to have exerted force to prevent rearmament is long past. If that is now attempted it will probably result in the loss of millions of soldiers. Since Germany has been allowed to rearm, it seems to me that we should be prepared to face the logical consequences of that rearmament, including the readjustment of her eastern borders and the eventual obtaining of colonial interests as the opportunity presents itself." He thought the Germans were "an extremely intelligent and able people, close to our own, and it seems that there should be a way of working with them rather than against them." He considered the formation of the German-Italian Axis to be one of the "most serious blunders in all English diplomacy."[18]

In December, 1937, Charles and Anne secretly sailed back to the United States to visit and to take care of accumulated personal and business matters. They returned to England and to their sons aboard the German liner *Bremen* three months later, just as Hitler was taking over Austria in the *Anschluss*. In the spring and summer of 1938, Lindbergh and Carrel completed their book, *The Culture of Organs*. Anne finished writing her book, *Listen! the Wind,* about the couple's flight across the South Atlantic from Africa to South America five years before. They had a varied social life with friends and officialdom in

England and France, including a royal ball at Buckingham Palace and dinners at Lord and Lady Astor's Cliveden. In June, they gave up Long Barn and moved from England to their lovely island of Illiec off the coast of France. Charles made a special effort to spend as much time as possible with his family on Illiec that summer "because conditions in the world are such that one should not count too definitely on summers in the future."[19]

During the last two weeks of August, 1938, Lindbergh and his wife made their strenuous tour of European Russia, with visits to Moscow, Rostov, Kiev, and Odessa. On their return flight they stopped over for a week in Czechoslovakia (including a meeting with President Eduard Beneš), less than a month before that country was compelled to yield its Sudetenland to Nazi Germany after the Munich Conference. Through all that, Lindbergh's interest in Germany in no way diminished, and his concern about developments in Europe mounted.[20]

Shortly after Munich, invitations on behalf of the Lilienthal Society, the Air Ministry, America's new Ambassador, Hugh R. Wilson, and Major Smith once again brought Colonel and Mrs. Lindbergh to Germany, for a nineteen-day stay from October 11 to 29. Ambassador Wilson hoped the visit would help him develop personal contacts with Goering. Once again Lindbergh toured aircraft factories, consulted key people in the Air Ministry and Luftwaffe, and inspected and flew aircraft.

Of particular importance were the Junkers 88 and, again, the Messerschmitt 109. With the approval of Goering and Udet, Lindbergh was the first American permitted to examine the Luftwaffe's newest and best bomber, the JU-88. And he got the unprecedented opportunity to pilot its finest fighter, the ME-109. He was highly impressed by both airplanes and knew "of no other pursuit plane which combines simplicity of construction with such excellent performance characteristics" as the ME-109. In his visits to Germany from 1936 through 1938, Colonel Lindbergh closely inspected all the types of military aircraft that Germany was to use against Poland, Denmark, Norway, the Netherlands, Belgium, France, and England in 1939 and 1940.

## Preparation

The ME-109 and JU-88 were first-line German combat planes throughout World War II. And Lindbergh's findings about those various planes found their way into American air intelligence reports to Washington long before the European war began.[21]

His earlier tours of Germany had not provoked much criticism of Lindbergh in the United States. An episode during his 1938 visit, however, became the focal point for controversy and a basis for increasingly vehement criticism of the aviator. That episode involved the presentation to him of a high German medal by Field Marshal Hermann Goering.

# 5/That German Medal

AT 8:30 on Tuesday evening, October 18, 1938, Ambassador Hugh R. Wilson gave a stag dinner at the American Embassy in Berlin in honor of Colonel Charles A. Lindbergh and Field Marshal Hermann Goering. The dinner came only two and one-half weeks after the Munich Conference, at which France's Premier Edouard Daladier and Britain's Prime Minister Neville Chamberlain had sought "peace for our time" through "appeasement" of Hitler's ambitions by yielding Czechoslovakia's Sudetenland to Nazi Germany. It was during that transient moment of increased hope for peace that the Lindberghs were once again visiting Germany. And the Ambassador hoped his dinner might improve his dealings with the number-two man in the leadership of Nazi Germany.

Among the Americans attending, in addition to Wilson and Lindbergh, were Truman Smith, now a Lieutenant Colonel; his Assistant Attaché for Air, Major Arthur Vanaman; the aircraft designer Igor Sikorsky; the Consul General, Raymond Geist; and the Second Secretary of the American Embassy, the Naval Attaché, and the Assistant Naval Attaché for Air. Among the Germans, in addition to Goering, were General Erhard Milch, General Ernst Udet, the aircraft designers Dr. Ernst Heinkel and Dr. Willy Messerschmitt, and the Chief of the Air Research Division of the Air Ministry. Also at the dinner were the Italian and Belgian Ambassadors to Germany.[1]

The corpulent Marshal Goering, wearing a newly designed

41

blue uniform, and his aides arrived last. Ambassador Wilson presented the German leader to his various guests, and he shook hands with each in turn. When they reached Lindbergh, Goering handed him a small red box and spoke to him in German. Consul General Geist translated the remarks. To the surprise of the Americans, Goering had "in the name of the Fuehrer" awarded the aviator the Service Cross of the Order of the German Eagle with the Star, a high German decoration for civilians. Goering said the decoration was for Lindbergh's services to aviation, including his historic solo flight across the Atlantic in 1927. Lindbergh accepted the award, and the guests applauded.

A few hours earlier, the Air Ministry had notified Colonel Smith's office that Goering intended to confer the medal at the dinner. The secretary who took the message, however, failed to deliver it until the next morning. None of the Americans at the dinner knew of the award beforehand. But if they had been informed, they probably would not have changed their conduct significantly. To have refused the medal in that setting would have embarrassed America's Ambassador, offended a top leader in their host country, and worsened German-American relations at a moment when they showed a possibility of improvement.

At dinner, Ambassador Wilson sat at the head of one table and Lindbergh at the head of another. During the meal Lindbergh spent much of the time talking to General Milch about aviation. After dinner he spoke for a time with the Italian Ambassador. Later Goering suggested that he and Lindbergh go into the next room and talk. Ambassador Wilson served briefly as interpreter and then turned that task over to Geist and Smith. In response to Goering's questions, Lindbergh told of his experiences and observations on his tour of the Soviet Union in August, comparing conditions there unfavorably to those in Germany, France, and England. Goering then began talking about Germany's accomplishments and plans in aviation. That was when he first told Lindbergh of the new JU-88, citing figures on its high performance. Until then the Americans had not even known of the existence of that secret new German twin-engine bomber. Lindbergh remained a few minutes after Goering left

the Embassy that evening and then returned with Colonel Smith
to the Military Attaché's apartment.

At the time, neither Lindbergh nor Smith had been upset by
the presentation of the medal. On their arrival at the Smith
apartment, however, both their wives immediately anticipated
its consequences. Mrs. Lindbergh quietly labeled it "the Alba-
tross." Mrs. Smith repeatedly told her husband that the medal
would "surely do Lindbergh much harm."[2]

Newspapers reported the episode, but they did not at first
offer much criticism of Lindbergh for accepting the medal.
Three weeks after the dinner, however, Nazi Germany violently
stepped up its persecution of the Jews. With the growing totalitarian oppression within Germany, with Germany's mounting
threats to peace and security, with the critical reactions in the
United States to those developments, and with Lindbergh's
efforts to discourage war in Europe and his opposition to
American involvement in that war, his acceptance of the medal
came under increasing attack.

Particularly prominent in the attacks on Lindbergh was
Harold L. Ickes, Secretary of the Interior in President Franklin
D. Roosevelt's Cabinet. In an address before a Zionist meeting
in Cleveland, Ohio, a month after the dinner, Ickes berated
Lindbergh for accepting "a decoration at the hands of a brutal
dictator who with that same hand is robbing and torturing
thousands of fellow human beings." Ickes would later repeat his
criticisms of Lindbergh many times, once referring to him in a
public address as a "Knight of the German Eagle." That particular assault, in 1941, finally provoked Lindbergh to defend
himself.[3]

In an open letter to President Roosevelt on July 16, 1941,
Lindbergh wrote that he had "received this decoration in the
American Embassy, in the presence of your Ambassador, and
. . . was there at his request in order to assist in creating a
better relationship between the American Embassy and the
German Government, which your Ambassador desired at that
time." He thought he deserved an apology from the President's
Cabinet member.[4] He never got that apology.

Despite his letter to the President, Lindbergh privately

minimized the importance of the medal episode. He saw "nothing constructive gained by returning decorations which were given in periods of peace and good will. The entire idea seems to me too much like a 'child's spitting contest.' " Believing that "there was no sensible alternative to accepting the decoration under the circumstances in which it was presented," Lindbergh would have taken "exactly the same course again, under those circumstances, even though I were able to foresee all the wartime hysteria and propaganda that lay ahead."[5] Writing ten years after the end of World War II, Lindbergh still insisted that the German decoration had never caused him "any worry," and he doubted that it had caused him "much additional difficulty." He thought his opponents had simply used it as "a convenient object of attack" and that "if there had been no decoration, they would have found something else." Lindbergh never returned the medal. Instead, he gave it, along with his many other decorations, to the Missouri Historical Society in St. Louis.[6]

In his continuing efforts to learn and understand "more about everything German," Colonel Lindbergh seriously considered moving his family to Berlin for part of the winter of 1938–39. He even got so far as preliminary house hunting there. He won high-level help in that effort from the Air Ministry and from Albert Speer, head of city planning for Berlin. Lindbergh consulted Ambassador Wilson on October 25 to determine if he had any objections. The Ambassador had none and thought the move might contribute a "certain amount of good" for German-American relations. He warned, however, that Lindbergh "would probably be attacked in the United States for choosing Germany as a residence." The Ambassador was sufficiently concerned about the growing newspaper assaults on the aviator to ask if he had ever tried to work out a *modus vivendi* with the press. Lindbergh replied that he had tried in the past but had not succeeded. He added (as recorded in the Ambassador's diary) that "as far as attacks on him went he didn't give a damn."[7]

After the Nazis sharply increased their violence against German Jews on November 9, 1938, the Department of State ordered Ambassador Wilson to return to Washington "for consultation." His departure proved to be permanent; the United States never again sent an Ambassador to Nazi Germany. At the same time, press attacks on Lindbergh were becoming increasingly strident—including criticisms for accepting the medal and for thinking of moving to Berlin. In that emotion-laden atmosphere, his friends Colonel Smith and Dr. Carrel both advised him not to make the move. Writing from New York City, Dr. Carrel warned that newspapers had "published misleading articles" about Lindbergh's plan to stay in Berlin and that as a result there was "a great deal of ill feeling" against him. The situation was "serious." He wrote that both Gentiles and Jews were turning against him and illustrated the point by sending Lindbergh a critical item clipped from *The New Yorker*. Dr. Carrel thought it important that Lindbergh not lose his "moral authority" in the United States.[8]

Actually, with the mounting friction between the United States and Germany, Anne and Charles had decided not to move to Berlin. They had, instead, taken an apartment in Paris. Lindbergh regretted the necessity for changing their plans; he had hoped that by living in Germany he "might better understand the German viewpoint on the policies on which we disagree." He believed that Europe was "headed for a devastating war unless some understanding is reached with Germany, and the more difficult it is to have contact with that country, the more difficult an understanding will become. After all, contact does not necessarily mean support."[9]

In a personal handwritten letter to Dr. Carrel, Lindbergh said that his decision to take an apartment in Paris rather than Berlin was "not based on the antagonism of the press." He simply did "not wish to make a move which would seem to support the German actions in regard to the Jews." Also, he did "not wish to cause embarrassment to our government, or to the German government." As for the press attacks, the Colonel insisted that he was "not very much concerned by the stories printed in the newspapers"; he had "neither desire nor respect for a popularity which is dependent on the press." He had, he wrote, "found that it would be necessary to sell my character if I wished to maintain the friendship of modern journalism." He "preferred its enmity." Because of his experiences with newspapers after the baby's kidnapping, he had "not even desired their friendship."[10] Colonel Lindbergh's war with the press in the United States was already raging as the war among the countries of Europe approached ever closer. The American aviator made no effort to avoid his personal contest with newsmen, but he earnestly tried to use his influence to avert what he believed would be a tragic war in Europe.

# 6/Munich

COLONEL LINDBERGH'S determined efforts to see, to learn, and to understand as much as possible about developments, within and among the European states continued. But his interest was not just abstract curiosity, especially as the danger of war grew. He became convinced that a war would be a tragedy for Europe and for Western civilization. Particularly from September, 1938, after his trip to the Soviet Union, until his return to the United States in April, 1939, Lindbergh tried to use his knowledge and influence to discourage war in Europe. Some of those efforts were his own initiatives; some were responses to the initiatives of others. In the process he shuttled frequently between Paris and London, with side trips to Berlin.

Lindbergh believed that after World War I the British and French either should have kept Germany down, so that it could never become powerful enough to challenge them successfully, or they should have sought friendly accommodation as Germany re-established its power and position in Europe and the world. For them to acquiesce clumsily while Germany built its resentments and power, and then belatedly to attempt to restrain Germany after its power had reached formidable levels, seemed to Lindbergh to have been a terrible mistake. He believed the last opportunity England and France had to check Germany effectively without fighting a disastrous war was when Hitler remilitarized the Rhineland in 1936. After that it was too late.[1]

47

# Preparation

Never a pacifist, Colonel Lindbergh urged France, England, and the United States to speed their military and air preparations. He conceded the necessity for war in certain situations, but he saw no merit in fighting an unsuccessful war—even in the name of high principles. By the years 1938–1939 he was convinced that Great Britain and France did not command sufficient power—particularly air power—to beat Germany. Even if they should prove able to triumph after terrible sacrifices, he believed the costs would have been prohibitive. Similarly, he believed that, with the Maginot Line, the French Army, and the British Navy arrayed against it, Germany could not crush the British and French without horrible losses.[2]

In any event, Lindbergh became convinced that a war between Germany, on one side, and Britain and France, on the other, would be a tragedy whichever side won. It would, in his view, be a fratricidal conflict that could destroy the inherited genetic and cultural treasures slowly built by Western civilization over the course of countless centuries. The only beneficiaries, in his opinion, might be the Communists and the Soviet Union. If left to themselves, Lindbergh believed, the Germans under Hitler would turn east toward the Soviet Union, not west toward Britain and France. He did not view such a course with the same misgivings as he did a war in the west. Conceivably a Russo-German conflict would leave the ramparts of Western civilization secure against Communist Russia and the Asiatic hordes.[3]

Given his analysis of the European situation by 1938, Lindbergh urged Britain and France to build their military air power. And he almost pleaded with them to reach an accommodation with Germany in order to prevent war. He found the French receptive but ineffective; he found the English generally smug and unimpressed. Lindbergh was dismayed by many of the German actions at home and abroad, but he saw no viable alternatives for the western nations other than accommodation with Germany.[4] Though he did not use the term, both his emphasis on Germany's overwhelming air superiority and his appeals for accommodation with Hitler's Germany coincided with and may have encouraged appeasement policies at the time.

Colonel Lindbergh's attempts to prevent war included long letters to influential people in Europe and America. They included countless conversations with policy makers in both social and official settings. They even included the use of his "good offices" secretly between officials in different countries. His contacts ranged from old friends in aviation circles to the heads of governments, foreign offices, and air forces. And evidences of his activity found their way into the official diplomatic communications and reports of the United States, Great Britain, France, Germany, and other countries. Not all were impressed by his efforts (especially in England), but many were (particularly in France).

Among others, his contacts in Great Britain included the King and Queen, Prime Ministers Stanley Baldwin and Neville Chamberlain, Foreign Secretary Lord Halifax, former Prime Ministers David Lloyd George and James Ramsay MacDonald, the future Ambassador to the United States Lord Lothian, Minister for the Co-ordination of Defense Sir Thomas Inskip, Air Marshal Hugh Trenchard and other high Air officers, Geoffrey Dawson of the London *Times,* Lord and Lady Astor, and various Members of Parliament. In France he conferred with Premier Edouard Daladier, Minister of Justice Paul Reynaud, Minister of Air Guy La Chambre, the economist Jean Monnet, and many others. In Germany his secret conversations with Generals Milch and Udet were reported up to Goering and Hitler for action decisions. Among Americans he had dealings with Ambassadors William E. Dodd and Hugh R. Wilson in Berlin, Acting Ambassador Alexander Kirk in Moscow, Ambassador William C. Bullitt in Paris, Ambassadors Robert W. Bingham and Joseph P. Kennedy in London, through Kennedy with President Roosevelt and Secretary of State Cordell Hull, through Roosevelt with Army Chief of Staff Malin Craig and Chief of Naval Operations William D. Leahy, with Air Corps Chief General Henry H. Arnold, and with the Military and Air Attachés in Moscow, Berlin, London, Paris, and Spain.

## Preparation

For example, in mid-1936 King Edward VIII invited Anne and Charles to dinner. Prime Minister and Mrs. Stanley Baldwin were also there. When Lindbergh began talking about English aviation developments relative to those on the Continent, the Prime Minister seemed to prefer to change the subject. After Lindbergh's return from his first visit to Germany, Harold Nicolson arranged a small lunch in the Houses of Parliament for Lindbergh with former Prime Minister MacDonald and Sir Thomas Inskip. Lindbergh told them of his observations in Germany. They listened politely, but the only consequence of the conversation was a later invitation for him to speak on navigation to flying cadets at England's Cranwell. He found that a pleasant experience, but it did nothing to convince him that the British were alert to the dangers he saw.[5]

In the spring of 1938, after their return to England from their three-month visit to the United States, Anne and Charles were frequent guests of Lord and Lady Astor at Cliveden, their magnificent country estate, and in their London house. Through the Astors, the Nicolsons, and others, they visited socially with the high and the mighty. For instance, at a luncheon given by Lady Astor on May 5, 1938, they were in the company of George Bernard Shaw, Ambassador Kennedy, Ambassador Bullitt, an editor of the *Times,* and others. On May 17, the Kennedys gave a dinner at the Embassy for Lord and Lady Halifax and invited the Lindberghs. Before dinner Lindbergh talked with British Secretary of State for War Leslie Hore-Belisha and voiced his concern about English aircraft production in comparison with that of the Germans. On May 22, the Lindberghs had tea with Harold Nicolson and his wife; the Colonel's ardent presentation of the German case during the conversation probably did little more than alienate the Englishman. The Astors gave a dinner and ball on May 23 attended by the King and Queen, the Duke and Duchess of Kent, the Lindberghs, and many others. On June 1, the Lindberghs attended a formal ball at Buckingham Palace.[6]

So often in those conversations Colonel Lindbergh found his English listeners polite, complacent, and unimpressed. As he told an America First audience in St. Louis in the middle of 1941, "Time and time again, whenever the opportunity arose, I talked to members of the British government about military aviation in Europe. They were always courteous, but seldom impressed. . . . It is impossible for me to describe to you the feeling of frustration I had in England when I attempted to tell people there what was taking place in the air of Europe."[7]

The Lindbergh family moved to Illiec in June, 1938, and that gave the Colonel opportunities to confer with high aviation, diplomatic, and political leaders in France. On June 23, Lindbergh talked with Ambassador Bullitt and the American Military Attaché at the Embassy in Paris, and later he had lunch with America's Air Attaché to Spain.[8]

When on September 8, 1938, the Lindberghs got back to Paris from their trip to the Soviet Union and Czechoslovakia, Europe was in the midst of its most alarming crisis since World War I. Hitler was demanding the German-populated Sudetenland from Czechoslovakia and threatening to take it by force if necessary. The Soviet Union had urged Czechoslovakia not to yield and offered military assistance. The Soviet leaders were also urging Britain, France, and the League of Nations to resist the German threat. But if Hitler were not bluffing a firm stand by Britain and France would mean war. The probable actions of Germany, Britain, France, and Czechoslovakia depended substantially on their various analyses of the power each side could bring to bear in the situation. The power of the several states would be affected by geography (Hitler's planned move was to the east, where Britain and France could not effectively deploy their ground forces and their fortifications were useless), by national morale and spirit, by military and air preparations, and by the quality (or boldness) of leadership. If German, British, French, and Czech leaders and people became convinced that Britain, France, and the Soviet Union could not successfully check a German military move against Czechoslovakia, or that the costs would be prohibitive, Hitler would be able to add the Sudentenland to Greater Germany without war. That was what happened. And Colonel Lindbergh played a role in the developments of the three weeks before the British and French backed down by yielding the Sudetenland to Nazi Germany at the Munich Conference on September 30, 1938.

It was reasonable to credit Colonel Lindbergh with exceptional knowledge of European air power at that time. He had already made two major visits to study German air power. He had inspected aviation facilities in France, the Soviet Union, and Czechoslovakia. He knew much about British and United States air developments. And he earnestly and repeatedly told almost any who would listen that Germany's air power then was greater than that of all the other European countries combined, that France's was hopelessly inadequate, and that British and Soviet air power was not sufficient to match Germany's. Resistance would result in disaster.

On September 9, 1938, the day after they reached Paris, Ambassador Bullitt invited the Lindberghs to Chantilly, the magnificent estate he had rented near Paris. There Colonel Lindbergh talked at length with French Minister of Air Guy La Chambre. As Lindbergh saw it, the French situation was desperate. France could not catch up with Germany in air power for years, if at all. So far as he could determine, France was building fewer than 50 warplanes per month, while Germany was building 500 to 800 per month. Britain was making about 70 per month. Lindbergh firmly contended that the German air force was "stronger than that of all other European countries combined." He believed that the French "opportunity of stopping the extension of German control to the east passed several years" earlier; an attempt to do so at the present moment would "throw Europe into chaos." He believed the results "would be much worse than the last war and would probably result in a Communist Europe."[9]

Air Minister La Chambre was persuaded that Lindbergh's analysis was essentially correct. He communicated Lindbergh's account to Premier Daladier and Foreign Minister Georges Bonnet. As reported by the British Ambassador in Paris, Bonnet "was very upset and said that peace must be preserved at any price as neither France nor Great Britain were ready for war." Daladier thought Lindbergh's estimate of Soviet air power was too pessimistic, but he was certainly not sanguine about the possibility of war with Germany. The British Military Attaché in Paris, reporting on information supplied by the French Ministry of War, wrote that "the Fuhrer found a most convenient ambassador in Colonel Lindbergh, who appears to have given the French an impression of [German] might and preparedness which they did not have before, and who at the same time confirmed the view that the Russian Air Force was worth almost exactly nothing." The British Attaché reported the statement of a French colonel that France "could not face the risk of the German air threat—since their material was so superior that they (the French) were powerless to deal with it." Aware of Colonel Lindbergh's analysis, the Deputy Chief of the French General Staff on September 22 insisted (as reported by the British Military Attaché) "that French cities would be laid in ruins and that they had no means of defense." The Attaché clearly got "the impression that the French did *not* intend to fight."[10] One should not conclude that the French attitude was shaped solely or even largely by Lindbergh's analysis. But his view was noted seriously, it did circulate at the highest levels, and it did enter into French dealings with Britain during the crisis.

In response to an urgent telegram from Ambassador Kennedy, the Lindberghs went to London on September 20. The next day (after meeting six of the Kennedy children), Lindbergh conferred at length with the Ambassador and his Embassy Counselor, Herschel Johnson, about the European diplomatic crisis and the military and air power situation. On September 22, 1938, Lindbergh wrote a letter to Kennedy summarizing the statements he had made to the Ambassador the day before. Kennedy immediately cabled Lindbergh's document to Secretary of State Cordell Hull in Washington, and he made further reference to the Colonel's views in a telephone conversation with Hull on September 24. In his letter Lindbergh wrote: "Without doubt the German air fleet is now stronger than that of any other country in the world." He was "certain that German air strength is greater than that of all other European countries combined, and that she is constantly increasing her margin of leadership." He thought the United States was "the only country in the world capable of competing with Germany in aviation" but that Germany was "rapidly cutting down the lead we have held in the past." He believed Germany had "the means of destroying London, Paris and Prague if she wishes to do so" and that "England and France together have not enough modern war planes for effective defense or counterattack." Given the German air superiority, Lindbergh thought it "essential to avoid a general European war in the near future at almost any cost." He feared that "a war now might easily result in the loss of European civilization." A general European war, whatever its outcome, would "result in something akin to Communism running over Europe and, judging by Russia, anything seems preferable." He believed it "wiser to permit Germany's eastward expansion than to throw England and France, unprepared, into a war at this time." Whether that Lindbergh report, or summaries of it, reached President Roosevelt is not clear.[11] But the President did make last-minute overtures to urge the continuing of negotiations in Europe.

Ambassador Kennedy also arranged for Colonel Lindbergh to meet with British political and Air Ministry officials in London. On the evening of September 22, Lindbergh spent two hours at dinner with John Slessor of the Air Ministry (later Marshal of the Royal Air Force) and the private secretary of Sir Cyril Newall, Britain's Chief of the Air Staff. At the time Slessor described Lindbergh as "a man of outstanding character" who was "entirely sympathetic to the British, so much so that one occasionally forgot that one was not speaking to an Englishman." He also noted that Lindbergh had "an enormous admiration for the Germans and likes them personally, though he says, of course, that there is much in their policy and methods which he cannot forgive." Lindbergh told Slessor that the "only sound policy" was "to avoid war now at almost any cost." He "spoke with admiration of Mr. Chamberlain and said he felt that he had taken the only possible course." Colonel

Lindbergh described the German Air Force as "incomparably the strongest in the world, and stronger than that of France, the United Kingdom and the United States of America put together." Slessor did not know how much Lindbergh's views may have been "due to German propaganda and carefully staged arrangements to impress him; but it is easy to understand after talking to him, how he was able to impress the French authorities with the formidable nature of the German threat." Lindbergh told Slessor that the German Air Force could "flatten out cities like London, Paris, and Prague." Slessor concluded then that Lindbergh probably was "overestimating" the German capacity "and underestimating their difficulties to some extent, possibly owing to successful propaganda." He wrote later that he had taken some of what Lindbergh said "with a pinch of salt" but that "there was much truth in his story." The next day Lindbergh had lunch with Air Marshal Sir Wilfrid Freeman and also talked with others in the British Air Ministry and in Air Intelligence.[12]

Meanwhile the Lindberghs saw Londoners placing sandbags around doors and windows in anticipation of war; some were digging trenches. Like others, Anne and Charles had themselves fitted with gas masks as a precaution. They spent the night of September 26 at Cliveden, with the Astors, and there listened to a broadcast of Hitler's speech.[13]

Mutual friends arranged for Colonel Lindbergh to meet with David Lloyd George, Britain's Prime Minister at the close of World War I, at the Welshman's home on September 27. Since Lloyd George shared the general foreign policy views of Winston Churchill and Anthony Eden and had no confidence in Prime Minister Chamberlain, he was not likely to be receptive to Lindbergh's views. He believed war unavoidable and wanted to defend the "prestige of democracy." Lindbergh told the old statesman that he "did not see how democratic prestige would gain much from an unsuccessful war" and urged that war should "at least be postponed." When Lloyd George contended that the Nazi system was just as bad as the Soviet system, Lindbergh concluded that the former Prime Minister did not "seem to recognize any difference to England between an alliance with European Germany and Asiatic Russia. He apparently does not worry about the effect of Asia on European civilization." Clearly Lindbergh did.[14]

On the trip back to Cliveden after his fruitless session with Lloyd George, Lindbergh thought Hitler must be "actually mad if he starts a general war under these circumstances. No one can win anything worth having. The best blood of Europe will be dead when it is over." He had difficulty sleeping that night and woke up from time to time "thinking about England being bombed."[15]

With news of the impending Munich Conference between Hitler, Mussolini, Chamberlain, and Daladier, Lindbergh was "very much relieved." But he still wondered "whether England would wake up after the experience she has gone through." He was convinced that "If she does not wake up now, there is no hope." Throughout the crisis, Lindbergh was favorably impressed by Joseph Kennedy's performance and believed that the Ambassador had "taken a large part in bringing about the conference."[16] With Munich, Hitler got the Sudetenland, Chamberlain got "peace for our time," and Lindbergh gained a few more months for his efforts to speed air preparations in Britain, France, and the United States.

# 7/French Failures

A FEW hours before the statesmen concluded their agreement at Munich, Ambassador William C. Bullitt telephoned Colonel Lindbergh asking him to come to Paris from London for a conference at the American Embassy on the morning of September 30. Lindbergh promptly complied. Bullitt even arranged for the airman to stay in the same Embassy room he had had after his transatlantic flight in 1927.

The Colonel quickly learned the purpose of the Ambassador's summons. Bullitt and the French Air Minister, Guy La Chambre, had been wrestling with the problem of building air power so that France would not in the future be in the hopelessly weak position that had seemed to make the Munich appeasement so essential. In their deliberations Bullitt had proposed the building of huge airplane factories for France in Canada near the border of the United States. The arrangement would by-pass the neutrality legislation that prohibited American sale of arms and munitions to belligerents. But it could take advantage of North American production facilities, and locating the factories near Detroit and Buffalo would permit them to draw on the trained labor force in those cities. Bullitt and La Chambre proposed that the project be directed by Jean Monnet, Colonel Lindbergh, and a French air production expert. Bullitt secretly cabled the idea to President Franklin D. Roosevelt, and also got in touch with Monnet and Lindbergh.

The Colonel listened as Bullitt, Monnet, and La Chambre

outlined the plan, but he did not commit himself. He agreed on the necessity for building French and British air strength, of course, but he doubted whether the French had the necessary spirit, morale, and leadership even if military planes could be provided from Canada. The discussions continued on Saturday, October 1. The French also let Lindbergh fly their latest and finest fighter, the Moran 406. On Monday, October 3, Premier Daladier, just back from Munich, entered into the deliberations, which ended the following day. Lindbergh had doubts about the idea, but he returned to Illiec to think about it before meeting once again with Monnet on Sunday, October 9.[1]

In the tranquil setting of his little island, Lindbergh drafted a memorandum summarizing his understanding of the project. And he composed a fourteen-page letter to Monnet outlining the reasons he thought it inadvisable for him to take an active part. Lindbergh believed the plan could produce needed aircraft for France. But, with or without those airplanes, he was convinced that a war with Germany would nevertheless be a disaster, with "something akin to communism over-running Europe." Consequently, he believed "the most important objective" remained "the avoidance of a European war." In his opinion, "Victory itself would be of little value, for it would leave no civilization able to appreciate or take advantage of it." The Colonel regarded "an agreement with Germany as essential to the future of Europe." If Britain and France tried "to keep Germany weak," he could see "little hope of avoiding a disastrous war."

Lindbergh feared that his participation in the project "could succeed only through failure." That is, if Canadian-made planes successfully helped prevent war in Europe, he would be criticized for helping spend French money for planes made in North America that never fought. Only if the planes eventually were used in war against Germany would his participation win approval, but he was convinced that such a war would be a disaster whatever its outcome. He could enter the project only if he were prepared to suffer abuse for his role. The fact that he was an American made him more vulnerable than a Frenchman might be.

He had other objections as well. His personal participation would inevitably bring premature publicity to the project. It would disrupt his family plans and his hopes for further study of Germany and the European situation during the winter of 1938–39.[2]

Jean Monnet did not like Lindbergh's letter and tried unsuccessfully to persuade him to withdraw it. But the Frenchman concurred with Lindbergh's decision not to participate. A few days later Monnet sailed for America. While in the United States he hoped to explore the idea further, and Lindbergh had suggested the names of airplane manufacturers he might consult. But the whole idea fizzled out and came to nothing.[3] France bought some military airplanes in the United States. But they did not prevent war in 1939. And they did not save France from defeat when Hitler turned his blitzkrieg west in the spring and early summer of 1940.

Two days after his final session on the matter with Monnet, the Lindberghs' third major visit to Germany began. The Colonel's observations during that trip, which lasted from October 11 to 29, 1938, further strengthened the convictions he had advanced repeatedly before. On November 2, he wrote to General Henry H. Arnold, Chief of the United States Army Air Corps, urging him to visit Germany in the near future to observe developments there. Arnold promptly replied that he had wanted to make such a trip to Germany three months earlier, "but for diplomatic reasons it was called off." Lindbergh's letter led Arnold to take up the matter again with the Chief of Staff and Secretary of War, but "the political situation" made the trip inadvisable. After the anti-Jewish violence erupted in Germany on November 9, Lindbergh agreed that it was "not an opportune time to send a mission to Germany."[4]

The deliberations in Paris on the "Canadian Plan" produced another scheme, which brought Colonel Lindbergh back to Berlin for two brief visits in December and January. In the course of his sessions with Bullitt, Monnet, La Chambre, and Daladier, Lindbergh had suggested that France might buy military airplanes from Germany. The idea produced shock and laughter initially, but Lindbergh was serious. And Daladier was not so startled by the thought as some of the others. On his return to Paris from Berlin at the end of October, Lindbergh again discussed the idea with La Chambre. The Air Minister suggested that, instead of entire planes, just the aircraft engines might be purchased from Germany. Lindbergh offered to help investigate the possibilities of such a purchase.

After Lindbergh moved his family from Illiec to an apartment in Paris for the winter of 1938–39, La Chambre asked if he could find out unofficially whether the Germans would be willing to sell airplane engines to France. Bad flying weather had compelled the Lindberghs to leave their plane in Berlin on their departure from Germany at the end of October; the need to return for the plane provided a convenient cover for that secret mission in the middle of December. Even Colonel Smith was not to know the purpose of the visit. Lindbergh explained the proposal to Generals Milch and Udet. Though France wanted the engines, Lindbergh told Udet, "the policy was more important than the actual value of the engines and . . . it might be used as a step toward a closer relationship between the two countries." The matter had to be referred to Goering and possibly to Hitler for decision, and both were away at the time. Consequently Lindbergh returned to spend Christmas with his wife and sons in Paris. The Luftwaffe Generals promised to notify him as soon as they learned the reactions of Goering and Hitler to the idea. Bad weather again kept his airplane in Berlin, providing an excuse for an additional trip there.[5]

When word arrived from Germany, Lindbergh returned to Berlin on January 16, 1939. It proved to be his last visit to Germany until the close of World War II, in 1945. Milch and Udet had obtained authority from Goering and Hitler to sell 300 airplane engines to France under certain conditions—including secrecy, payment in currency instead of goods, the engines to be delivered about December, 1939, or January, 1940. Lindbergh (this time flying his plane) returned to Paris from Berlin with the information. The French government made plans for going ahead with the transaction. In the process La Chambre and Daladier informed Ambassador Bullitt of the scheme—explaining that they liked the idea less for the value of the engines than for "the improvement that might be produced by such an order in the diplomatic relations between France and Germany, and because the news of such a deal would tend to make the Italians less sure of German support."

Before going ahead, however, Premier Daladier wanted to know from President Roosevelt whether the purchase of the engines "would produce an unfortunate effect on public opinion in the United States." Bullitt had misgivings about the project and did not believe that "there is any real approach by Germany toward friendship with France." In March, the Ambassador informed La Chambre that President Roosevelt could not predict the effect of the purchase on American opinion. The same month, Hitler, in violation of his promises at Munich, took over the rest of Czechoslovakia. President Roosevelt's noncommittal response and Hitler's renewed expansion killed the whole idea.[6]

By April, 1939, Colonel Lindbergh believed that "the atmosphere of war" was "constantly growing" and that it would "only take an incident or two to start trouble."[7] With Europe soon to be inflamed by war, Lindbergh returned to the United States. That voyage ended his self-imposed exile abroad and inaugurated new phases of his prewar and antiwar activities.

# II

"The Truth
Without Prejudice
and Without Passion"

# 8/Home Again

WHEN the liner *Aquitania* eased from the harbor at Cherbourg, France, that spring day of April 8, 1939, it carried a full load of passengers. Many were refugees. Among the passengers was Colonel Charles A. Lindbergh, returning home to the United States after living for nearly three and one-half years in England and France. The Old World had provided him, his wife, and their children a degree of privacy, personal security, and freedom from newsmen that their native America had denied them. It had also provided the aviator with unique opportunities to observe closely the mounting storm clouds of war. The conflagration that he feared would destroy Western civilization was drawing inexorably closer.

Lindbergh dreaded the barbarism of newsmen, press photographers, and curiosity seekers that he was certain to encounter in the United States; he worried about the safety of his wife and sons if he brought them back to America. But they had been away a long time. And if war erupted, their place was in America. Their plans for the future were not firm; if circumstances abroad improved, he would return to Europe. But they did not improve. And Lindbergh saw his responsibilities to be in the United States. His wife and sons followed later in April. They stayed briefly at her family's home in New Jersey before locating at Lloyd Neck, Long Island.[1]

Circumstances were to bar Lindbergh's return to Europe for more than six years, until after the nightmare of World War II there had ended. During those years he served his country in various ways. Some of that service before and during the war was to be in the familiar patterns of aviation and flying. But part of it was to be in the unfamiliar (and, for him, the much less pleasant) arena of political action as he earnestly tried to persuade Americans that the United States should not and need not become involved in the European war. Lindbergh saw his noninterventionist effort as patriotic service to his country. But it proved to be more traumatic than any Lindbergh experience before or later, save only the unspeakable ordeal of the kidnapping and murder of their first-born. It was far more damaging to his image and reputation than any other part of his career. But Lindbergh had as much courage in public affairs as he had always had in the skies. And he proved ready to pay the price exacted by a cause that he believed to be paramount in the years 1939–1941.

As usual, scores of newsmen and photographers swarmed on Colonel Lindbergh when he left the ship in New York, pushing, shoving, shouting, falling over each other, and exploding flash bulbs in his face. Dozens of uniformed police and plainclothesmen formed a wedge so he might get through. Even then his party, including Dr. and Mme Carrel, was separated from him by the mob. Lindbergh thought it "a ridiculous situation when one cannot return to one's own country without having to go through the roughhousing of photographers and the lies and insults of the press." For him it took "the sweetness from the freedom of democracy and makes one wonder where freedom ends and disorder begins." It was, as he wrote in his diary, "a barbaric entry to a civilized country." Mrs. Lindbergh and their sons went through a similar ordeal when they arrived two weeks later. Newsmen, photographers, curiosity seekers, and crackpots hounded them wherever they went, much as they had four years before; police and guards were almost as necessary in 1939 as they had been in 1935. Understandably, Lindbergh missed "the privacy and decency of Europe."[2]

Others greeted Lindbergh's return with more civilized and responsible approaches. While he was still at sea, he received a radiogram from Congressman Sol Bloom, Democratic Chairman of the House Committee on Foreign Affairs, inviting him to testify on the neutrality legislation it had under consideration (after deliberation, Lindbergh respectfully declined). A communication invited him to attend a forthcoming meeting of the National Advisory Committee for Aeronautics, of which he was a long-time member (and he accepted). A radiogram from General Henry H. Arnold asked Lindbergh to contact him as soon as he could after reaching the United States. The Colonel immediately radioed an acknowledgment. He telephoned the Air Corps Chief the night of his arrival and made an appointment to meet him at West Point the next day, Saturday, April 15, 1939.

To avoid the newsmen who had bedeviled him the night before, Lindbergh had lunch alone with General and Mrs. Arnold in the main dining room of the Thayer Hotel at West Point, which had been cleared and closed to the public to guard their privacy. For some three hours the two military aviators discussed air preparations in Europe and America. When waiters restlessly indicated their need to prepare the room for the evening meal, the three adjourned to the grandstand of the Military Academy's baseball field, where Army was playing Syracuse. There, in the midst of spirited cadets, Lindbergh continued briefing Arnold on Hitler's Luftwaffe. Seated in front of them was a row of reporters from New York newspapers, totally unaware that their prey was behind them. General Arnold later wrote that Lindbergh gave him "the most accurate picture of the Luftwaffe, its equipment, leaders, apparent plans, training methods, and present defects" he had received up to that time.[3]

The Air Corps Chief asked Colonel Lindbergh to go on active duty with the Air Corps to study aeronautical research facilities and to make recommendations for improving those facilities and using them in the development of American air power. Arnold specifically asked him to take into account the comparable developments in foreign military aviation. Lindbergh promptly accepted; on April 18, General Arnold issued the formal order activating him. Officially Lindbergh was on active duty for only two weeks, but from May until September, 1939, he continued to perform the same function, without pay, on an "inactive-active status." The Air Corps assigned him a P-36A fighter for his use in flying to aviation research, development, and manufacturing facilities all over the United States in the performance of his duties. In connection with this work, he served on various committees, most notably on the board headed by Brigadier General Walter G. Kilner to propose priorities for Air Corps research and development programs during the period 1939–1944. In some degree reflecting Lindbergh's influence, the Kilner Board's final report gave high priority to the development of powerful liquid-cooled aircraft engines and to superior fighter planes comparable to Britain's Spitfire and Germany's ME-109. Arnold found the value of the Board's work to be "inestimable."[4]

On April 20, after going on active duty with the Air Corps, Colonel Lindbergh had his only meeting with President Franklin D. Roosevelt. The appointment was arranged by Lindbergh's cousin and friend Admiral "Jerry" Land, Chairman of the United States Maritime Commission. During their fifteen-minute visit at the White House, Lindbergh found the President likable and an interesting conversationalist, but "there was something about him" that he "did not trust, something a little too suave, too pleasant, too easy." He saw Roosevelt as "mostly politician" and thought the two of them "would never get along on many fundamentals." He resolved to work with the President as long as he could, but had "a feeling that it may not be for long." Many years later, Lindbergh recalled that the experience was like talking to a person wearing a mask.[5]

On May 17, at General Arnold's request, Lindbergh testified before the House of Representatives Appropriations Committee on behalf of funds for the Air Corps in general and aviation research programs in particular. He said the United States had lost its lead in military aviation and urged that it "push ahead" as fast as possible. He testified that Germany had "greater research facilities than any other country in Europe" and "several times as much in the way of basic research facilities" as the United States had at the time. Because it was protected by geography from direct assaults by unfriendly states, he urged that the United States give priority to the development of high-quality military aircraft, rather than to the accumulation of huge numbers of airplanes.[6]

In addition to his activities for the Air Corps, Lindbergh also devoted much time to the National Advisory Committee for Aeronautics. As with the Air Corps, his work for NACA focused particularly on aviation research and development programs. He served as chairman of a major committee dealing with NACA and university aeronautical research facilities. He testified before the House Appropriations Committee on behalf of funds for NACA research programs. He drafted his committee's report recommending that new NACA laboratories be located at Moffett Field, near Sunnyvale, California. Both NACA and the Air Corps valued his work and sought his continued help.[7] Important as his duties with them were, however, other less congenial responsibilities beckoned that seemed to him even more important.

# 9/The Battle Begins

DURING the summer of 1939 Colonel Lindbergh focused most of his time and energies on Air Corps and NACA matters. But his concerns about developments in Europe continued, and tensions abroad steadily mounted. Hitler increased his pressures to get the Polish Corridor for Nazi Germany. Britain and France firmed up their commitments to Poland and determined to yield no further to Hitler's demands. War seemed increasingly imminent. Consequently, in the latter part of August, Lindbergh's attention returned more and more to the dangers of war in Europe, to America's policies toward such a war, and to deciding his own course in the event of a European war.

Conversations with friends and associates often centered on those worrisome matters. He talked with Dr. and Mme Carrel and with Colonel Truman Smith, who was now back in the United States. He conferred with the conservative Democratic United States Senator from Virginia, Harry Byrd, whom he had known for years through their common friendship with Harry Guggenheim. Technical dealings with people in the Air Corps and the aviation industry spilled over into discussions of international affairs. And, as always, he particularly valued quiet, thoughtful talks with Anne.

William R. Castle played a role in the beginning of Lindbergh's battle against intervention in World War II. Castle, born in Hawaii and with long associations with Harvard University, had served prominently in the Department of State after World

War I. He was Chief of the State Department's Division of Western European Affairs during the administrations of Warren G. Harding and Calvin Coolidge. He was United States Ambassador to Japan briefly in 1930 and served as Under Secretary of State during the last two years of Herbert Hoover's administration. A conservative, devoted to Hoover, and strongly Republican politically, Castle had jaundiced views of Franklin D. Roosevelt's Democratic administration on both domestic and foreign affairs. He actively served the Republican National Committee on foreign policy matters in the 1930's. Lindbergh had known him since Castle helped Anne and Charles with diplomatic arrangements for their flight to the Orient in 1931. Early in 1939, Castle and Lindbergh had exchanged letters on European developments. When the Colonel returned to America in April, Castle invited him to stay in his home whenever he was in Washington, and wanted very much to discuss "the European situation" with him.[1]

Lindbergh had dinner with the Castles in mid-July. In the course of their conversation, Lindbergh wondered if it might not be wise, should war erupt, to have a small group ready to become active in opposition to American entry into any European conflagration. Castle wanted to follow up on the idea and proposed bringing Fulton Lewis, Jr., into their discussions. Lewis was a conservative radio commentator whose broadcasts were carried regularly by the Mutual Broadcasting System. Lindbergh's aviation duties were absorbing his energies at the time, but Castle renewed the suggestion a short while later.[2]

On August 23, with the probability of war in Europe increasing, the Colonel had dinner with Castle and Lewis. In the course of their conversation, Castle suggested that Lindbergh speak out against American involvement in any European war. Fulton Lewis offered to make arrangements for the network broadcast of such an address. Lindbergh fully shared the conviction of the other two men that the United States should not enter a European war, but he was reluctant to take on the role of a spokesman. He had disliked politics ever since observing his father's political career a quarter of a century before. Noninterventionist speeches would thrust him into the limelight again, and he had already had more of newsmen and publicity than he wanted.[3]

Nonetheless, he thought seriously about what part he should play. He turned the P-36 he had been using back to the Air Corps and began commuting by train between New York and Washington. It gave him "a greater independence of action than before." (To avoid attracting attention, he sometimes wore horn-rimmed glasses without lenses.) "Constantly thinking about war," he wondered whether anything he "could say in a radio address would be of constructive value, even in a minute way." He worried that events may "have gone too far on the other side for words to have any effect. Better not to speak at all in that case."[4]

On September 1, 1939, Hitler's military forces attacked Poland in eastern Europe, and two days later Britain and France responded by declaring war on Germany. The European war was a reality. Lindbergh was shocked by the whole business. If Britain and France "wanted to fight a German eastward movement, why in heaven's name pick this particular set of circumstances to fight over? They are in a hopeless position militarily." He was convinced that if the Allies tried "to break the German Western Wall," they would lose, "unless America enters the war." If the United States entered, Europe would be "still more prostrated" after the war ended. And he feared the consequences in America by that time. "The future of the human world hangs in the balance today. This war will change all of our lives."[5] It certainly changed his!

By September 7, he had prepared rough drafts of an article and two speeches but was not satisfied with them. He wrote in his private journal that day: "I do not intend to stand by and see this country pushed into war if it is not absolutely essential to the future welfare of the nation. Much as I dislike taking part in politics and public life, I intend to do so if necessary to stop the trend which is now going on in this country." On Sunday, September 10, he telephoned Castle and Lewis, and reached the decision to make a radio broadcast the following week. Fulton

Lewis, Jr., made arrangements for the Mutual Broadcasting System to carry the address live on Friday evening, September 15, 1939. The National Broadcasting System and the Columbia Broadcasting System also carried it, providing full national coverage.[6]

During the days before that first noninterventionist broadcast, Lindbergh worked at drafting his speech and also continued his duties with the Air Corps and NACA. On Thursday, September 14, the day before the broadcast, he told General Arnold of his intention to speak out, though Arnold already knew (and may have privately shared) Lindbergh's general view on the subject. The two officers agreed that Lindbergh should discontinue his "inactive-active" status with the Air Corps, but Lindbergh offered to help in the future if the General wished. The Colonel let Arnold read the draft of his radio address, and the General saw nothing improper in it so far as Lindbergh's connection with the Air Corps was concerned. Lindbergh did not, however, permit Secretary of War Harry Woodring (or anyone else in the Roosevelt administration) to see the speech before the broadcast. His noninterventionist activities never diminished the friendship and mutual respect that he and Arnold had for each other. Secretary Woodring (though a noninterventionist himself) was displeased when he learned that Lindbergh planned to speak. He would have prevented it if he could.[7]

Colonel Lindbergh spent Friday morning, September 15, at a long meeting of the National Advisory Committee for Aeronautics. In the early afternoon he returned to his Washington apartment for lunch with Anne and Fulton Lewis. Later, he closeted himself with Truman Smith, who had been trying to reach him all day. Smith, it turned out, was the unenthusiastic errand boy for an administration attempt to "buy off" Lindbergh with the promise of a high government position. The offer came through Secretary of War Woodring to General Arnold and through Arnold to Smith (though neither Arnold nor Smith expected Lindbergh to accept). The proposal, as it reached Lindbergh from Colonel Smith that afternoon, was that if he would cancel his radio address and not publicly oppose the administration's foreign policies, the position of Secretary of Air in the President's Cabinet would be created and Lindbergh appointed to fill it. Lindbergh, of course, did not accept the "offer," but the episode further increased his misgivings about the Roosevelt administration.[8]

Castle had suggested that he and newsman Frank Kent look over Lindbergh's speech before he delivered it to assure its effectiveness, but Lindbergh did not turn to them. It was his practice to write all of his own noninterventionist speeches and articles, and he spent much time in their preparation. Anne had read that first address carefully in advance and had suggested improvements; she did so with most of his speeches and articles. Arnold, Truman Smith, and Fulton Lewis saw the draft in final form.[9]

At 9:45 that evening, standing before six microphones in a small room in the Carlton Hotel in Washington, D.C., Colonel Lindbergh broadcast his speech on "America and European Wars." He spoke without great oratorical flourishes, in a clipped, even-paced, slightly nasal tone. The three networks carried the address nationwide. After listening to a rebroadcast later that evening at the Lewis home, Anne and Charles took a late train for New York.[10] His battle against intervention was formally launched; it did not end until the Japanese attack on Pearl Harbor brought the United States into World War II twenty-seven months later.

Many newspapers and commentators criticized the speech (interventionist Dorothy Thompson portrayed him as the pro-Nazi recipient of a German medal), and he received abusive mail. Lindbergh himself was not satisfied with his delivery. But the address also won much editorial praise and thousands of laudatory letters. Among those, General Arnold sent a brief note telling the Colonel that Secretary Woodring (and he) thought the address "was very well worded and very well delivered."[11]

Other noninterventionists were encouraged by the aviator's action and hoped he might serve a leadership role in unifying and strengthening the movement to keep the United States out

74

of World War II. For example, former President Herbert Hoover wrote congratulating him for his "really great address." On Hoover's initiative, the two met at the Waldorf-Astoria Hotel in New York City on September 21 to discuss foreign policy and the possibility of organizing a nonpolitical committee to keep the country out of war. (Lindbergh was skeptical and Hoover optimistic about the utility of committees.) Through Hoover and Castle, the Colonel later met other leading Republicans and noninterventionists. He thought them able and responsible, but too conservative, too political, and not the caliber of leader that America required. Senator Byrd arranged for Lindbergh to meet some of his Senate colleagues, including Walter George of Georgia and Hiram W. Johnson, an old progressive and isolationist from California. Lindbergh also visited at length with the aging Senator William E. Borah of Idaho, a noninterventionist and the ranking Republican on the Foreign Relations Committee. The two men (both proudly independent) liked and respected each other immediately, and lunched together again later. Borah startled Lindbergh with the suggestion that the aviator would make a good candidate for President—neither the first nor the last time that idea would be broached, and neither the first nor the last time Lindbergh would reject it.[12]

The responses of noninterventionists encouraged Lindbergh to continue his active opposition to American involvement in the European war. The swift and terrifying military successes of Germany's blitzkrieg in Poland, the ineffectiveness of British and French military efforts, and the spirited controversy in the United States over revision of neutrality legislation also encouraged his further efforts. Speaking on "Neutrality and War," he made his second nationwide noninterventionist broadcast on Friday evening, October 13, 1939. As he correctly anticipated, it provoked more criticism than the first speech. But he thought it "desirable to get people thinking about fundamental problems," and he considered the resulting criticisms to be "of very secondary importance."[13]

In November, 1939, *Reader's Digest* published his controversial article "Aviation, Geography, and Race." *Reader's Digest* also carried Anne Lindbergh's "Prayer for Peace," in its January, 1940, issue. The Colonel's "What Substitute for War?" was in the March, 1940, issue of *Atlantic Monthly*. On May 19, 1940, as Hitler's blitzkrieg was smashing British and French military resistance in western Europe, Colonel Lindbergh made a major radio address on "The Air Defense of America." In the middle of June, just before the French surrender and when the American political parties were preparing their platforms and planning to choose their presidential candidates, Lindbergh broadcast on "Our Drift Toward War." In August, in Chicago, he addressed his first major public rally. In October, in the midst of the American presidential campaign and while the Battle of Britain was raging in the skies over England, he broadcast "A Plea for American Independence." That same month he addressed a meeting at Yale University organized by Kingman Brewster, Jr., who would later be President of the University, and other students. Anne's controversial little book, *The Wave of the Future,* was published in October, and in December she broadcast an appeal for "Relief in Europe."

Early in 1941, Colonel Lindbergh testified against the Roosevelt administration's lend-lease bill before both the House Committee on Foreign Affairs and the Senate Committee on Foreign Relations. And in March, 1941, after enactment of lend-lease, *Collier's* published his "A Letter to Americans."[14]

Thus during the first year and a half of World War II in Europe, *before* he joined the America First Committee, Colonel Charles A. Lindbergh had already made five nationwide radio broadcasts, addressed two public meetings, published three articles in popular national magazines, testified before two major legislative committees, and consulted with numerous noninterventionist leaders. Countless millions of Americans had heard him on the radio, had read his articles, had read newspaper accounts of his speeches, or had heard or read endorsements or criticisms of him and his views. He had become the most praised, the most damned, the most controversial, and the most tenaciously independent of the major opponents of the Roosevelt administration's policies toward the European war.

Each of his speeches and articles had its own distinctive emphases. However, certain themes and patterns of thought recurred again and again in his writing and public statements. So far as he was able, Colonel Lindbergh told "the truth without prejudice and without passion."

# 10/The European War and Western Civilization

DRAWING on his experiences and observations during some four or five years abroad in Europe, Asia, Africa, and Latin America, Charles A. Lindbergh provided Americans with a portrait of the European war that differed substantially from the one conceived by the Roosevelt administration and by so-called interventionists in the United States. He did not see the conflict as basically a war for democracy or morality. He was skeptical of the ideological and moral righteousness of the British and French. He conceived of morality in international affairs as relative to time, place, circumstances, and power. His approach was, in effect, more understanding of the Germans (without approving of what they did) and more skeptical of the Allies than the conventional view in the United States. Lindbergh saw a divided responsibility for the origins of the European war, rather than an assignment of the total blame to Hitler, Nazi Germany, and the Axis states. He did not view Germany, Britain, and France as implacable foes with irreconcilable differences that could be resolved only by war; he saw them all as parts of Western civilization. And he conceived of the European war as a fratricidal struggle (like the wars between Athens and Sparta in ancient Greece) that could destroy Western civilization. Conceptions of race were conspicuous in his analyses, as were his concerns about the challenge of Asiatic hordes to the survival of Western civilization. Like later American "realists," Colonel Lindbergh attached great weight to the role of power in international relations and in prevailing definitions of morality.

In his second noninterventionist broadcast Lindbergh said he did not believe that the conflict abroad was "a war for democracy." Instead, he saw it as "a war over the balance of power in Europe—a war brought about by the desire for strength on the part of Germany and the fear of strength on the part of England and France." And he thought that the longer the war lasted and the more destructive it became, the less hope there was for democracy.[1]

In his *Atlantic Monthly* article, published early in 1940, Lindbergh contended that neither side in Europe had "a monopoly of right—except the kind of right which is judged by its own particular and rather momentary standards." He saw the war as "a continuation of the old struggle among western nations for the material benefits of the world." "The ideologies of the opposing sides are," he wrote, "but in keeping with the conditions in the countries they represent." That is, Britain and France embraced ideologies "that come with luxury, and stable times, and the desire to enjoy rather than to acquire." In contrast, Germany had a political system and ideology that sprang from its recent "great hardships and chaotic times" and involved "rigid discipline and the subordinating of individual freedom to the strength of a recuperating state—a state whose people must acquire before they can enjoy." Both sides were "fighting for a right"—that is, "the right of conquest against the right of possession." Lindbergh wrote: "Measured by their own standards of today, or by their enemy's standards of yesterday and tomorrow, the Germans are as much in the right as the English and French, for right is not an absolute quality; it is relative to outlook, and outlook changes with conditions— varies from year to year, and from generation to generation." He did not think the "vital need" was "to decide who is at fault in the war in Europe, or to criticize the vacillating policies that caused it, or to argue over our concepts of right or wrong."[2] Speaking in Chicago in 1940, six weeks after the fall of France, Lindbergh insisted that nothing was to be gained "by shouting names and pointing the finger of blame across the ocean." He said: "Our accusations of aggression and barbarism on the part of Germany, simply bring back echoes of hypocrisy and Versailles."[3]

The European war was, as Lindbergh saw it, a war among states within Western civilization, a war between members of the "white races." Such a war could destroy the heritage of centuries and open the floodgates to Asiatic challenges from the Russian border. In a much-quoted statement in his first noninterventionist broadcast, Colonel Lindbergh said: "These wars in Europe are not wars in which our civilization is defending itself against some Asiatic intruder. There is no Genghis Khan or Xerxes marching against our Western nations. This is not a question of banding together to defend the White race against foreign invasions. This is simply one more of those age old quarrels within our own family of nations—a quarrel arising from the errors of the last war—from the failure of the victors of that war to follow a consistent policy either of fairness or of force."[4] In his *Reader's Digest* article two months later, he saw it as "a war within our own family of nations, a war which will reduce the strength and destroy the treasures of the White race, a war which may even lead to the end of our civilization." He thought it essential "to turn from our quarrels and to build our White ramparts again." He believed Western civilization depended "on a united strength among ourselves" and on "a Western Wall of race and arms which can hold back either a Genghis Khan or the infiltration of inferior blood; on an English fleet, a German air force, a French army, an American nation, standing together as guardians of our common heritage, sharing strength, dividing influence." He believed that Germany was just as essential as England and France to that effort, for Germany alone could "either dam the Asiatic hordes or form the spearhead of their penetration into Europe." The flyer also considered aviation "a tool specially shaped for Western hands" and "another barrier between the teeming millions of Asia and the Grecian inheritance of Europe—one of those priceless possessions which permits the White race to live at all in a pressing sea of Yellow, Black, and Brown." Western civilization should "not commit racial suicide by internal conflict. We must learn from Athens and Sparta before all of Greece is lost." He insisted that America's "bond with Europe is a bond of race and not of political ideology." If the white race were "ever seriously threatened, it may then be time for us to take our part in its protection, to fight side by side with the English, French, and Germans, but not with one against the other for our mutual destruction." He was convinced that neither the United States nor Western civilization would "gain by a continuation of this struggle in Europe." In all that line of reasoning, Lindbergh saw the Soviet Union as an Asian power.[5]

Writing more than thirty years later, Charles A. Lindbergh explained his racial views in the following terms: "I think race is an important and valuable quality, and that our world would be a much poorer place to live on if its various races did not exist. I think a man should be proud of his race or of his mixture of races. Certainly I am. I would like to see racial pride encouraged, but also the freedom of mixture between races according to individual desire. In my opinion, we should encourage racial differences, but discourage racial prejudices. As to superiority, I think that can be claimed validly only in relation to the framework of the race claiming it (as a carpenter is superior to a bricklayer in the field of carpentry). It seems to me that the average intellectual superiority of the white race, for instance, is countered by the sensate superiority of the black race. Even though I was born and live in the framework of the white race, I believe it is quite possible that the black race will achieve a better balance of life eventually. I believe that each race must protect its own security territorially and otherwise, and that it would be unfortunate for mankind if any race obtained too great predominance. This does not mean that I believe the status quo should always be, or can always be maintained. It goes without saying that no pure race exists. Nevertheless racial differences are obvious. As H. A. L. Fisher wrote, 'We know a European when we see one.' I become more and more doubtful that the superiority in science and technol-

**81**

ogy of European man is leading him to a better life than that achieved by other peoples." In another letter, General Lindbergh wrote that "certain races have demonstrated superior ability in the design, manufacture, and operation of machines." He had in mind particularly the North Americans, British, Germans, Dutch, and Swedes. "The growth of our western civilization has been closely related to this superiority. Whether or not it will eventually be advantageous to our peoples is yet to be shown."[6]

Speaking to the American people in September, 1939, Lindbergh contended that if World War II brought "more Dark Ages to Europe," the United States might better serve the Western heritage by staying out of the war than by getting in. "The German genius for science and organization, the English genius for government and commerce, the French genius for living and the understanding of life—they must not go down here as well as on the other side. Here in America they can be blended to form the greatest genius of all."[7]

As he moved from the general to the specific in his analysis of the European war, Colonel Lindbergh told Americans essentially what he had previously told the British, French, and American officials in private, before he left Europe. He said that air power worked to Germany's advantage in Europe, that it worked to the disadvantage of Great Britain, that German air power greatly surpassed that of other European countries, that Germany's expansionist ambitions appeared to lie to the east in Europe, that Britain and France were not militarily capable of defeating Germany, and that the proper course for them was accommodation or a negotiated settlement in Europe. At the time of Munich, he said, England and France should have divided "European influence with Germany along the Siegfried and Maginot Lines."[8]

The first year of World War II in Europe seemed to confirm the accuracy of Lindbergh's analysis. Germany's blitzkrieg quickly crushed Poland in the early fall of 1939. Britain and France were not able to provide effective military assistance to their eastern European ally. Though the Soviet Union eventually triumphed, Finland's early military successes and the Soviet Union's difficulties in downing its small neighbor in the Winter War of 1939–1940 seemed to sustain Lindbergh's unfavorable impressions of Soviet military strength. And in the spring and early summer of 1940, Nazi Germany's blitzkrieg quickly over-ran Denmark, conquered Norway, swept through the Low Countries of Holland and Belgium, drove British forces off the European continent at Dunkirk, and forced the French sur-render on June 22, 1940. Germany's mechanized land forces, effectively supported by the Luftwaffe's terrifying tactical air power, had swept away all military resistance in central and western Europe. With Fascist Italy under Benito Mussolini sharing in the final defeat of France, and with Spain under the dictatorship of Generalissimo Francisco Franco, fascists con-trolled central and western Europe. Only the Soviet Union in eastern Europe and Great Britain on its island redoubt offered any hope of effective resistance in Europe to the Nazi jugger-naut. But the Soviet Union had been neutralized by the Nazi-Soviet Pact of August, 1939, and its performance in the Russo-Finnish War provided little cause to believe that its forces could defeat Nazi Germany. After Britain's evacuation of its troops from the European continent at Dunkirk, its capacity to survive an all-out German assault was in doubt.

Not until the Battle of Britain, in the fall of 1940, were the armed forces of any country able to demonstrate in combat that Nazi Germany was anything less than invincible militarily. Winston Churchill provided Great Britain with the courageously inspiring leadership it needed to resist assaults from the air and the sea. German bombers wrought terrible damage on English bases, ports, and cities. But Royal Air Force Hurricane and Spitfire fighters inflicted heavy losses on the Luftwaffe and successfully denied Germany control of the air over Britain. The German air power that had been so terrifyingly successful against the comparatively small and obsolete air forces it en-countered on the Continent proved less effective against RAF fighters. Goering and his top Luftwaffe officers provided less able direction of the strategic air war against Britain than they had given the tactical operations against continental adversaries. For the first time, Hitler's expansion was checked successfully by force. Whether Britain would be able to survive prolonged assaults in the future remained to be seen. And whether the British would be able to defeat Nazi Germany on the European continent was open to question.

Neither in his public addresses and articles nor in his private letters and journals did Colonel Lindbergh comment much about the Battle of Britain. In a personal letter in October, 1940, he doubted the capacity of the English people to "stand the present strain indefinitely." If Germany were not "seriously hampered by a shortage of food or raw material," Lindbergh thought, "England would be forced to meet German terms eventually, even without an actual invasion." In that same letter, he wrote that America's "encouragement of England and France, both in bringing and carrying on the present war," had "complicated the re-adjustment that had to take place in Europe." In another letter, written a month later, Lindbergh pointed out that "the relative vulnerability of London and their industrial areas, and the numerical superiority of the German Air Force," worked against the British. To Britain's advantage, however, was "the fact that most of the fighting is over British soil and all German planes and crews brought down are lost, whereas many of the British crews shot down escape with their lives and sometimes even without serious damage to their machines." Writing many years later, Lindbergh insisted that the outcome of the Battle of Britain did not conflict with his analysis of air power in Europe. "The German Luftwaffe had not been organized for the purpose of attacking England. No serious attempt at the invasion of England was ever made." In any event, the Battle of Britain did not change Lindbergh's conviction that the European war was a terrible mistake, which should be ended quickly by a negotiated settlement. And it did not, in the slightest, alter his determined opposition to American involvement in the European war.[9]

By early 1941, Britain had prevailed in the Battle of Britain and was bracing for the long haul in its struggle with Nazi

Germany. In his testimony against lend-lease before the House Committee on Foreign Affairs in January, 1941, Colonel Lindbergh contended that aviation strengthened American defenses but made more difficult any attempt to invade Europe. As he saw it, "aviation decreases the security of nations within a continent against each other, but increases the security of the continent as a whole against foreign invasion."[10]

Over and over again, in public addresses during 1941, Lindbergh emphasized that he "never wanted Germany to win this war." Repeatedly he said it would "be a tragedy to the entire world if the British Empire collapses." But just as often he insisted that "England and France were never in a position to win this war." Even if a British victory were possible, he thought it would require years of fighting and the loss of millions of lives, and "would create prostration, famine, and disease in Europe—and probably in America—such as the world has never experienced before." He thought the consequences would be "the downfall of all European civilization, and the establishment of conditions in our own country far worse even than those in Germany today." There could be no real winners of such a war, he feared, "except Russia and Japan." Believing that, Lindbergh charged that those who had urged Britain and France to wage war to stop Germany had "pushed two great nations to disaster" and were "pushing all Europe into chaos." Consequently, Lindbergh repeatedly and consistently urged "a negotiated peace" to end the European war as quickly as possible. He opposed having the United States send aid-short-of-war to England, believing "that it has weakened our position in America, that it has added to bloodshed in European countries, and that it has not changed the trend of the war." In his opinion, "The alternative to a negotiated peace is either a Hitler victory or a prostrate Europe, and possibly a prostrate America as well." Therefore he preferred "a negotiated peace to a complete victory by either side." He believed that "the only way European civilization can be saved is by ending it quickly."[11]

An early negotiated peace might save Europe from self-destruction; he repeatedly urged such a settlement. But once the war erupted in 1939 and began to rage through its devastating course, Colonel Lindbergh's main emphasis went to advocating the construction of American defenses in the Western Hemisphere and to urging the United States to stay out of the European war.

# 11/Air Power and American Defense

CHARLES A. LINDBERGH shared many of the views of other noninterventionists in opposing American entry into World War II. But his personal knowledge, experience, and expertise gave special weight to the significance of air power (its potential and its limitations) in his analyses. He firmly insisted that air power, properly maintained, strengthened America's defensive position in the Western Hemisphere.

Like others on both sides in the foreign policy debate before Pearl Harbor, Lindbergh cited the "lessons of history" to bolster his arguments. He quoted George Washington's "Farewell Address," and he pointed to the lessons to be learned from the consequences of American involvement in World War I. "The last war demonstrated the fallacy of sending American soldiers to European battlefields." He found significant warnings for America in the experiences of ancient Rome.[1]

Like other noninterventionists, Lindbergh denied that he wanted literal isolation or that the word "isolationism" accurately described the course he urged for the United States. He repeatedly called, instead, for "an independent destiny for America." In October, 1940, he delivered a nationwide radio broadcast entitled "A Plea for American Independence." In his second America First address, in April, 1941, he said: "It is a policy not of isolation, but of independence; not of defeat, but of courage." In May, he told a Madison Square Garden audience that "an independent destiny for America" did not mean "that we will build a wall around our country and isolate ourselves from all contact with the rest of the world. But it does mean that the future of America will not be tied to these eternal wars in Europe." As he defined "independent destiny," it meant that American "soldiers will not have to fight everybody in the world who prefers some other system of life to ours." And it also meant that Americans "will fight anybody and everybody who attempts to interfere with our hemisphere."[2]

Like other noninterventionists, Lindbergh feared the consequences for Americans if the United States entered the war abroad. In his first radio broadcast, he warned: "We are likely to lose a million men, possibly several million—the best of American youth. We will be staggering under the burden of recovery during the rest of our lives. And our children will be fortunate if they see the end in their lives, even if, by some unlikely chance, we do not pass on another Polish Corridor to them. Democracy itself may not survive. If we enter fighting for democracy abroad, we may end by losing it at home." He insisted that "Our safety does not lie in fighting European wars. It lies in our own internal strength, in the character of the American people and of American institutions." He repeated those warnings many times later. In October, 1940, he told students and faculty at Yale University: "I believe very firmly that our involvement in this war would be a disaster both for our own country and for Europe." He believed that "if democracy is to be saved, it will not be by the forceful imposition of our ideals abroad, but by the example of their successful operation at home."[3]

On those and other themes he expressed views that most noninterventionist speakers advanced in varied forms. But when Colonel Lindbergh turned to matters of air power and military defense, he spoke with firsthand knowledge and experience that other noninterventionist leaders could not equal. It was on considerations of air power and national defense that his arguments carried their greatest authority. He touched on the subject in each of his speeches and articles. But he provided his most concentrated analyses in a nationwide radio broadcast on

May 19, 1940, in his testimony against lend-lease before the House Foreign Affairs Committee on January 23, 1941, and in his address before the America First rally in Oklahoma City on August 29, 1941.

Colonel Lindbergh repeatedly insisted that air power worked to the disadvantage of Great Britain, that it enhanced Germany's power in Europe, that it increased the difficulty of invading Europe, and that it strengthened America's defensive position in the Western Hemisphere. Even more than Germany, Lindbergh contended, the United States was in "a singularly fortunate position" so far as air power was concerned. Americans had, he believed, "natural ability in the design, construction, and operation of aircraft." He pointed out that "Our highly organized industry, our widely separated centers of population, our elimination of formalities in inter-state travel, all contribute to the development of American aviation." He had personally flown the ocean approaches to the United States and insisted that geography and the oceans enhanced America's defense relative to the "warring armies of Europe and Asia." If the United States properly formulated its defense policies, if it constructed and maintained the land, sea, and air forces required by those policies, and if it operated from appropriate defense bases, it could be virtually impregnable militarily at that time. "The Air defense of America is as simple as the attack is difficult."[4]

Lindbergh believed that the United States should construct and maintain air bases "in Newfoundland, Canada, the West Indies, parts of South America, Central America, the Galapagos Islands, the Hawaiian Islands, and Alaska." He favored gaining the co-operation of other countries in the Western Hemisphere to get the needed defense bases. Though "secondary bases" might be located in Greenland, he thought Greenland was "not of primary importance from the standpoint of aviation bases." For the Philippines, Lindbergh believed the United States "should either fortify these islands adequately, or get out of them entirely." He did not think Iceland or the Cape Verde Islands were essential to America's defense, and he ridiculed the idea that America's defensive frontiers lay on the Rhine or anywhere in Europe.[5]

He thought it unwise for the United States simply to build huge numbers of military airplanes without consideration of what its defense policies and goals should be. For the policies he envisaged, he thought "a total air force of about ten thousand thoroughly modern fighting planes plus reserves" would be sufficient. He would give priority to long-range bombers that could attack approaching fleets at great distances from America's shores and to fast defensive pursuit planes to strike down attacks from the air. He thought it "obvious . . . that air power made it costly, if not impossible, for naval forces to operate within effective bombing range of an enemy coast adequately protected by aircraft." Consequently, "troops could not be landed and maintained on any coast where an enemy had strong supremacy of the air."[6]

Colonel Lindbergh readily conceded that even at the then-prevailing level of aviation technology it was possible to build bombers capable of flying from Europe across the Atlantic Ocean, delivering their bombs on targets in the United States, and making the return flight to Europe nonstop. But he thought "The cost of trans-oceanic bombing would be extremely high, enemy losses would be large, and the effect on our military position negligible." Though the damage from such attacks could be large by peacetime standards, it would be totally ineffectual for the purpose of accomplishing the military invasion of the United States. In any event, "not a single squadron of trans-oceanic bombing planes exists anywhere in the world today."[7]

Furthermore, Lindbergh contended that no country could successfully invade and conquer another country across oceans using air power alone; it would still be necessary at that time to transport invading troops by sea. He told the House Foreign Affairs Committee, in January, 1941, that "If air invasion alone could be successful, it would have been used by the Germans against England many months ago." He thought that "If England is able to live at all with bases of the German air force less than an hour's flight away, the United States is not in great danger across the Atlantic Ocean." He believed an "air invasion across the ocean" was "absolutely impossible at this time, or in any predictable future."[8]

Lindbergh conceded that there would be scientific and technological developments in the future that would force reconsideration of America's defensive position. But he insisted that "No generation can entirely safeguard the future for those that follow. They must meet their own problems as those problems arise. The greatest inheritance we can pass on to our children is a reasonable solution of the problems that confront us in our own time—a strong nation, a lack of debt, a solid American character free from the entanglements of the Old World." He told the America First audience in Oklahoma City "that we have enough problems to solve in our own generation; and that if our grand children insist on splitting atoms and building rockets, it must be upon their own responsibility."[9]

Believing that Britain and France could not defeat Germany in Europe, believing that American aid-short-of-war simply added to the bloodshed and destruction in Europe without changing the course of the war, and believing that the United States should build its own military power for the defense of the Western Hemisphere, Lindbergh consistently opposed the sending of arms to the belligerents fighting abroad. He wanted the United States to keep the military equipment it manufactured for its own defense forces at home.

In the fall of 1939, President Roosevelt asked Congress to revise the neutrality law by repealing the arms embargo then in effect and re-enacting the system of cash-and-carry that had expired four months before the European war began. The changes the President wanted would enable Britain and France to buy military equipment from American producers, providing they paid cash and carried it away from the United States in non-American ships. British control of the seas would, in effect, deny the Axis powers access to American munitions.

Lindbergh did not attach great importance to neutrality legislation. His position on the changes being debated in the fall of 1939 was influenced a bit by former President Herbert Hoover. In his second radio broadcast, on October 13, Lindbergh urged the continuation of the embargo on the sale of offensive armaments to belligerents. So far as defensive arms were concerned, he favored "supplying European countries with as much as we can spare." He did "not want to see American bombers dropping bombs which will kill and mutilate European children, even if they are not flown by American pilots." But he was "perfectly willing to see American anti-aircraft guns shooting American shells at invading bombers over any European country." Like most noninterventionists, he urged the re-enactment of cash-and-carry. That is, he thought "The only safe course for neutral shipping at this time is to stay away from the warring countries and dangerous waters of Europe," and he believed "The extension of credit to a belligerent country is a long step toward war, and it would leave us close to the edge."[10] Nevertheless, after exhaustive debate, Congress did as President Roosevelt wanted: it re-enacted cash-and-carry, and it repealed the entire arms embargo (not just the embargo on defensive weapons, as Lindbergh and Hoover had proposed).

By the latter part of 1940, Britain's financial resources were rapidly becoming depleted. In a long letter to President Roosevelt on December 8, Prime Minister Winston Churchill warned that the time was coming when Britain would "no longer be able to pay cash." Roosevelt responded by describing, at a press conference on December 17, his plan "to eliminate the dollar sign" in aiding Great Britain. In a fireside chat on December 29, the President dramatically described the disastrous consequences he feared might befall the United States if Britain were defeated or agreed to a negotiated peace. He called upon Americans to make the United States "the great arsenal of democracy." On January 6, 1941, the President urged Congress to enact his lend-lease idea. During the next two months that proposal was the subject of one of the most spirited and important debates in the history of American foreign affairs.

Colonel Lindbergh's opposition to lend-lease was clear and unequivocal. Both the House Committee on Foreign Affairs and the Senate Committee on Foreign Relations invited him to testify on the proposed legislation. Some who shared his general views thought he took more controversial positions than were necessary. But he handled himself extremely well in responding to the questions of Committee members, and he was the star witness for the noninterventionists. His appearances packed the Committee rooms and got detailed press coverage.

On January 23, in some four and one-half hours before the House Committee, Lindbergh emphasized particularly the role of air power in American defense. In an even more prolonged appearance before the Senate Committee on February 6, he repeated some of his earlier testimony, but he particularly stressed that aid to Britain would weaken America's defenses rather than strengthen them. He told both Committees that he opposed lend-lease because it would be a step away from America's traditional system of government and because he feared it would weaken the United States and move it closer to war. He told the House Committee that America's position was "greatly strengthened for defense and greatly weakened for attack" by air power. He told the Senate Committee that America's aid-short-of-war policy in the form of lend-lease involved "giving up an ideal defensive position in America for a very precarious offensive position in Europe." He favored "building strength in America" because he thought the United States could "be successful in this hemisphere." He opposed "placing our security in an English victory" because he thought such a victory was "extremely doubtful." He feared that the policy represented by lend-lease would "lead to failure in war, and to conditions in our own country as bad or worse than those we now desire to overthrow in Nazi Germany." Lindbergh opposed aid to Great Britain that would carry the United States into the war or would weaken America's forces in the Western Hemisphere. He believed lend-lease could do both.[11]

As was usually the case, however, Roosevelt and his followers triumphed; Lindbergh and the noninterventionists were beaten. Congress passed the Lend-Lease Act, and President Roosevelt signed it into law on March 11, 1941. It essentially resolved the problem of financing American aid to Britain and other countries fighting the Axis Powers abroad. But it did not diminish Lindbergh's opposition to entry into World War II or his conviction that the United States could successfully defend itself within the Western Hemisphere.

Convinced that the United States had "the most perfect defensive position of any nation," Colonel Lindbergh, in August, 1941, asked his America First audience in Oklahoma City: "Shall we now give up the independence we have won, and crusade abroad in a utopian attempt to force our ideas on the rest of the world; or shall we use air power, and other advances of modern warfare, to guard and strengthen the independence of our nation?"[12] In the summer of 1941, Lindbergh's arguments against intervention were strengthened when Hitler turned his back on England and struck east to begin the massive Russo-German war.

# 12/The Russo-German War

ON June 22, 1941, Adolf Hitler hurled his German legions east against the gigantic Russian bear. Though most experts predicted defeat for the Soviet Union, the Russo-German war proved to be a disaster for Nazi Germany. Hitler's panzer divisions and Luftwaffe drove deep into the Soviet Union and wrought terrible destruction and death there. But they were checked at the gates of Moscow; they failed to take Leningrad; and they were defeated at Stalingrad in some of the worst fighting of World War II. Joseph Stalin's Communist Russia gobbled up Hitler's men and equipment faster than the efficient but comparatively small German state could supply them. Russia had been too much for Napoleon's France to down; it proved too much for Hitler's Germany more than a century later. Napoleon's reverses in Czarist Russia set the stage for his subsequent defeats at Leipzig and Waterloo; Hitler's reverses in Communist Russia set the stage for D-Day, on June 6, 1944, and for V-E Day, on May 8, 1945. The men and matériel that Nazi Germany squandered against the Soviet Union in eastern Europe were not available for use against Great Britain and the United States in the west; the millions of lives and tens of thousands of tanks and planes that the Soviet Union consumed in defeating Germany were, in effect, lives and equipment that Britain and the United States did not have to consume. Though the human and material costs for the Soviet Union were fantastically huge (and partly because they were huge), Stalin's Soviet

Union greatly expanded its power and empire during and after World War II. The Soviet successes helped make victory over the Axis possible; they also helped pave the way for the Cold War later.

The eruption of the Russo-German war strengthened Colonel Lindbergh's conviction that the United States should stay out of the European war. And it reinforced his belief that Hitler's expansionist ambitions lay to the east in Europe, rather than to the west. The visits he and his wife made to the Soviet Union in 1931, 1933, and 1938 had given them an affection for the Russian people, a dislike for the Soviet system, and an unfavorable impression of Soviet technological and military development. He thought the Soviet system would collapse sooner or later. He was not favorably impressed by the aviation developments they saw there in August, 1938. But the Soviet Union had enough land, people, and machines to present real problems for any assailant.

Though his German hosts in 1936, 1937, and 1938 generally had not talked about military and diplomatic strategy, Lindbergh had gotten a clear impression that Nazi Germany intended to expand east rather than west.[1] Given his conception of the comparative military and air power of the various states, Lindbergh had believed that Britain and France could not successfully war against Germany if Hitler turned east. Furthermore, in terms of wisdom and statecraft he thought Britain and France should not do so. He believed that the only European beneficiaries of a war between the Allies and Germany might be Communist Russia.

On July 1, 1941, just nine days after Hitler began the Russo-German war, Colonel Lindbergh addressed a large America First Committee rally in San Francisco, California. In that speech, he leveled his forensic guns at Anglo-American policies relative to the war in the east. If the European war was to be viewed as a struggle for freedom and democracy, he found it a bit confusing. At the beginning of the war, Communist Russia and Nazi Germany aggressively shared in dismantling Poland, over objections from Britain and France; by July, 1941, the

Soviet Union was to be cheered and aided as Britain's partner in the struggle for freedom. During the winter of 1939–40, American sympathies went out to Finland fighting against the Soviet Union; by 1941, American sympathies were supposed to go to the Soviet Union and against the Finns. "The murderers and plunderers of yesterday are accepted as the valiant defenders of civilization today; and the valiant defenders of yesterday have become the wicked aggressors of today." He thought it incongruous that "the idealists who have been shouting against the horrors of Nazi Germany, are now ready to welcome Soviet Russia as an ally." It seemed to him that they were "ready to join with a nation whose record of cruelty, bloodshed, and barbarism" was "without parallel in modern history."[2]

But if the Russo-German war compounded the ideological confusion, in Lindbergh's opinion it also dramatized the diplomatic and military blundering of the British and French. By contesting Hitler's moves east they had brought Germany's might down upon themselves. Lindbergh told his San Francisco audience that he had seen Soviet bombers on Czech airfields in September, 1938, and he insisted that "Russia and Germany would have been at each others throats two years ago had it not been for the interventionist interference of England and France." Anglo-French appeasement at Munich (where "Russia was not even represented") had restrained German forces that "were prepared to march eastward." Then, a year later, Britain and France "beguiled Poland into a futile war." As Lindbergh explained it, "Intervention by England and France in the war between Germany and Poland did not save Poland; it postponed the war between Germany and Russia, and brought the defeat of France and the devastation of England." Similarly, with Japan undecided whether to fight the Soviet Union to its north or the United States in the Pacific, American policies had driven Japan "into the arms of the Axis" and were drawing its hostilities against the United States.[3]

Speaking on the basis of his firsthand knowledge of conditions in Europe, Lindbergh told his America First audience that he opposed any American alliance with either England or

Germany. But he said that he "would a hundred times rather see my country ally herself with England, or even with Germany with all of her faults, than with the cruelty, the godlessness, and the barbarism that exist in Soviet Russia." He thought such an alliance "should be opposed by every American, by every Christian, and by every humanitarian in this country."[4]

He closed his address with a renewed appeal for nonintervention. "Why give up an impregnable position in America for a hazardous and untenable position in Europe? Why bring to this country the chaos, the intolerance, and the hatred that will inevitably come with a foreign war?" He said: "It is not a question of whether Hitler would like to invade America. It is not a question of trusting promises that may be broken. I never have, and I do not now recommend basing the security of our nation on the promises of any man, or any foreign government. Our security should rest on the strength, the character, and the arms of our own people." As he saw it, "The real defeatist in America is the man who says that this nation cannot survive alone." He called for "a unified nation behind an impregnable defense, and an independent destiny for America."[5]

In his very last noninterventionist address, before an America First rally in New York City on October 30, 1941, Lindbergh said that "If Germany had been permitted to throw her armies eastward against Russia in 1939 instead of in 1941, the picture in Europe would be far different today. Whether or not Germany would have turned west after conquering Russia is debatable. But even if she had done so, a weaker Germany would have faced a stronger England and France."[6]

Most American noninterventionists shared Lindbergh's general views on the significance of the Russo-German war for the United States.[7] But the Roosevelt administration, the interventionists, and the majority of the American people disagreed. They continued to see Nazi Germany as the principal threat and favored aid to the Soviet Union as a way of contributing to the essential defeat of Hitler.[8]

One has no difficulty singling out both accurate and inaccurate predictions in Charles A. Lindbergh's analyses of international affairs (and in the analyses of those who opposed his position). Nevertheless, any evaluation of his views should properly take into account the Russo-German war.

The ease and efficiency with which the German military forces crushed Poland, Denmark, Norway, the Netherlands, Luxembourg, Belgium, and France suggest that Lindbergh was not entirely mistaken in his evaluation of Germany's military power on the European continent. Britain's RAF fighters were more successful and Germany's Luftwaffe less effective in the Battle of Britain than Lindbergh's analysis would have led one to expect. And, contrary to his predictions, Britain did defeat Germany. But it did not do so alone. When one takes into account the magnitude of the total military effort that ultimately proved essential to accomplish the final defeat of Nazi Germany in Europe, it does not seem entirely unreasonable to have questioned Great Britain's military capacity to accomplish that defeat of Germany alone—or even with American aid-short-of-war. Surely Britain could not have defeated Nazi Germany by itself without vastly greater losses than it actually suffered in the war.

Superficially, Lindbergh's forecast that the United States was "likely to lose a million men, possibly several million," if it attempted to defeat Germany in war seems excessive. During World War II the United States suffered "only" 1 million casualties and "only" 300,000 killed in helping to defeat Germany, Italy, and Japan. But before the final surrender by Nazi Germany, in May, 1945, a total of more than 12 million soldiers on all sides died in the European war. When one adds civilian deaths, the total increases to more than 25 million. The overwhelming majority of those died in the Russo-German war in eastern Europe. If any substantial proportion of the losses suffered by the Soviet Union had been shifted to Great Britain and the United States, Lindbergh's alarming estimates would not have been excessive. And if the resultant human, economic, and material losses had been added to those actually suffered by the countries of western Europe and North America, one might reasonably suspect that their political systems, economies, and civilizations would have been much more damaged by World War II than they were. Without the Russo-German war, Lindbergh's frightening forecasts about the difficulties and costs of defeating Nazi Germany in the west might have proved tragically accurate.

# III

The Battle of the Committees

# 13/Veterans and Legionnaires

THE heated debates in the United States on policies toward the European war were part of democracy in action, with all its vitality and imperfections. Mass pressure groups played colorful and important roles in those debates, in the so-called "battle of the committees." Citizens have organized foreign policy pressure groups throughout American history. In the years 1940–1941, such groups tried to arouse support for or opposition to particular policies by means of advertisements, pamphlets, radio speeches, public rallies, and motion pictures. They also tried to influence government policy-making through letters, petitions, and lobbying. Though much criticized, those committees helped to clarify issues and crystallize existing attitudes. They informed the public, organized public opinion, and made it vocal. They helped to convert general attitudes into demands for action on particular measures. In that sense they were agencies for the democratic process in the making of American foreign policies. Such committees organized on all sides in the foreign policy debates before Pearl Harbor. And Charles A. Lindbergh somewhat reluctantly became a prominent figure in that "battle of the committees."

Throughout his noninterventionist efforts Lindbergh was his own man. He wrote his own speeches and articles. He advanced his own ideas. He controlled his own moves. He did not trim his statements and actions to win popularity, to please friends, or to appease foes. He pridefully guarded his independence and integrity. He was not an organization man. In spite of (or because of) his previous experiences with committees and boards, he was skeptical of the effectiveness of committees to accomplish practical goals.

At the same time, however, he recognized the necessity for working with others in the common effort to keep the United States out of World War II. And other noninterventionists eagerly sought Lindbergh's help in organizing and leading the opposition to entry into the war. There were far more efforts to draw him into organizational roles than he could possibly have honored even if he had wished. Some approached him through his known associates, such as William R. Castle, Truman Smith, and Juan Trippe of Pan American Airways. Some he met through his friendships with various legislators, including Senator Harry Byrd of Virginia and Senators Henrik Shipstead and Ernest Lundeen of his old home state of Minnesota. Some simply wrote to him without prior contacts. And each new acquaintance brought him into contact with still others in the noninterventionist movement. At one time or another he was in touch with virtually every leading opponent of American entry into the war, and with countless lesser figures in that effort. Most were transient contacts (though name-droppers, newspapers, and interventionists often made them seem more substantial than they were). A few developed into friendships that endured long after the Japanese attack on Pearl Harbor brought their common strivings against the war to an abrupt end.

Since his earlier activities had centered on aviation and science, Lindbergh had not previously known most of those with whom he worked in opposing involvement in the war. The noninterventionist movement (like the interventionist movement) attracted support from a wide range of groups and viewpoints within the American population. Lindbergh recognized that diversity. Without compromising his own views, he tried to work with individuals and groups who held widely varying views on other matters but who shared a common opposition to involvement in the war abroad. Those who sought his help spanned nearly the entire spectrum of the noninterventionist movement, from the right to the left and from militarists to pacifists. But he won greater enthusiasm from conservative and Republican circles than from liberals, socialists, or pacifists within the noninterventionist movement.

William R. Castle brought him into contact with Dean Carl W. Ackerman of the Columbia University Graduate School of Journalism and with Merwin K. Hart, a Harvard classmate of Roosevelt and president of the ultraconservative New York State Economic Council. They were more generous with ideas for tasks for the Colonel to undertake than he wanted. Castle also arranged for Lindbergh to meet with John Cudahy, a noninterventionist who had served as Roosevelt's diplomat in Poland, Belgium, and the Irish Free State. Lindbergh's friend Juan Trippe introduced him to Douglas Stewart and George T. Eggleston, publisher and editor respectively of the conservative noninterventionist magazine *Scribner's Commentator*. Truman Smith arranged for him to meet Lawrence Dennis, a former Foreign Service Officer who edited the right-wing *Weekly Foreign Letter*. Through President Alan Valentine of the University of Rochester, Lindbergh visited with the famed historian Charles A. Beard. The aviator had known Henry Ford, the noninterventionist Michigan industrialist, for many years and had given the multimillionaire his first airplane ride. A letter from the energetic writer and journalist O. K. Armstrong of Missouri near the end of 1939 eventually brought the Colonel into the turmoil surrounding Verne Marshall's No Foreign War Committee a year later.[1]

Identification with reputable organized groups could serve a helpful function in Lindbergh's efforts to reach the American people. Through radio broadcasts, published articles, and testimony before legislative committees, he reached many millions. But to address public meetings in cities across the land called for local organization. It was difficult for him to determine the character and responsibility of individuals and groups that approached him to address such meetings. A continuing association with an established organization could relieve him of such concerns in arrangements for addressing public rallies.[2]

The need for such assistance became apparent in the circumstances surrounding the first two or three public meetings he addressed.

Veterans' groups were divided within themselves on the proper course for the United States relative to wars abroad. Like Colonel Lindbergh, the American Legion and the Veterans of Foreign Wars favored building America's military defense forces. Many of their leaders and members opposed entry into wars abroad. And in the summer of 1940, individuals prominent in the Legion and the VFW sought Lindbergh's help in marshaling those organizations against involvement abroad. Bennett Champ Clark, Democratic United States Senator from Missouri and a founder and former national commander of the American Legion, conferred at length with him on the matter. James E. Van Zandt, Republican Congressman from Pennsylvania and also a former commander of the Legion, was brought into the deliberations, as was the head of the VFW. O. K. Armstrong had been active in the Legion and was a member of its Committee on Foreign Relations.[3]

Late in June, Senator Clark asked Lindbergh to address a major antiwar rally in Chicago. After checking on its sponsors, Lindbergh agreed. Though ostensibly representing veterans' groups, the rally was sponsored by the Citizens Keep America Out of War Committee. It was a local Chicago organization headed by Avery Brundage of the American Olympic Association and Judge William J. Grace, a Republican politico.[4]

The rally was originally scheduled for July 7, but Democratic leaders in Chicago forced its postponement until Sunday, August 4, after the major presidential nominating conventions were over.[5] It was the first public rally that Lindbergh addressed in his noninterventionist effort. It came only six weeks after Hitler's Germany and Mussolini's Italy had forced the surrender of France; the Battle of Britain was already beginning in the skies and seas around England. The Democratic Party had nominated Franklin D. Roosevelt for an unprecedented third term as President of the United States. The Republican Party had rejected noninterventionist contenders and had, instead, nominated the corporation executive and internationalist from Indiana and New York, Wendell L. Willkie. It was a crucial time both at home and abroad.

Lindbergh abhorred Roosevelt, and he was not enthusiastic about Willkie. But he was pleased with "the so-called 'isolationist' planks which have been adopted in both party platforms." Indeed, he momentarily allowed himself to wonder if "the danger of our military intervention in Europe is past." Perhaps the Chicago "Keep America Out of War" rally "might be an anticlimax."[6] That optimism did not last long, however, and his speech in Chicago provoked more criticism than any earlier statement in his battle against intervention.

The Citizens Keep America Out of War Committee had secured the huge Soldier Field for its rally. With lots of free publicity from Colonel Robert R. McCormick's *Chicago Tribune,* the Committee hoped for an overflow attendance. It was to be disappointed. Still, some 35,000 to 40,000 people filled half the seats on that hot Sunday afternoon to hear speakers on American foreign affairs (a much better turnout than Chicagoans generally gave their beloved Cubs or White Sox in their ball parks). Brundage, Van Zandt, and Senator Patrick A. McCarran, Democrat from Nevada, shared the speaking honors with Lindbergh. He was not displeased by the attendance, and was not really surprised by the vehement criticism that his speech provoked among interventionists. As he told his Chicago audience, "I prefer to say what I believe, or not to speak at all."[7]

On his Chicago trip Lindbergh met with others who would share in the noninterventionist effort. He was a house guest of Colonel McCormick. At dinner after the rally Lindbergh visited at length with Bob and Barbara Stuart, who were in the process of converting their tiny Yale student group into the national America First Committee. Stuart, a young, idealistic New Dealer, was a bit put off by the conservatism of Lindbergh and the sponsors of the Chicago rally. He had misgivings about Lindbergh's hope that the veterans' groups might be suitable vehicles for opposing entry into World War II. As Stuart saw it, those groups were so conservative and nationalistic that many people might identify them with an American brand of fascism. On Lindbergh's return trip from Chicago, he stopped off for a visit with Henry Ford in Dearborn, Michigan.[8]

O. K. Armstrong of Springfield, Missouri, had been in the middle of Lindbergh's explorations of the possible use of the American Legion and other veterans' groups for opposing American entry into the war. He was a talented magazine writer, whose boundless energies and great enthusiasms often outdistanced his judgment and organizational talents. He had triggered the discussions that Lindbergh had in the summer of 1940 with Senator Clark, Congressman Van Zandt, Theodore Roosevelt, Jr., and others of the Legion.[9] In September, 1940, Armstrong used his position as a member of the Foreign Relations Committee of the Legion to plan a conference opposing involvement in the war. But the national commander of the Legion, Raymond J. Kelly, promptly repudiated the action and helped force Armstrong's resignation from its Foreign Relations Committee. Though it included many isolationists, the Legion increasingly moved in interventionist directions. At the national conventions in Boston in 1940 and in Milwaukee in 1941, the isolationists were badly beaten, and the Legion's utility as a noninterventionist vehicle evaporated.[10]

The second public meeting Colonel Lindbergh addressed during this period was a smaller affair than the first had been, with fewer complications. On the evening of October 30, 1940, he spoke to a full house in Yale University's Woolsey Hall. The meeting came near the close of the presidential campaign, as Willkie and Roosevelt were trying to outdo each other in their speeches against involvement in the war. Kingman Brewster, Jr., then a Yale undergraduate, organized the meeting on behalf of the local student group that had been the nucleus out of which the national America First Committee had emerged. Lindbergh's thirty-minute address was the longest he had so far delivered on foreign affairs. It won a good reception, including unequivocal plaudits from Yale's distinguished diplomatic historian, Samuel Flagg Bemis, and its international law authority, Edwin Borchard.[11]

# 14/No Foreign War Committee

LINDBERGH'S friend O. K. Armstrong was a hard man to down. After the American Legion convention in Boston had turned its back on him and his fellow noninterventionists, he revived his call for an Emergency Peace Conference to meet in Washington on Monday and Tuesday, October 21 and 22, 1940. He rounded up support for the meeting from leaders of major organizations "interested in keeping our country at peace." Among those included were such prominent pacifists as Frederick J. Libby of the National Council for Prevention of War and Dorothy Detzer of the Women's International League for Peace and Freedom. It also included such nonpacifist noninterventionists as R. Douglas Stuart, Jr., of the America First Committee, the young man Lindbergh had visited with in Chicago.[1]

In an unannounced appearance, Colonel Lindbergh spoke briefly at a dinner meeting of the Conference. His was an appeal for unity and co-operation in the common effort to keep the United States out of the war. "Some, in which I include myself, believe that we should build strong military forces for defense. Others among us believe that war can best be prevented by more peaceful answers. This viewpoint I respect, as I hope they will respect mine. The essential point is that all of us oppose America's involvement in this war, and believe that such involvement can and must be prevented." He concluded that "Our methods may differ, but our objective is the same, and it is important enough to necessitate co-operation among us." He hoped the meeting would "help to bring that co-operation about."[2]

The Conference created a No Foreign War Campaign, with Armstrong as temporary chairman. Its officers ranged from conservative isolationists, such as Douglas M. Stewart of *Scribner's Commentator,* to religious pacifists, such as Dr. Charles F. Boss, Jr., of the Methodist World Peace Commission and Frederick J. Libby. It planned its own ornate sponsoring committee. Theoretically it was designed to co-ordinate the non-interventionist efforts of the already established pacifist and isolationist groups.[3]

In operation, however, the activity in the No Foreign War Campaign centered with Armstrong and the conservative isolationists around him (including Stewart, George Eggleston, and Charles S. Payson, all of *Scribner's Commentator* ). They—particularly Armstrong—identified with Lindbergh, though he was not formally a member. In November and December, Verne Marshall of the Cedar Rapids, Iowa, *Gazette* became increasingly prominent. Marshall had been an ambulance driver for the French at Verdun in 1916, and had joined the American Army after the United States entered World War I. As a newspaperman he specialized in exposing skulduggery and corruption in high places. He had a flair for publicity, inexhaustible energy, plenty of courage, and intense patriotism, but erratic judgment. He was active in the Republican Party, nominated Iowa's Hanford MacNider for President in 1940, and campaigned for Willkie against Roosevelt. In the course of the campaign, Marshall became privy to documents on a proposed peace conference allegedly obtained from top Nazi leaders in October, 1939, and brought back to the United States by oilman William Rhodes Davis. Davis claimed to have gone to Europe at Roosevelt's behest to consult German leaders, but the President and his Secretary of State, Cordell Hull, refused to see him on his return. Marshall had tried unsuccessfully to persuade Willkie to use the information against Roosevelt in the Republican presidential campaign. He believed the documents were authentic, and he was convinced that they further proved the duplicity and warlike intentions of President Roosevelt.[4]

Despite his original willingness to participate in the No Foreign War Campaign, young Stuart of the America First Committee quickly became disenchanted with it. He was convinced that Armstrong was trying to build a competing noninterventionist organization. Flurries of consultations, inquiries, and correspondence deepened Stuart's misgivings. Stewart and Eggleston of *Scribner's Commentator* seemed too conservative, in his opinion, and Marshall was too erratic, political, and injudicious. Also, he worried about evidences of anti-Semitism in the group.[5] The Armstrong-Marshall-Stewart group in turn distrusted the liberal and New Deal leanings of some in America First—including Stuart. Hanford MacNider of America First, an Iowa manufacturer with a distinguished combat record in World War I, wanted nothing to do with the likes of pacifist Frederick J. Libby. And though most pacifists were not enthusiastic about America First, they found the conservative-nationalist tone of the Armstrong-Marshall-Stewart group to be even less acceptable.[6]

In the fall and winter of 1940, Colonel Lindbergh was not formally a member of any of the organizations—and did not want to be. But he wanted to encourage organization and promote co-operation in the common effort to keep the United States out of the war. He wrote Stuart that Armstrong's No Foreign War Campaign would "not conflict with the work of the America First Committee." He thought it "desirable to encourage all possible organizing against our involvement in the war." And he believed that nonpacifists could "afford to cooperate with the 'Peace Groups' against involvement in war without jeopardizing our national rearmament program, or altering our own stand in favor of building an adequate defense."[7]

In early December, 1940, the America First leaders decided definitely not to work with Armstrong's No Foreign War Campaign. Armstrong and Marshall tried to draw MacNider and Castle into leadership positions—and failed. After conferring with Marshall in New York, General Robert E. Wood, national chairman of America First, concluded that he did not "question his sincerity, his enthusiasm and his energy, but he would be a difficult man to control and I would be afraid to lend my name to the committee while he had direction of the work of the committee." Instead, Wood and Stuart assigned the responsibility for co-ordinating America First activities with the various pacifist organizations to Sidney Hertzberg, the America First publicity director. Hertzberg, Jewish, a pacifist and a socialist, had good relations with the peace organizations and was vastly more acceptable to them than Armstrong or Marshall could be.[8]

With the collapse of the No Foreign War Campaign, Verne Marshall, O. K. Armstrong, and their associates promptly organized a No Foreign War Committee and announced it to the public on December 17, 1940. With financial backing from some of the same people who were behind *Scribner's Commentator,* the No Foreign War Committee might concentrate its strength in the eastern United States, while America First focused on the Middle West. It also hoped to do a better job of reaching the man in the street than the more aloof America First Committee might.[9]

Verne Marshall insisted (then and later) that Colonel Lindbergh had personally persuaded him to accept the chairmanship of the No Foreign War Committee. Lindbergh insisted (then and later) that he had not done so. Lindbergh was close to Armstrong, Stewart, and others in the Committee, and he participated in the discussions that culminated in its formation.[10] He had agreed to address a rally in St. Louis to be organized by Armstrong and sponsored by the No Foreign War Campaign (later Committee), providing Armstrong made no commitments or announcements without prior approval by Lindbergh. Armstrong and Marshall pressed ahead, however, with arrangements that were not acceptable to him. In the ensuing confusion, Lindbergh called off the St. Louis meeting at that time. He thought the arrangements might have gone satisfactorily "if Armstrong had not allowed his enthusiasm to push him quite so fast."[11]

At the same time, Marshall and Armstrong were parting ways. Both were energetic, impulsive, courageous, patriotic, aggressive, emotional, "banty rooster" types. Both pushed themselves too hard. Each thought the other was trying to upstage him; each questioned the judgment and good faith of the other. Passions mounted. Marshall's emotions became strained to the breaking point. He said things he should not have said. Finally, Armstrong resigned from the No Foreign War Committee on January 13. The next day the America First national committee formally approved the earlier decision by General Wood to disassociate America First from "Verne Marshall and his organization."[12]

On January 16, 1941, Colonel Lindbergh telegraphed a statement to the press services that, while he had "attempted to cooperate with all American organizations opposed to our entering the war in Europe," he had "no connection with the No Foreign War Committee." In his statement he said that he had "attended a number of conferences when . . . the No Foreign War Committee, was being formed" but found himself "unable to support the methods and policies adopted by the new organization." He pointed out that he had "at no time been a member of the Committee" and had not "contributed to its financial support." At the same time, he pledged his continued opposition to American entry into the war.[13]

Marshall, abandoned all around and his nerves shot, collapsed along with his Committee. Charges of every sort rained on him, including allegations that he was anti-Semitic and pro-Nazi. The disintegration was so complete as to be almost pathetic. At the end of January, Stuart wrote: "Both Mr. Marshall's committee and his financial backers have deserted him. He has been smeared from 'hell to breakfast' and is on the verge of a nervous breakdown." The No Foreign War Committee formally disbanded in April, 1941. Verne Marshall was hospitalized in May for a nervous collapse and spent many weeks recovering his health.[14]

The fiasco conceivably may be attributed both to Marshall's indiscretions and bad judgment and to the effectiveness of his interventionist assailants. The whole traumatic experience made Lindbergh even more wary of working with committees. But it also increased his awareness that a responsibly led organization could help him constructively in his battle against intervention.

O. K. Armstrong retired from the battleground briefly to lick his wounds, but he was soon back in the thick of things. In May, 1941, the America First Committee hired him to organize noninterventionist meetings in the interventionist South—with strict orders to undertake only projects specifically assigned to him. But his style did not change. In his typical manner, he wrote Stuart that he was "ready to be used anywhere, anytime, in any way, and you know that. On to Atlanta! We'll take that town like Sherman never dreamed of." Again, things did not go right. Other America First organizers also had difficulties in the South, but Armstrong failed spectacularly in trying to organize a meeting in Atlanta. He blamed his failure on "the stupendous difficulties thrown in our way in the interventionist south." Difficulties there were, but the America First leaders concluded that some of them were of Armstrong's own making. They fired him after only two months on the payroll.[15] Charles A. Lindbergh, however, was to have a much longer run with America First.

# 15/America First

FROM September, 1940, until December 7, 1941, the America First Committee was the most powerful isolationist or noninterventionist pressure group in the United States. And from the time he joined, in April, 1941, until Pearl Harbor, nearly eight months later, Charles A. Lindbergh was the Committee's most popular and controversial speaker.

The America First Committee grew out of an earlier student organization at Yale University led by R. Douglas Stuart, Jr., a twenty-four-year-old law student and son of the first vice-president of the Quaker Oats Company. During the summer of 1940, young Stuart won the support of prominent middle western business and political leaders for a national organization. On September 4, 1940, the Committee announced its formation, with national headquarters in Chicago.[1]

General Robert E. Wood, chairman of the board of Sears Roebuck and Company, served as national chairman of America First, and Stuart was national director. Wood, born in Kansas in 1879, was graduated from West Point in 1900. He served in the Philippines during the insurrection and in Panama while the canal was being built. During World War I he was Acting Quartermaster General. After the war he retired from the Army and became vice-president of Montgomery Ward and Company, before moving to Sears Roebuck as vice-president in 1924. He became president of Sears in 1928 and chairman of the board in 1939. Though a Republican and a businessman, Wood considered himself a liberal. He voted for Roosevelt in 1932, supported much of the early New Deal, and with growing misgivings voted for Roosevelt again in 1936.[2] A skilled administrator, he commanded the respect of other America First leaders and tempered differences among them that might have reduced the Committee's effectiveness.

Young Stuart had studied government and international relations at Princeton University, graduating in 1937. He spent several months traveling in Europe before entering the Yale University Law School in 1938. He held an Army Reserve Officers Training Corps commission. Handsome, personable, and idealistic, Stuart gave to the limits of his capacities in the Committee's battle against intervention.[3] Some criticized his youth and lack of administrative experience, but his judgment on matters of policy generally was sound.

General Wood, Stuart, and five others from the Middle West (mostly businessmen) formed the executive committee that shaped and supervised America First policies. More than fifty prominent individuals served at one time or another on a larger national committee. Among the more noted members of the national committee were John T. Flynn, Hanford MacNider, William R. Castle, George N. Peek, Chester Bowles, Mrs. Bennett Champ Clark, Mrs. Burton K. Wheeler, Alice Roosevelt Longworth, Edward Rickenbacker, Kathleen Norris, and Lillian Gish Henry Ford was a member of the national committee for a time in the fall of 1940, but the Committee dropped him in an effort to reduce its vulnerability to the charge of anti-Semitism.

The Committee financed its battle against intervention through voluntary contributions. William H. Regnery of Chicago, president of the Western Shade Cloth Company and a member of the America First executive committee, was the largest financial backer. Altogether the America First national headquarters received around $370,000 from approximately 25,000 contributors. Local chapters were largely self-supporting through voluntary contributions and were more dependent on small contributions than was the national headquarters.

In the fall of 1940, the Committee placed full-page advertisements in major newspapers and sponsored radio broadcasts. Though most of its leaders and members were Republicans, it also included many Democrats and earnestly tried to be nonpartisan. America First took no official position on the presidential election of 1940, but General Wood hoped that its newspaper advertisements would help inject the foreign policy issue into the campaign.

In November, the Committee began to organize local chapters in cities and towns all over the country. The chapter system took advantage of local enthusiasm for the noninterventionist view, and it decentralized the financing of the battle against intervention. The Committee's greatest growth occurred between December, 1940, and May, 1941. By December 7, 1941, the America First Committee had approximately 450 chapters and subchapters. Its total national membership was around 800,000 to 850,000. The Committee had members in every state and organized chapters in most of them, but it won its greatest strength in the Middle West. It was least successful in the interventionist South. Among the more prominent and active of the speakers at major America First rallies were Senator Burton K. Wheeler, Democrat from Montana, and Senator Gerald P. Nye, Republican from North Dakota.

Its original public announcement, in September, 1940, included the following statement of the America First Committee's Principles:

"1. The United States must build an impregnable defense for America.

"2. No foreign power, nor group of powers, can successfully attack a *prepared* America.

"3. American democracy can be preserved only by keeping out of the European war.

"4. 'Aid short of war' weakens national defense at home and threatens to involve America in war abroad."

Early in 1941, the Committee battled against enactment of lend-lease. After President Roosevelt signed lend-lease into law on March 11, 1941, it crusaded against the use of the American

Navy to escort convoys to Britain, fearing shooting incidents that might drag the United States into the war.[4]

Colonel Lindbergh was not a member of America First during the first half of its existence. He repeatedly encouraged its organizational efforts, and he was in touch with some leaders of the Committee even before it was created. But he preferred to keep his own efforts independent of the constraints that organizational affiliation might have imposed. For reasons of his own, neither did Stuart want the America First Committee to identify too closely with Lindbergh.

As early as November, 1939, Stuart's student group at Yale had written to Lindbergh asking him to address a mass meeting—but got no response. In July, 1940, O. K. Armstrong served briefly as a communications intermediary between Stuart's group and the aviator. Stuart and Lindbergh first met early in August, 1940, when the Colonel was in Chicago to address the Keep America Out of War rally, and when Stuart was in the process of developing his student group into a national organization. In conversation at dinner at that time, Stuart found Lindbergh to be "a most attractive guy and a very clear thinker." He thought Lindbergh was "a very sincere and courageous American who has the habit of sticking his neck out." Stuart was uneasy about the extreme conservatism of some around the Colonel. He feared that if the America First Committee were to identify publicly with Lindbergh, it would bring attacks and "smears" that could discredit the new organization and reduce its effectiveness. Consequently, Lindbergh's frequently expressed desire to remain independent made it easy for Stuart to avoid inviting him to join the Committee.[5]

The eagerness of interventionist critics, in the fall of 1940, to seize on any opportunity to identify Lindbergh with America First strengthened Stuart in his original conviction. When Lindbergh agreed to speak at Yale in October, Stuart urged Kingman Brewster to "handle the public relations carefully." He wanted it made clear that the invitation came from the local group at Yale rather than from the national America First Committee. Both Stuart and Lindbergh attended O. K. Arm-

strong's Emergency Peace Conference in October, and in different ways both were concerned over the controversies surrounding the No Foreign War Campaign and the later No Foreign
War Committee. Those experiences further increased Stuart's
misgivings about some of the conservative isolationists identified with Lindbergh.[6]

For his part, Colonel Lindbergh was pleased with the development of America First and tried to be helpful. When individuals sent him contributions to support his noninterventionist
activities, Lindbergh returned the checks, enclosed an America
First circular, and suggested that the Committee needed all the
help it could get. His discussions with Henry Ford played a
major role in the industrialist's decision to serve on the America
First national committee. Lindbergh contributed $100 to the
Committee and allowed his name to be included when the
Committee made public a list of its contributors. His testimony
against lend-lease before the Senate Foreign Relations Committee and his "A Letter to Americans" in *Collier's* were both
printed in the *Congressional Record*. Congressmen and Senators could legally send bulk packages of franked reprints from
the *Record* to an addressee, who could then address them to
individuals and remail them free, using the legislator's frank. In
that way the America First Committee mailed out many thousands of copies of the Lindbergh items to people on its mailing
lists.[7]

Though Stuart thought it wiser not to have Lindbergh as a
member of America First, General Wood thought differently.
Wood and Stuart had very real affection and respect for each
other. They held essentially the same foreign policy views, and
they shared a determination to guard the respectability of the
Committee, in order to enhance its effectiveness. But General
Wood was less cautious than Stuart in that regard, he was more
conservative in his views, and he felt a growing need to solicit
Lindbergh's help in the leadership of the Committee. General
Wood's responsibilities in directing Sears Roebuck left him with
less time and energy for active leadership of America First than
were required. He was uneasy lest his Committee activities

harm the corporation he headed. He repeatedly asked to step down. And he hoped that Lindbergh might succeed him as national chairman of America First.

General Wood and Colonel Lindbergh first met in the offices of Harry Bennett at the Ford Motor Company's River Rouge plant in Michigan, on September 16, 1940, not long after the formation of America First. They and Stuart were there to recruit Henry Ford as a member of the national committee. From the first, Wood and Lindbergh liked and respected each other. Throughout his dealings with America First, Lindbergh communicated most frankly and confidentially with General Wood. After their first meeting they exchanged views in private correspondence. They consulted personally on December 12, 1940, when Wood was in New York for a meeting of the National Association of Manufacturers and also to confer on relations between the America First and No Foreign War organizations. They visited when Wood was again in New York late in January, 1941.[8]

At a meeting of the America First executive committee on March 28, 1941, General Wood again emphasized his desire to step down from the chairmanship and his belief that the Committee needed a full-time chairman. He thought Colonel Lindbergh was the best man for the position. Lindbergh "had emerged as the real leader of our point of view, with a tremendous following amongst the people of this country." Stuart "admired Colonel Lindbergh and thought him a very great citizen," but he believed "the smear campaign which had been leveled against him throughout the country removed him as a possible head of this Committee." After thorough discussion, the executive committee authorized General Wood to write Lindbergh asking if he would serve as chairman of America First, subject to approval by a majority of the national committee. In his letter to the Colonel, General Wood wrote: "Your patriotism, your courage, your intellectual honesty have made you stand out as the head of all the elements that are opposed to our entry into this European conflict." Wood emphasized that he would continue as a member of the Committee and that his dedication to its cause was not diminished. But he thought America First was "seriously handicapped" by his inability to "devote the necessary time to it." General Wood and Stuart also went to New York, where they conferred privately with Lindbergh.[9]

Colonel Lindbergh was troubled when he discovered that word of his being considered for chairman of America First had leaked to members of the New York chapter even before he talked to Wood. And he feared that cleavages on the matter, along with festering friction within the New York chapter, might worsen if he were named chairman. He thought "it would be a great mistake, from every standpoint, for me to take a leading position in the America First Committee at a time when internal friction may come to a head." He feared that the interventionist opposition "would seize upon this immediately in an attempt to discredit the Committee and to nullify, as far as possible, the unifying effect we are striving for among anti-interventionist forces." As an alternative, Lindbergh suggested that he become a member of the national committee, address an America First meeting, and urge noninterventionists to rally to the Committee "in a unified effort to counteract the trend of intervention." He thought he "could help to increase the membership and influence of the Committee in this way without precipitating the friction and argument which apparently would be involved in my taking a leading position at this moment." He thought it "essential" for America First "to act with the utmost rapidity," because America's "decision on intervention" must be made "in the very near future."[10]

At a meeting of the America First executive committee on April 10, General Wood read a letter from Lindbergh declining the chairmanship but agreeing to become a member of the national committee. The executive committee promptly added Lindbergh to the national committee—the decision to be announced in connection with an America First rally in Chicago later in April.[11]

General Wood and Stuart concurred in the decision without abandoning their separate convictions on the matter. Wood continued to believe that Lindbergh was "the one man in the United States to head up this committee and rally . . . the sentiment in this country that is opposed to our entry into the war." He still hoped that "if the announcement [of Lindbergh's membership] is received with the enthusiasm" he expected, "by June 1st at the latest the time will be ripe" for Lindbergh to accept the chairmanship. In contrast, Stuart still had misgivings about the wisdom of adding Lindbergh to the Committee. He conceded that Lindbergh's membership would "give the Committee a big lift throughout the country," but he expected "the smearing to start."[12]

At the same time, some were advising Lindbergh not to tie up with America First. Judge William J. Grace of the Citizens Keep America Out of War Committee wrote Lindbergh complaining that America First was straddling the fence in its position on aid to Britain even though "aid to Britain means nothing else but war." Grace charged that America First had been unwilling to co-operate with his or other noninterventionist groups. He saw America First as "little more or less than an opportunity for some ladies and gentlemen of the social register to bask in limelight or public attention without mixing up with the hoi polloi in the matter of doing the front line soldier rough work which is necessary to win both in war as well as in peacetime activity." But Lindbergh responded that it was "essential to combine our forces against intervention" and that he tried "to cooperate with all reliable organizations opposing intervention." He believed that "In these times, one cannot search too long for perfection." He thought it "essential to act quickly."[13]

In practice, Charles A. Lindbergh's role in America First, from April to December, 1941, did give the Committee a boost. He was its most popular speaker. He won new members and rallied enthusiasm for the Committee and its cause. He had become the acclaimed leader for the noninterventionist movement. But the attacks on the Committee did increase greatly after he became a member. Critics seized on his statements to "smear" the organization and the movement. During the last half of 1941, interventionist attacks and "smears" won far more attention in the press than the efforts to prevent entry into the war did. One can only guess whether the patterns would have been substantially different if Lindbergh had never joined the Committee. Interventionists were gaining strength and boldness; noninterventionists were falling under the domestic and foreign avalanche that was to destroy them. Late in May, General Wood again urged Lindbergh to become chairman of America First, and once again Lindbergh declined.[14] General Wood continued as national chairman of the Committee until it disbanded after Pearl Harbor.

Colonel Lindbergh addressed his first rally as a member of America First at the Chicago Arena on April 17, 1941. Ten thousand people crowded in to hear him, with an overflow of some 4,000 outside. The enthusiastic audience interrupted him with applause and cheers some thirty times in a twenty-five-minute speech. He urged support for America First whatever the listener's views on aid to Britain were (America First approved it if it were truly aid-short-of-war; Lindbergh thought aid unwise both for Britain and the United States). He referred to America First as "a purely American organization founded to give voice to the hundred odd million people in our country who oppose sending our soldiers to Europe again." His two-day stay in Chicago also included consultations with America First and noninterventionist leaders in the area—including General Wood, Stuart, Judge Grace, and President Robert M. Hutchins of the University of Chicago.[15]

Altogether, Lindbergh addressed overflow audiences at thirteen America First rallies in almost every part of the United States. No other speaker attracted such huge crowds, won such enthusiastic acclaim, or was subjected to such vehement criticism from interventionists. He spoke at huge America First rallies in New York City in April, May, and October. In May he also addressed meetings in St. Louis, Minneapolis, and Philadelphia. In June he spoke before that huge audience in the Hollywood Bowl, near Los Angeles. In July he spoke in San Francisco. In August he addressed meetings in Cleveland and Oklahoma City. In September he gave a highly controversial speech in Des Moines. The Fort Wayne chapter, by winning an America First membership drive, won a Lindbergh rally in October. He delivered his final America First address in New York's Madison Square Garden on October 30, 1941. He had planned to speak in Boston on December 12, but by then Pearl Harbor had brought the United States into the war.[16] He wrote all his own speeches, taking great pains to compose them carefully. And he paid all his own expenses in his noninterventionist activities.[17]

In addition, dozens of other America First chapters sought him to address their meetings. Many of them conducted major drives to persuade America First to give them a "Lindbergh rally." As Stuart wrote him, "If you can just arrange to divide yourself into 118 equal parts, all the America First representatives will be happy."[18]

Lindbergh also advised on Committee policy, particularly through correspondence and consultation with General Wood and Stuart. The Committee reached its peak of strength and controversy while he was a member. But the interventionists also stepped up their opposition; they concentrated their attacks on America First in general and on Colonel Lindbergh in particular. At the core of that opposition was President Franklin D. Roosevelt's administration.

# 16/The Roosevelt Administration

FRANKLIN D. ROOSEVELT the political statesman and Charles A. Lindbergh the aviator were two of the most charismatic Americans of the twentieth century. Each inspired the worshipful adoration of millions; each aroused passionate hatred from others. So long as they performed in separate spheres there was no contest between them. But when either invaded the domain of the other (as when the Roosevelt administration canceled commercial air mail contracts in 1934, or when Lindbergh spoke out on foreign affairs from 1939 to 1941), the result was a battle of the giants.

In most respects Roosevelt and Lindbergh provided a study in contrasts. Though each was widely traveled, Lindbergh's family roots were in the rural and small town Middle West; Roosevelt's were in the Northeast. Neither had distinguished himself academically, but Roosevelt's studies at Groton, Harvard, and Columbia provided him with more impressive credentials than Lindbergh possessed from his attendance at scattered public elementary and secondary schools and his unenthusiastic stay of less than two years at the University of Wisconsin. Neither was a pacifist, but Roosevelt's great love was the sea and the Navy; for Lindbergh it was aviation and the Air Corps. Roosevelt loved politics and was the supreme master of the art; Lindbergh had disliked politics since childhood and disdained the political arts. Roosevelt enjoyed the limelight and delighted in playing to his audience; Lindbergh was the most private of individuals and thought it demeaning to make a play for popularity. Roosevelt could be intuitive, clever, and devious; Lindbergh was direct, candid, and honest. Lindbergh had an obsession for technical precision and factual accuracy; Roosevelt could be loose with details but alert to political possibilities and limitations. Each was a "doer," a man of action.

Despite the charges made against each of them at the time, Roosevelt was not pro-Communist and Lindbergh was not pro-Nazi. But Roosevelt was anti-German, while Lindbergh found much to admire in the Germans. Roosevelt viewed Nazi Germany as a vastly more dangerous menace to America and the world than Communist Russia; Lindbergh saw Germany as a barrier for the West against challenges from Asia spearheaded by the Soviet Union. Roosevelt thought no peace with Hitler's Germany could endure; Lindbergh repeatedly urged a negotiated settlement in Europe. Roosevelt favored aid-short-of-war to the victims of Axis aggression; Lindbergh believed that aid would prolong the war abroad and weaken America's defenses without altering the course of the European war. Roosevelt believed the defeat of Nazi Germany to be essential for peace and security; Lindbergh thought that a war sufficiently massive to defeat Germany could also destroy Western civilization and benefit Communist Russia. By 1941, both men realized that Charles A. Lindbergh was the most formidable adversary of President Roosevelt's policies toward the European war. They acted accordingly.

In December, 1933, Roosevelt had wired his congratulations to Anne and Charles Lindbergh on the completion of their flight exploring potential commercial air routes across the Atlantic.[1] Early in 1934, however, the President was troubled by the Colonel's public criticism of Postmaster General James A. Farley's cancellation of air mail contracts. Lindbergh charged that Farley's action condemned "the largest portion of our commercial aviation without just trial." He declined an invitation from Secretary of War George H. Dern to serve on a special committee to report on Army aviation in relation to national defense. He wanted nothing to do with the promulgators of the executive action that had compelled the Army to take over the commercial air mail system.[2]

Lindbergh never voted for Roosevelt in any election. The Colonel unenthusiastically cast his ballot for Herbert Hoover against Roosevelt in 1932; he was out of the country in 1936 and did not vote at all; he voted for Wendell Willkie against Roosevelt in 1940, and for Thomas E. Dewey in 1944.[3]

Colonel Lindbergh had co-operated closely with Truman Smith and Ambassador Hugh R. Wilson in Berlin, with Ambassador Joseph P. Kennedy in London, with Ambassador William C. Bullitt in Paris, with General H. H. Arnold of the Air Corps, and with others of President Roosevelt's appointees. But however valuable his help may have been, the dealings of those officials with Lindbergh did not enhance their status with the President. Roosevelt's call for 50,000 military airplanes a year was consistent with Lindbergh's emphasis on building American air power. But the President's sensational focus on numbers departed from the priority Lindbergh gave to research and development.

President Hoover had appointed Colonel Lindbergh to the National Advisory Committee for Aeronautics in 1931. He continued to serve on NACA under Roosevelt, until he resigned on December 1, 1939. In 1938, Lindbergh had been approached about an appointment as Chairman of the new Civil Aeronautics Authority, but he had declined. The Colonel and the President had met personally only once, at the White House, when the aviator went on active duty with the Air Corps in April, 1939. Just before his first noninterventionist broadcast he had been approached indirectly about a position as Secretary of Air in the President's Cabinet. Late in September, 1939, Mrs. Roosevelt had urged Mrs. Lindbergh to address a Democratic luncheon in Philadelphia, but Anne had graciously declined.[4] The President and the Colonel were warily stalking each other as Lindbergh began his active opposition to Roosevelt's foreign policies.

Initially, Roosevelt did not honor Lindbergh's opposition with any public references. But in personal conferences, letters, and public addresses the President skillfully guided American public opinion away from isolationism toward internationalism of an aid-short-of-war variety. He encouraged interventionists to organize against the isolationists. In private conversations and correspondence he criticized Colonel Lindbergh, Senator Burton K. Wheeler, Senator Gerald P. Nye, and others who opposed his foreign policies. And by 1941 his feuds with Lindbergh and Wheeler were headlined across the land.

In December, 1939, President Roosevelt invited the mellow old Kansas Republican newspaper editor William Allen White to spend a night at the White House. The President wanted the newsman's help in getting "the American people to think of conceivable consequences [of the war in Europe and Asia] without scaring the people into thinking that they are going to be dragged into this war." A direct result of that overture was the formation of the Committee to Defend America by Aiding the Allies, under White's chairmanship. Among all the foreign policy pressure groups that existed before Pearl Harbor, the so-called White Committee was the principal adversary of America First. In 1940 and the early months of 1941, its leaders consulted frequently with administration policy makers. Its stand on foreign affairs corresponded closely to President Roosevelt's public positions at the time. Though its influence waned during the last half of 1941, it continued active until after Pearl Harbor.[5]

May 20, 1940, was the day that White publicly announced the formation of his Committee; it was the day after Lindbergh's broadcast on "The Air Defense of America"; it was a few days before Britain evacuated its forces from Europe at Dunkirk; and it was only a month before France surrendered to Hitler's Germany. On that date, President Roosevelt confided to his Secretary of the Treasury, Henry Morgenthau, Jr.: "If I should die tomorrow, I want you to know this. I am absolutely convinced that Lindbergh is a Nazi." The next day the President wrote Henry L. Stimson, who was soon to join his Cabinet as Secretary of War, that he was worried "by 'fifth column' activities over here." He wrote: "When I read Lindbergh's speech I felt that it could not have been better put if it had been written by Goebbels himself. What a pity that this youngster has completely abandoned his belief in our form of government and has accepted Nazi methods because apparently they are efficient."[6] Interventionists increasingly used that tactic of identifying isolationists with Nazism to discredit Lindbergh and other noninterventionist opponents of the administration's foreign policies.

On the same day as the Stimson letter, May 21, 1940, the President authorized the Attorney General "to secure information by listening devices direct to the conversation or other communications of persons suspected of subversive activities against the Government of the United States, including suspected spies." Many telegrams received at the White House criticizing the President's defense policies were being referred to J. Edgar Hoover, Director of the Federal Bureau of Investigation. In May, 1941, correspondence endorsing Lindbergh's opposition to the use of American ships to escort convoys was removed from White House files and "sent to Secret Service." In November, 1941, the President asked his Attorney General "about the possibility of a Grand Jury investigation of the money sources behind the America First Committee."[7]

The White House helped arrange for Senators and others to broadcast critical replies to Lindbergh's noninterventionist speeches. It obtained the services of Assistant Secretary of State Adolf A. Berle and the Democratic National Committee's Director of Radio to help with those replies. For example, Democratic Senator James Byrnes of South Carolina broadcast a vigorous attack on Lindbergh after his radio address of May 19, 1940. The White House got Democratic Senator Key Pittman of Nevada to broadcast "the same sort of beating that JB gave him" after Lindbergh's speech of June 15. Democratic Senator Scott Lucas of Illinois answered Lindbergh's speech of August 4 in Chicago, and Senator Claude Pepper of Florida vehemently denounced the Colonel from the Senate floor. Adolf Berle helped former Assistant Secretary of War Louis A. Johnson write the speech that he broadcast in response to Lindbergh's address of October 14, 1940.[8]

President Roosevelt's pugnacious Secretary of the Interior,

Harold L. Ickes, began his spirited public attacks on Lindbergh as early as December, 1938. He repeated them often thereafter, with increasing ferocity. To keep track of what Lindbergh was saying, Ickes maintained a complete indexed file of all the airman's noninterventionist speeches. Ickes strongly urged the administration to organize propaganda to build national unity and to combat the isolationists. Late in 1940, Roosevelt named him to chair a Cabinet committee to consider the matter. On December 19, the President's Cabinet had "a long talk over the alarming growth of the appeasement movement headed up by General Wood and Lindbergh and various others, which is assuming dangerous proportions." Secretary of War Stimson thought "It would be shocking if these people, who have no morals on international affairs, should succeed in stalling all action."[9]

Speaking at Columbia University around that time, Secretary Ickes called Colonel Lindbergh a "peripatetic appeaser who would abjectly surrender his sword even before it is demanded." On April 13, 1941, four days before Lindbergh gave his first address as a member of America First, Ickes spoke at a dinner in Chicago sponsored by the Jewish National Workers' Alliance of America. In his speech, Ickes accused Lindbergh of being the "No. 1 Nazi fellow traveler" in the United States and "the first American to raise aloft the standard of pro-Naziism." He said the aviator was "the proud possessor of a Nazi decoration which has already been well earned." Ickes described Anne Lindbergh's little book, *The Wave of the Future,* as "the bible of every American Nazi, Fascist, Bundist, and appeaser." In his opinion, the America First Committee should have been re-named "the America Next" Committee. He insisted that it attracted "antidemocrats, appeasers, labor baiters, and anti-Semites" and that Hitler was "enthusiastic about it."[10]

President Roosevelt asked the news commentator Jay Franklin (John F. Carter) to do some research for him on the Civil War Copperheads. Franklin did his work and submitted a fifty-page report to the President on April 22. The Copperheads were northerners with pro-southern sympathies who had been critical of Abraham Lincoln and his policies during the Civil War. In his memorandum Franklin compared Colonel Lindbergh to the Civil War General George B. McClellan as similarly "giving the sanction of professional prestige to the doctrines of defeatism." At his press conference three days later (the day after Lindbergh addressed a New York America First rally), newsmen asked Roosevelt why Colonel Lindbergh had not been called into active military service. In his response the President compared Lindbergh to Clement L. Vallandigham, the leading Civil War Copperhead.[11]

The allusion delighted most interventionists and infuriated noninterventionists. John T. Flynn, chairman of the America First chapter in New York, issued a scorching statement defending Lindbergh and excoriating the President. But others praised the President. One of the latter telegraphed the President urging that Lindbergh "be given one way transportation to Germany." Another wired: "Future of democracy more important than half baked views of aerial acrobats mesmerized by the German air force."[12]

The most important response came from Lindbergh himself. In a letter to the President on April 28, 1941, Lindbergh resigned his commission as a Colonel in the Army Air Corps Reserve. Since the President, his Commander in Chief, had "clearly implied" that he was "no longer of use to this country as a reserve officer," and since he had, in effect, questioned Lindbergh's loyalty, character, and motives, the Colonel believed he had "no honorable alternative" to resigning his commission. He took the action "with the utmost regret," because his "relationship with the Air Corps is one of the things that has meant most to me in life." He placed it "second only to my right as a citizen to speak freely to my fellow countrymen, and to discuss with them the issues of war and peace which confront our nation in this crisis." He promised to continue to serve the United States "as a private citizen." Colonel Lindbergh also wrote to Secretary of War Stimson formally resigning his Air Corps commission. In his private journal Lindbergh reflected on the irony of finding himself "opposing my country's entrance into a war I *don't* believe in, when I would so much rather be fighting for my country in a war I *do* believe in." He was "stumping the country with pacifists and . . . resigning as a colonel in the Army Air Corps, when there is no philosophy I disagree with more than that of the pacifist, and nothing I would rather be doing than flying in the Air Corps."[13]

Responses to his resignation were predictable: silence from the White House; denunciations from interventionists; praise from noninterventionists. Senator Robert A. Taft of Ohio wrote Lindbergh congratulating him on his foreign policy stands and criticizing the President's "cowardly" attack on the airman. As Taft saw it, the President "lacks the courage to come out openly for a declaration of war, while taking every possible step to accomplish that purpose, and yet threatens those who oppose his policy, as if the country were at war." Oswald Garrison Villard, a long-time pacifist and civil liberties crusader, wrote a formidable defense of Lindbergh. Some undergraduate students at the University of Southern California formed a "Campus Copperhead" organization supporting Lindbergh.[14]

On July 14, 1941, in an address in New York, Secretary Ickes again flailed away at Lindbergh. "No one has ever heard Lindbergh utter a word of horror at, or even aversion to, the bloody career that the Nazis are following, nor a word of pity for the innocent men, women and children, who have been deliberately murdered by the nazis in practically every country in Europe." Ickes had "never heard this Knight of the German Eagle denounce Hitler or nazism or Mussolini or fascism." He had not even "heard Lindbergh say a word for democracy itself." As he saw it, "all of Lindbergh's passionate words are to encourage Hitler and to break down the will of his own fellow citizens to resist Hitler and nazism."[15]

Lindbergh saw no advantage in contesting with Ickes, but he tried to assign responsibility for the Cabinet member's remarks to the President. On July 16, Lindbergh wrote to Roosevelt concerning Ickes's repeated charges that he was connected with a foreign government and the criticism of him for accepting the German medal in 1938. Lindbergh reminded the President that he had received the decoration "in the American Embassy, in the presence of your Ambassador," and "was there at his request in order to assist in creating a better relationship between the American Embassy and the German Government, which your Ambassador desired at that time." Lindbergh wrote that if Ickes's statements and implications were false, he had "a right to an apology" from the President's Secretary of the Interior. He maintained that he had "no connection with any foreign government" and had "had no communication, directly or indirectly, with anyone in Germany or Italy" since he had left Europe in 1939. Lindbergh offered to open his files for the President's investigation and to answer any questions that the President might have about his activities. He asked the President to give him "the opportunity of answering any charges that may be made against" him. But he insisted that "unless charges are made and proved," as an American citizen he had "the right to expect truth and justice" from the members of the President's Cabinet. The only response Lindbergh got from the White House was a memo from Stephen T. Early, the President's secretary, verbally spanking him for releasing his letter to the press before it reached Roosevelt.[16]

Ickes seemed pleased by Lindbergh's letter. He wrote in his diary: "Up to that time I had always admired Lindbergh in one respect. No matter how vigorously he had been attacked personally he had never attempted to answer. He had kept determinedly in the furrow that he was plowing. I had begun to think that no one could get under his skin enough to make him squeal. But at last I had succeeded. I suspect that it was my reference to him as a 'Knight of the German Eagle' that got him." In a reply carried in Frank Knox's *Chicago Daily News,* Ickes wrote: "Neither I nor anyone in this administration ever charged that Mr. Lindbergh had any connection with any foreign government or that he was in communication with any representative of a foreign government. But it is a notorious fact that he has been devoting himself to a cause which, if it should succeed, will be of immeasurable benefit to Hitler." In his article, Ickes suggested that Lindbergh could "put himself right by championing the cause of democracy and civilization. He can denounce Hitler and his brutal aggressions. He can cheer on England. He can unite with those who are prepared to defend American institutions."[17] In effect, Ickes was saying that Lindbergh could cleanse himself if he would abandon his noninterventionist opposition to Roosevelt's foreign policies and join with Ickes in support of intervention. That Lindbergh would not do.

Despite its vigorous opposition to Lindbergh and the other isolationists, the Roosevelt administration did not create the aggressive government propaganda organization that Secretary Ickes repeatedly urged. Lowell Mellett of the White House staff headed an Office of Government Reports, which performed an "information" function. But his operation was much too bland and restrained to suit Ickes and other interventionists.[18]

On May 20, 1941, President Roosevelt appointed Mayor Fiorello H. La Guardia of New York City to be Director of a new Office of Civilian Defense. One of his responsibilities was "to sustain national morale." And the President explicitly defined the "morale" aspect to include "the whole subject of effective publicity to offset the propaganda of the Wheelers, Nyes, Lindberghs, etc." Under La Guardia the Office of Civilian Defense did undertake anti-isolationist efforts. It also encouraged and co-operated with private groups in their campaigns against isolationism. The total effort by the Roosevelt administration to defeat the isolationists was massive, many-faceted, and effective. But it fell far short of the wishes of Secretary Ickes and other extreme interventionists. La Guardia was fully as interventionist as Ickes, but his tremendous energies were spread much too thin. So far as the Office of Civilian Defense was concerned, La Guardia focused most of his attention on narrowly civil defense matters. In the end, the Roosevelt administration's interventionist crusade against the isolationists depended heavily on the activities of private individuals and interventionist pressure groups (often encouraged and aided by the administration).[19]

Nevertheless, the tone that Secretary Ickes had set in attacking Lindbergh and America First increasingly became the general tone of the "Great Debate" in the last half of 1941. In some respects it was much like that of the McCarthy era ten years later. The guilt-by-association, the charges that individuals were serving a dangerous and evil foreign totalitarian cause by not sufficiently voicing their opposition to that cause, were devastating in destroying the reputations and effectiveness of Lindbergh, America First, and other noninterventionists. But those tactics were by no means limited to members of the Roosevelt administration. Interventionist pressure groups, special interest groups, newspapers, and individual interventionists joined in bludgeoning Charles A. Lindbergh and his fellow noninterventionists. Figuratively, it became a bloody brawl during the last half of 1941.

# 17/The Interventionists Organize

DURING the year and a half before Pearl Harbor, the two most powerful interventionist pressure groups were the Committee to Defend America by Aiding the Allies and Fight for Freedom, Incorporated. Those two groups reflected a cleavage and the different tendencies within the interventionist camp, and within the Roosevelt administration. The White Committee adhered to President Franklin D. Roosevelt's public aid-short-of-war approach; the Fight for Freedom Committee believed aid-short-of-war would not be enough to defeat the Axis and favored full United States involvement in the war. The Fight for Freedom Committee also was more aggressive than the Committee to Defend America in its attacks on the isolationists.

The Committee to Defend America by Aiding the Allies, organized in May, 1940, maintained its national headquarters in New York. William Allen White, the respected Republican editor of the *Emporia Gazette,* was national chairman, and Clark Eichelberger was executive director. Like interventionists in general, the White Committee insisted that it was more important to assure a British victory over the Axis than to keep the United States out of the war. Following the lead of the President, the White Committee opposed a negotiated peace and favored all-out aid-short-of-war. It conducted major campaigns for the destroyer deal with England in 1940, for lend-lease early in 1941, and for the use of American ships as convoy escorts.[1]

## The Interventionists Organize

In December, 1940, Britain's Prime Minister Winston Churchill was appealing for more aid from the United States, and President Roosevelt was beginning the moves that culminated with passage of the Lend-Lease Act a few weeks later. And, in December, the White Committee suffered a major internal crisis. White, from Kansas on the Great Plains, recognized and understood the mixed feelings of most Americans—their sympathy for Britain, their opposition to the Axis, and their continued desire to stay out of the war. Indeed, he shared those feelings. (A later generation of Americans could have its own antiwar sentiments and at the same time find it incomprehensible that pre-Pearl Harbor Americans were reluctant to enter World War II.) White was increasingly troubled by the strength and restiveness of the more extreme interventionists in his Committee. They were particularly vocal in the New York chapter and centered in the so-called "Century Club group" there. White's age, health, and Kansas responsibilities made it hard for him to cope with them. Charges by isolationists that the warlike "Century group" represented the true views of his Committee made his situation more difficult.

On December 23, 1940, White dropped a bombshell that threatened to blow his Committee apart. In response to an inquiry from Roy W. Howard of the Scripps-Howard newspapers, White wrote from Kansas that "The only reason in God's world I am in this organization is to keep this country out of war." He opposed repeal of the Johnson Act and did not want American ships to carry contraband into the war zone. "If I was making a motto for the Committee to Defend America by Aiding the Allies, it would be 'The Yanks are not coming.' " He thought it unfair to criticize his Committee because some of its members were more warlike. He wrote: "Any organization that is for war is seriously playing Hitler's game."[2]

White's statement pleased the moderates in his Committee, infuriated the extreme interventionists, disturbed those in his Committee who feared its divisive effects, and delighted Lindbergh and the noninterventionists. Colonel Lindbergh immediately released a statement: "Mr. White has rendered a great service to this country by clarifying his position, and the position of his Committee. He has given us new hope for a united America at a time in our history when unity is essential." Differences between them still existed on aid to Europe, he wrote, but those remaining differences were less important than that Americans could unite "on the necessity of building strength at home, and keeping out of war abroad." General Robert E. Wood and other noninterventionists responded in similar ways.[3]

Extreme interventionists, however, were much less pleased. Fiorello La Guardia charged White with "doing a typical Laval." He wrote to White suggesting that the Committee divide: "You could continue as Chairman of the 'Committee to Defend America by Aiding the Allies with Words' and the rest of us would join a 'Committee to Defend America by Aiding the Allies with Deeds.'" At La Guardia's request, a copy of his letter was brought to President Roosevelt's attention, and others kept the White House informed as the controversy developed in the Committee. The New York chapter rubbed salt in White's wounds by promptly inviting La Guardia to be its honorary chairman. In the turmoil, White resigned as national chairman on January 2, 1941, though he stayed on as honorary national chairman and pledged his continued support for the Committee.[4]

The crisis weakened the Committee to Defend America, but it did not really benefit Lindbergh and the noninterventionists. Neither Senator Ernest W. Gibson of Vermont nor Clark Eichelberger, who in turn succeeded White, satisfactorily filled his shoes as national chairman. But Americans did not draw together in opposition to war, as Lindbergh had hoped. Interventionists from the Northeast strengthened their positions in the Committee to Defend America.

In April, 1941, extreme interventionists organized Fight for Freedom, Incorporated. The new organization, drawing support from many who had backed the White Committee earlier, insisted that aid-short-of-war would not be enough and urged the United States to enter the European war as a full belligerent. Episcopal Bishop Henry W. Hobson of southern Ohio was national chairman, and Senator Carter Glass of Virginia was honorary chairman. It reflected the attitudes of Secretary of War Henry L. Stimson and Secretary of the Navy Frank Knox in the President's Cabinet. It won its greatest support in states along the Atlantic seaboard.[5]

Fight for Freedom gained strength as the more moderate program of the Committee to Defend America seemed less and less adequate for the task of defeating the Axis. And it gained as the "war now" wing of the interventionist forces grew in relation to the "aid-short-of-war" wing. During 1941, the Committee to Defend America continued its activities—and its opposition to the isolationists. But it seemed bland in comparison with the more strident tone of Fight for Freedom and its no-holds-barred assaults on the isolationists. The increasingly vicious attacks on Charles A. Lindbergh, Burton K. Wheeler, Gerald P. Nye, and other noninterventionists were devastatingly effective. The consequences of those methods are still evident in the shattered careers and reputations of prewar noninterventionists.[6]

In addition to those two major groups, whose primary concern was foreign policy, there were many other organizations that added their weight to the crusade against the isolationists in general and against Lindbergh in particular. Especially prominent and effective was an organization called Friends of Democracy, Incorporated. Described as "a non-partisan, non-sectarian, non-profit, anti-totalitarian propaganda agency," Friends of Democracy was formed in Kansas City in 1937 and moved its main headquarters to New York City in 1939. Its founder and national director was the Reverend Leon M. Birkhead, a Unitarian minister. Its national chairman was the author Rex Stout. It attacked both rightists and leftists, but Birkhead believed fascism was a much greater threat to American democracy than communism was. Friends of Democracy claimed to take no foreign policy position, but Birkhead and Stout were both dedicated interventionists. Birkhead had been aroused against Nazism on visits to Europe in the 1930's, and he had favored an American declaration of war against Nazi Germany even before the European war began. Stout was a sponsor of Fight for Freedom, and both Birkhead and Stout addressed meetings of the Fight for Freedom Committee. Friends of Democracy raised funds to conduct major campaigns against Charles A. Lindbergh, the America First Committee, Henry Ford, Father Charles E. Coughlin, Hamilton Fish, and others. Early in 1941 it published an elaborate brochure entitled *The America First Commitee—The Nazi Transmission Belt.* It called America First "a Nazi front. . . . by means of which the apostles of Nazism are spreading their antidemocratic ideas into millions of American homes!" Friends of Democracy co-operated with Fight for Freedom and the Committee to Defend America, both of which purchased and distributed its pamphlets attacking Lindbergh and America First. One of its investigators was John Roy Carlson, author of the book *Under Cover,* which attacked prewar isolationists.[7] In New York, the Council Against Intolerance in America, headed by George Gordon Battle, was another of the non-foreign policy groups that turned its guns on Lindbergh and America First in 1941.[8]

Countless newspapers, magazines, journalists, and columnists added their might to the assaults on Lindbergh and America First. Some were as dignified and responsible as the *New York Times;* others were as extreme and vitriolic as Marshall Field's *PM* in New York. Critical columnists ranged from Walter Lippmann to Dorothy Thompson and Walter Winchell. Newsreels portrayed the isolationists and their activities in unfavorable light.

Some writers and speakers, particularly in 1940 and earlier, kept their arguments on a high plane. They presented the case for intervention positively, and they argued against the reasoning of the noninterventionists. There was no significant violence on either side in the foreign policy debate before Pearl Harbor. But as it dragged on emotions mounted. Self-restraint was harder to maintain. Individuals on both sides found it increasingly difficult to see their opponents as honest people who happened to hold different opinions. Attacks on both sides became more personal, more vicious, and more destructive. It became easier

Colonel and Mrs. Lindbergh, with their son Jon, disembarking from the *American Importer,* Liverpool, England, December 1935

Lindbergh and Major Truman Smith during an inspection trip in Germany, 1936

Luncheon guests of Hermann Goering, 1936: far left, Captain Koenig, American Air Attaché; third from left, Lindbergh; center, Goering; fourth from right, Frau Goering; third from right, Anne Morrow Lindbergh

Lindbergh and Michel Détroyat, French aviation expert, conferring during inspection of a German airplane factory

*National Archives photograph*

Lindbergh piloting the Mohawk, built to his specifications in England, that he and his wife flew on various trips to France and Germany; to Italy, Yugoslavia, and India in 1937; and to Czechoslovakia and the Soviet Union in 1938

*nal Archives photograph*

*Wide World Photos*

In a Curtiss P-36 before take-off, Moffett Field, San Jose, California, July 4, 1939

Return to America: disembarking from the *Aquitania*, New York, April 1939

On the speakers' platform at America First rally, Madison Square Garden, New York, May 23, 1941: from the left, Senator Burton K. Wheeler, Lindbergh, Kathleen Norris, and Norman Thomas

Lindbergh addressing the America First rally in Hollywood Bowl, California, June 20, 1941

General Robert E. Wood

Lindbergh and Henry Ford,
Dearborn, Michigan,
April 1942

Lindbergh testifying against the lend-lease bill before the House
Foreign Affairs Committee, January 23, 1941

(*Above*) America First rally, Madison Square Garden, New York, October 30, 1941, at which Lindbergh spoke; (*facing page, top left*) American Indians, members of the Non-Sectarian Anti-Nazi League, picketing the America First Committee's New York office to protest the rally

*(Left)* Lindbergh
at the rostrum
in Manhattan Center,
New York,
April 23, 1941, and
*(above, right)* the crowd
outside

In the Pacific during World War II: *(above)* with General Robert B. McClure in the Solomons, 1944; *(below, left)* with Major Thomas B. McGuire on Biak, 1944; *(below, right)* with Lieutenant General George C. Kenney, Commanding General of the Far East Air Command, in Brisbane, Australia, July 1944

to see one's adversaries not just as mistaken but as evil, and possibly motivated by selfish, antidemocratic, or even subversive considerations. By the last half of 1941, the debate on America's policies toward the European war was being conducted on a much lower level than one might prefer in a democracy. And in that contest Charles A. Lindbergh and the America First Committee took a terrible beating.

# 18/"Is Lindbergh a Nazi?"

FEW Americans have been so lavishly praised as Charles A. Lindbergh; few have been so severely denounced as he, for his opposition to American entry into World War II. Some simply criticized his foreign policy analyses and found them mistaken or unwise. Many questioned his qualifications to speak on foreign affairs. But increasingly, especially in 1941, critics challenged his loyalty, his patriotism, and his dedication to democracy. In the eyes of millions of Americans then and later he was seen as little better than a Nazi. The effectiveness of such charges seriously undermined the noninterventionist movement before Pearl Harbor.

The increasingly vicious attacks on Lindbergh were partly a calculated tactic to defeat the opposition by whatever methods seemed most effective. The long feud between Lindbergh and the press made many newsmen ready agents for destroying him. But there were other variables in the compound. The foreign policy debate that took place before Pearl Harbor was tremendously important for the world, for the United States, and for the very lives and futures of individual Americans. From the highest to the most obscure, most Americans felt intensely on the subject. Because the issues were so fundamental and important, emotions heightened on all sides. As passions mounted, it was increasingly more difficult to see adversaries as "honorable though mistaken." The emotional tendencies encouraged the questioning of the motives and morality of those who advanced

142

conflicting views. A few extremists on each side provided provocations inviting extreme responses from the other. The patterns escalated. And, as the premier spokesman for noninterventionism, Charles A. Lindbergh attracted both the enthusiasm of its devotees and the enraged enmity of its adversaries. He was ever so visible—and vulnerable. His triumph might be the defeat of the Roosevelt administration's foreign policies; his destruction could bring the whole noninterventionist cause down as well.

The intensity of such emotions is increased when they are part of cataclysmic world conflicts. That has often been true in the history of American foreign affairs, whether the conflicts abroad were the Wars of the French Revolution, the Napoleonic Wars, or the Cold War with the Communist states after World War II. Noninterventionists could (and did) charge interventionists with being more interested in foreign causes than in American interests. They could (and did) charge interventionists with being Anglophiles who wanted to crawl back into the British Empire. After the beginning of the Russo-German war they could (and did) charge interventionists with advancing the cause of atheistic communism. But with Hitler's Nazi Germany, Mussolini's Fascist Italy, and militarist Japan aggressively threatening to triumph in a world-wide assault on freedom and democracy, the isolationist charges were not terribly effective. To urge any policy that was less than unqualified opposition to Hitler and Nazi Germany could be (and was) interpreted as positive support for Hitler and the Nazis. Such was Lindbergh's experience.

It obviously was in Germany's interest to prevent American entry in the war on the side of Great Britain. All German propaganda agents and agencies in the United States opposed American entry into the war. There were striking similarities between the foreign policy views of American isolationists and Nazi propaganda in the United States. In August, 1940, *Facts in Review,* the leading German propaganda publication in the United States, quoted Field Marshal Hermann Goering as saying that there were no planes in Germany that, when loaded with bombs, could fly to America and return. Goering continued: "America simply cannot be invaded by air or sea. That is particularly true if her armaments and national defense are appropriate to or commensurate with the country's size, population, resources and industrial production, not to mention the spirit of the people. . . . If American defenses are what they should be, particularly if America's air force is properly developed, built up, organized and strategically based, America can defy any group of powers. No one would be so idiotic as to attempt an invasion."[1] Those views were almost identical to the ones Lindbergh was advancing at the time.

In its reports to Berlin, members of the German Embassy staff claimed to have contact with some around Lindbergh and America First, but they recognized that it would be the "kiss of death" for American isolationists to identify with Nazi Germany. German officials in the United States repeatedly urged their government in Berlin to avoid giving any public endorsements of Lindbergh or other leading noninterventionists. In May, 1940, the German Military Attaché in Washington insisted that "what Lindbergh proclaims with great courage, is certainly the highest and most effective form of propaganda." He thought: "The slightest sign of activity on the part of German agents would dash the weapons from the hands of these men." In July he repeated that view. In October, he and Hans Thomsen, the German Chargé d'affaires in Washington, urged "that Lindbergh, his speeches and his connections with leading German personages not be mentioned in the press, in speeches and discussions, etc." In December, Thomsen advised that the work of the isolationist committees "be passed over in silence in the German press and radio as far as possible." The German Foreign Ministry in Berlin warned that statements by American isolationists, including those by Lindbergh, "must not in any case be incorporated in the propaganda bulletin and distributed by the Mission because it is to be feared that the isolationist spokesmen will be compromised with the American public as a result of this."[2] But those precautions were not sufficient. It was in the German interest for the United States to stay out of the European war; the tiny pro-Nazi contingent in America (including the German-American Bund) did urge noninterventionist policies for the United States; and the interventionists had no difficulty contending that in urging nonintervention Lindbergh was ("consciously or unconsciously") serving the cause of Nazi Germany.

Some of Lindbergh's friends and fellow noninterventionists tactfully advised him to tailor his statements to reduce his vulnerability to attacks. After the Colonel's first Chicago address, in August, 1940, William R. Castle wrote him that his influence was "so terribly important in this whole struggle to keep out of the war that we must make every effort to let nothing happen which will destroy that influence." Castle thought it "immensely important" that Lindbergh "somehow be cleared of the charge of being pro-German." He volunteered "to look over an address purely from the point of view of the English, as the words may affect your audience," if Lindbergh wished—which he did not. In reply, Lindbergh said that he wrote his speeches "without an attempt to gain popularity and with the feeling that it is desirable for someone to speak frankly and as he actually feels." He thought America already had "far too many of the type of articles and addresses that bend with the changing winds of popular opinion." The Socialist noninterventionist Norman Thomas also wrote to Lindbergh, urging: "(1) Emphasize your personal opposition to the cruelty, intolerance and tyranny of fascism. (2) Make it clear that at the very least, a desirable peace would mean the continuance of Great Britain and her self-governing dominions as absolutely independent nations with real power, not as puppets to Hitler. (3) Clarify your own position on co-operation by us with the winner of this war. I do not think you mean to imply that American business is temporarily to share with the German state the profits of exploitation, yet some of your enemies so interpret your remarks." Historian Charles A. Beard advised Lindbergh that he was "doing great damage to the cause of staying out of war by repeatedly saying in public that Britain has lost the war." Beard thought "the declaration may make more enemies to our cause than friends."[3]

In the middle of 1941, when Lindbergh urged "new leadership" for America, General Robert E. Wood wrote to him pointing out that the statement "might be misconstrued by some extremists as advocating a revolution." Wood realized that was "far-fetched," but he feared that "our opponents are anxious to hang anything they can on us." Lindbergh did issue a statement clarifying his meaning, but he wrote Wood that he did not think there was "any way of preventing an antagonistic press from removing sentences from their context. One can only attempt to avoid giving our opposition the opportunity to do this more than is necessary." Through General Wood, George N. Peek advised Lindbergh to say that "he and America First are for defense of constitutional Americanism against Communism, Fascism, Nazism, Imperialism or any other alien isms that threaten from within or without the integrity of our form of government and way of life." Peek thought such a statement could silence the "whispering campaigns that he is pro-Nazi."[4] Lindbergh did not make the statement Peek suggested; and the campaigns were not just whispered, but were shouted.

Lindbergh correctly understood those and other pieces of advice to be the well-intentioned urgings of friends of his cause. But he did not bend. He spent long hours composing his speeches, carefully choosing his words to express exactly what he wanted to say. He was not willing to advance views only to please his friends, to win applause from his audiences, or to appease his adversaries. Early in 1941, he wrote in his private journal: "I prefer adventure to security, freedom to popularity, and conviction to influence." Many years later, he said that before Pearl Harbor it had become "such a fetish to damn the enemy that I got disgusted with it."[5] His interventionist opponents compelled him to pay a high price for his stance.

An editorial in the *New York Times,* commenting on Lindbergh's radio address of May 19, 1940, used the words "peculiar," "ignorant," and "blind" in analyzing the Colonel's views and concluded that "Colonel Lindbergh remains a great flier." Democratic Senators James F. Byrnes of South Carolina, Key Pittman of Nevada, and Claude Pepper of Florida were among the many who charged him with being America's number-one

## "Is Lindbergh a Nazi?"

"Fifth Columnist." Senator Pepper thought the airman wanted to see American life regimented in Hitler's way. Professor William Y. Elliott of Harvard University accused him of cowardice in his plea for appeasement and co-operation with Germany. Henry A. Wallace, the Democratic vice presidential candidate, called him "the outstanding appeaser of the nation battling for the Republican party." In December, 1940, Robert E. Sherwood, the distinguished playwright and a speech writer for President Roosevelt, told a White Committee rally that Lindbergh was "simply a Nazi with a Nazi's Olympian contempt for all democratic processes—the rights of freedom of speech and worship, the right to select and criticize our own government and the right of labor to strike." Professor James H. Sheldon of the board of directors of the Non-Sectarian Anti-Nazi League charged that Lindbergh was "the kind of person who would have advised George Washington to quit at Valley Forge." Hostile and abusive letters, both signed and unsigned, reached him by the thousands. In August, 1940, a handwritten letter to "Dear Nazi Lindbergh" demanded that he stop his antiwar speeches and retract his earlier statements "or else you will not see your other baby alive within three weeks from today." Many urged that he be deported to Hitler's Nazi Germany.[6] Those and countless other charges and denunciations preceded his affiliation with the America First Committee in April, 1941. From then on things got worse!

One may get some idea of the difficulties Lindbergh faced by focusing on the first two America First rallies he addressed in New York, one in Manhattan Center on April 24, 1941, and the other in Madison Square Garden on May 23. At the earlier rally the speakers included Democratic Senator David I. Walsh of Massachusetts and novelist Kathleen Norris, in addition to Lindbergh. John T. Flynn, chairman of the New York chapter of America First, presided. Some 10,000 people crowded into the auditorium, with an overflow of several thousand. Leon M. Birkhead's Friends of Democracy and other groups had organized opposition picketing of the meeting. Birkhead charged in advance that the rally would be "the largest gathering of pro-

**147**

Nazi and pro-Fascists, of both domestic and imported brands, since the German American Bund rallies in Madison Square Garden." In the crowd outside, the Non-Sectarian Anti-Nazi League distributed copies of a circular on "What One Hitler Medal Can Do." The speeches were broadcast locally by one radio station; the station also carried replies by Rex Stout and James P. Warburg, which were sponsored by the Fight for Freedom Committee.[7]

The newspaper *PM* reported the meeting as including "a liberal sprinkling of Nazis, Fascists, anti-Semites, crackpots and just people. The just people seemed out of place." It charged that "Lindbergh followed the Nazi line to a 't' " and that "Audience reaction would have pleased even Joe Goebbels, the Nazi Propaganda Minister." Walter Winchell referred to America First as "the America Last Outfit" and contended that "every hate spreader they could find showed up for that meeting." He charged that "What Lindbergh and that group want is no opposition. No supporters of dictators can stand opposition!" In his broadcast reply, Stout maintained that Lindbergh "would be acceptable to Hitler as an American gauleiter, or two and two no longer make four." Not long after the meeting, Birkhead told organizers of Fight for Freedom in Cincinnati that Lindbergh had "already been selected by Hitler as the 'Fuehrer' of America."[8]

Lindbergh's appearance on May 23 attracted some 23,000 people into Madison Square Garden, with perhaps 10,000 more listening outside. Senator Burton K. Wheeler, Kathleen Norris, and Norman Thomas also spoke at the meeting. John T. Flynn again presided. From the platform Flynn denounced Joseph McWilliams, a local pro-fascist in the audience, and said such people were not wanted at America First meetings. Before the rally, the New York chapter of the Committee to Defend America by Aiding the Allies charged that those attending would "mingle with Nazis, Fascists and Communists" and "with persons of all shades of opinion subversive to the United States and the democratic way of life." Friends of Democracy distributed handbills outside the meeting linking Lindbergh with the Nazis. The Henry Luce publications *Time* and *Life* carried pictures of Lindbergh, Wheeler, and the other speakers at the rally with arms raised giving the Pledge of Allegiance, and commented on the similarities to the Nazi salute.[9]

The reporting on the character of the audience there varied widely. John Roy Carlson, in *Under Cover,* described Flynn's denunciation of Joseph McWilliams at the rally, but he insisted that *"the Coughlinite mob burst into applause for Joe!!!"* According to Carlson, it took Flynn several minutes to quiet the applause. He said there was a "weak, unconvincing round of boos" against McWilliams. A writer in the interventionist *PM* reported: "The bulk of the Garden throng seemed sympathetic to Flynn's attack on McWilliams. There was only a smattering of applause for the Yorkville Fuehrer." That writer, however, contended that many Coughlinites attended the rally. Concerning the latter point, Edwin S. Webster, Jr., secretary of the New York America First chapter, asserted: "Although certain of the people mentioned were probably at our rally they were in the very small minority. No press tickets or tickets of any sort are given to the people in question. It has been remarked frequently by people coming to our rallies that they have seldom seen such a fine looking crowd of Americans." Writing many years later, Lindbergh remembered that he had agreed in principle with the denunciation of McWilliams but thought Flynn had "attacked with far too much emotion and excitement." Flynn's tone "spread quickly," and the audience's "first angry shouts merged into a somewhat alarming roar." Police moved into position to protect McWilliams, but the uproar subsided; there was no violence. Lindbergh did not "recall any indication of support for McWilliams," but he doubted "that any pro-McWilliams shouting could have been heard during that antagonistic roar."[10] Whatever one may conclude about the meeting, the most critical reports were not necessarily the most accurate.

In June, 1941, *PM* carried a major article by Ralph Ingersoll and James A. Wechsler charging that "to the men and movements which compose the pro-Fascist front and imperil democracy at home, Charles A. Lindbergh has brought hope; and their offensive against democracy threatens our future." The columnist Dorothy Thompson repeatedly charged "that Lindbergh is pro-Nazi, and that he shares the Nazi philosophy." She insisted that "the entire pro-Nazi mass movement in this country is behind Lindbergh—the whole kit and kaboodle of them." The City Council in Charlotte, North Carolina, changed the name of Lindbergh Drive to Avon Avenue. When the chairman of the Norwalk, Connecticut, America First chapter proposed a public debate on foreign affairs, the Connecticut state chairman of Fight for Freedom responded that "instead of spending money hiring a hall" America First should hire "an aeroplane and a few parachutes and letting Messrs. Lindbergh, Wheeler, and Taft and some others do a Rudolph Hess into Hitler's Germany, which they are aiding so much by their present activities, and from which government Lindbergh received a military decoration and concerning the acts of which country he has never once uttered one word of condemnation. In our first fight for freedom we got rid of Benedict Arnold. In this fight for freedom let us get rid of all of the Benedict Arnolds."[11]

Lindbergh addressed a huge crowd in the Hollywood Bowl in June, 1941. When Wendell Willkie then addressed an interventionist rally there in July, his supporters went all out in their unsuccessful efforts to outdo America First and Lindbergh. As a part of that effort, Darryl F. Zanuck sent a memo to 20th Century-Fox Film Corporation department heads urging them to get personal pledges from all those in their departments that they would come to the Willkie rally and would bring their families with them. He directed each department head to report personally to him on the results of his efforts.[12]

Until June 22, 1941, American Communists were noninterventionists; on that date, the beginning of the Russo-German war, they immediately reversed themselves and became fervent interventionists. But both before and after the beginning of the Russo-German war the Communists were among Lindbergh's assailants. In January, 1941, the Communist *New Masses* called Lindbergh "our foremost Nazi." An editorial in the *Daily Worker* on April 25, 1941, labeled him "a reactionary imperialist, part and parcel of the same imperialist class which runs the show at Washington; he just happens to have a difference of opinion with them at the moment on how best to go about expanding the American Empire, and preparing for a war against the Soviet Union." After the Russo-German war converted the American Communists from isolationists into interventionists, William Z. Foster of the American Communist Party charged that Lindbergh and General Wood were "conscious Fascists who want to come to an agreement with Hitler at any cost, abolish the communist party and labor unions."[13]

In August and September, 1941, Friends of Democracy prepared an elaborate pamphlet entitled *Is Lindbergh a Nazi?* The Reverend Leon M. Birkhead thought the pamphlet would be "a major contribution to the cause of destroying the influence of Lindbergh." In its preparation, Friends of Democracy "had in mind those sections of the country where Lindbergh had his biggest following." To that end, they "left out personalities and stories about Lindbergh that might boomerang." Ulric Bell of Fight for Freedom thought his organization "would invest $500 in mailing costs." He believed it best "to concentrate in the isolationist states." In October, Birkhead sent Bell "a very confidential statement outlining our plans for our Lindbergh project." Friends of Democracy arranged a luncheon at Toots Shor's Restaurant in New York for fifty members of its motion picture division at which Birkhead sought $10,000 in contributions "for a publicity campaign branding Charles A. Lindbergh as a Nazi."[14]

The twenty-eight-page pamphlet, *Is Lindbergh a Nazi?*, missed no argument in its attempts to discredit Lindbergh. It charged that he had become "the American voice of the Berlin Propaganda Ministry." It saw him as "a very real threat to our democratic way of life." Charging that Lindbergh advocated "policies which, if carried out, will result in an American Hitler," it contended that "his words might have been written by Adolf Hitler." It printed some of Lindbergh's statements in columns parallel to similar statements by Hitler, the English fascist Sir Oswald Mosley, and Lawrence Dennis. For example,

Lindbergh was quoted as saying: "Neither I nor anybody else in the America First Committee advocates proceeding by anything but constitutional methods." In the parallel column it quoted Hitler's words: "Neither I nor anybody else in the National Socialist Party advocates proceeding by anything but constitutional methods." It was not entirely clear from the pamphlet whether its authors thought everyone else who advocated the use of constitutional methods was also a Nazi and pro-Hitler. The pamphlet concluded that Lindbergh had become "the voice of American Nazism." It was widely distributed by Friends of Democracy, Fight for Freedom, and other interventionist groups.[15]

In many respects, Charles A. Lindbergh's foreign policy views *were* similar to those advanced by Nazi propaganda in the United States. If his policies had been implemented, the consequences would have benefited Hitler's Germany. And if Nazi Germany had been defeated in World War II, the defeat would not have been accomplished by American men and equipment. German agents were pleased by Lindbergh's noninterventionist efforts, and profascists in the United States applauded him.

At the same time, however, Lindbergh did not like Hitler or Nazism. He did not favor a Nazi dictatorship either for Germany or for the United States. He did not want Nazi Germany to triumph in Britain or in the United States. Whatever one may think of his views, Lindbergh formulated them in terms of his own judgment of what was best for the United States and for Western civilization. He thought the United States should not be guided in its conduct of foreign affairs by the wishes of any foreign government (German, British, or Russian) but, rather, by what Americans thought best for the United States.

The methods used by interventionists in attacking Lindbergh in 1941 were fundamentally similar to those used by McCarthyites in attacking liberal internationalists in the early 1950's. The McCarthyites discredited their adversaries by associating them with Communist Russia; interventionists discredited their adversaries by associating them with Nazi Germany. Those "guilt-by-association-with-an-aggressive-totalitarian-power" methods were effective in destroying the careers and reputations of liberal internationalists in the 1950's; those same methods were even more effective in destroying the careers and reputations of Lindbergh and other leading isolationists in World War II. Those methods, both in 1941 and 1951, were unfair, intolerant—and effective. But they were even more effective in 1941 than in 1951. In the 1950's, McCarthyites were contesting with the so-called "liberal internationalist establishment," which finally triumphed over Senator Joseph McCarthy and his followers. It discredited both the Senator and his methods. In 1941, however, the "liberal internationalist establishment" shared in the use of those methods against the isolationists. Not only did it triumph, it did not even seriously object to the methods used to accomplish that victory. And, unlike its tone in the 1950's, it showed no pity for the victims of those methods during the World War II years. To be trite, it depended on whose bull was being gored.

The interventionist assaults on Lindbergh were becoming increasingly vicious and effective by the middle of 1941. But he, in effect, invited even more devastating attacks by a speech he delivered at an America First Committee rally in Des Moines, Iowa, on September 11, 1941.

# IV

"War Agitators" and
American Democracy

# 19/"Who Are the War Agitators?"

FROM the very beginning of his battle against intervention in 1939, Colonel Charles A. Lindbergh warned against propaganda by those who wanted to drag the United States into the war abroad. In the years 1940–1941, he repeatedly berated the "powerful elements" that were pressing the United States toward war. In his radio broadcast on May 19, 1940, nearly a year before he joined the America First Committee, Lindbergh said: "The only reason that we are in danger of becoming involved in this war is because there are powerful elements in America who desire us to take part. They represent a small minority of the people, but they control much of the machinery of influence and propaganda. They seize every opportunity to push us closer to the edge." He urged "the underlying character of this country to rise and assert itself, to strike down these elements of personal profit and foreign interest."[1] He repeated that general view many times in later speeches.

On June 15, he charged that an "organized minority in this country" was "flooding our congress and our press with propaganda for war" and was "pushing us closer and closer to the edge." On August 4, he told his audience in Chicago that there were "interests in this country and abroad who will do their utmost to draw us into the war." On April 17, 1941, in his first address as a member of America First, he complained that the United States had "been led toward war by a minority of its people, through misinformation and through confusion of the issues involved." When he spoke in New York less than a week later, he said: "We have been led toward war by a minority of our people. This minority has power. It has influence. It has a loud voice. But it does not represent the American people."[2]

Thomas W. Lamont of the Wall Street banking firm of J. P. Morgan and Company was an active internationalist and interventionist. He had been a partner of Dwight W. Morrow and a friend of his family, including his daughter Anne Morrow Lindbergh. Through the Morrows, Lamont was also a friend of Charles Lindbergh. After Lindbergh's radio address on May 19, 1940, Lamont wrote to the Colonel chiding and challenging him on the reference to "powerful elements" who wanted to involve America in the war. He asked Lindbergh to name names. Lamont insisted that he was "in contact with a good many different people and shades of opinion" but did not "know of any such elements." He admonished Lindbergh that "we must not broadcast suspicions and accusations unless we have complete basis for the charges." It was a friendly letter, and Lindbergh responded in kind. In his reply Lindbergh wrote that he "intentionally did not specify individuals, groups, or organizations" because he still hoped it would "not be necessary to do this." He thought it obvious that there were " 'powerful elements' in America who desire us to take part in the war," but he believed it to be "of vital importance for us to avoid the class antagonism and hatred which would arise from such accusations." Lindbergh feared that involvement in the European war would cause "chaotic conditions" that could destroy "the moderation we have known in America." He wanted "to avoid this at all costs" and believed "that the only possibility of avoiding it is for us to keep out of the war in Europe."[3]

Except for references to the Roosevelt administration, Lindbergh did not "name names" until less than three months before Pearl Harbor. His speeches and articles were notable for their lack of "name calling." He did, however, give the matter much thought, and he began to shape his views on the subject. For example, in August and September, 1940, he devoted many hours writing several drafts of "A Letter to Americans," which was to be published in *Collier's* late in March, 1941. His early versions, however, were much different from the published article. In those rough drafts he was, in effect, experimenting with variations of thoughts that he would voice publicly in his Des Moines address a year later. A handwritten version that he scribbled on August 18, 1940, was entitled "To the Capitalist, [the Intellectual] the Politician, and the Jew." Two days later he changed and called it "To the Capitalist, the Politician, and the Jew"; the intellectual had been dropped. He wrote to those groups: "Upon your shoulders more than any others rests the blame for America's trend toward war." A draft that he prepared a month later was again directed "To the Capitalist, the Intellectual, the Politician, and the Jew." And again he contended that those four groups "more than all others are causing this agitation for war." He charged that they had "sacrificed our American destiny to your idol of money, to your academic idealism, and to your selfish desires for power."[4] But Lindbergh was still shaping his thoughts and groping on his timing. No more weight should be given to those versions than to any other writer's discarded rough drafts. He did not use those versions for his final article, and he refrained from "naming names" for another year.

Colonel Lindbergh decided, however, that if it appeared that the United States would enter the war, he "would name the groups responsible for pushing us into it." The question was when to do so. It would have to be before Congress declared war. Lindbergh determined to continue his opposition to involvement up to the last moment, but he resolved to stop his noninterventionist efforts when war came. By September, 1941, he had concluded that America's participation was "practically inevitable" and that "an incident to involve us might arise on any day." Fearing that the United States could enter the war before his next address, Lindbergh decided to make a "for-the-record" speech identifying the war makers as he saw them. He correctly anticipated the uproar his speech would provoke and the abuse he would suffer for making it.[5]

General Robert E. Wood and other leaders of American First

urged Lindbergh to address a meeting in Des Moines, Iowa. Despite its location in the heart of America's agricultural Middle West, Iowa had lagged in the organization of local America First chapters. It was the home of Vice President Henry A. Wallace, who enthusiastically supported President Roosevelt's foreign policies. Furthermore, the state was blanketed by the Gardner Cowles newspapers, the *Des Moines Register* and *Tribune,* which actively supported the President's foreign policies. Committee leaders hoped a Lindbergh rally in Des Moines might spark the growth of America First in the state and dramatize the opposition to the interventionist views of the Cowles publications, Vice President Wallace, and the President.[6]

The *Des Moines Register* struck hard at Lindbergh in an editorial ten days before the rally. At the same time, the temporary chairman of the newly organized Des Moines chapter of the Fight for Freedom Committee gave a speech calling Lindbergh "the most valuable aid to Hitler of any man in America" and "public enemy number one of the U.S." He charged that if Lindbergh "were a paid agent of the German government he could not serve the cause of Hitler so well." Several local American Legion posts voted to bring another nationally known speaker to Des Moines to answer Lindbergh. An American Legion band scheduled to play at the rally withdrew because of the post's opposition. And interventionists organized heckling of the speakers at the meeting.[7]

Lindbergh labored long and hard in preparing his speech. Initially he entitled it "Who Are the Interventionists?" At the last moment, however, he changed it to "Who Are the War Agitators?," believing the new title was "stronger." As usual, no one but Lindbergh and his wife saw the speech before he delivered it. But both titles worried R. Douglas Stuart, Jr., and others of the America First staff who gathered in his suburban Chicago home to listen to the coast-to-coast broadcast of the speech.[8]

More than 8,000 people crowded into the Des Moines Coliseum to hear Lindbergh. President Roosevelt broadcast his "shoot-on-sight" speech earlier the same evening. In his talk the President announced that he had ordered the American Navy to attack German and Italian warships found within the Atlantic patrol zone without waiting for them to attack first. The organizers of the America First rally had arranged for the President's speech to be carried live to their audience at the start of the meeting. Lindbergh and his party came on the platform just after the President completed his powerful and moving address —a difficult act to follow. Noisy and organized hecklers in the audience made matters worse. The first speakers, Mrs. Janet Ayer Fairbank and Hanford MacNider, the national vice-chairmen of America First, handled the situation well, and the audience was far more receptive by the time Lindbergh gave his twenty-five-minute address.[9]

Lindbergh began his speech by referring to the "ever-increasing effort to force the United States into the conflict." He thought that effort had been "so successful that, today, our country stands on the verge of war." The main body of his speech focused on the question of who was "responsible for changing our national policy from one of neutrality and independence to one of entanglement in European affairs." He promised to speak "with the utmost frankness."

Lindbergh told his audience: "The three most important groups who have been pressing this country toward war are the British, the Jewish, and the Roosevelt Administration. Behind these groups, but of lesser importance, are a number of capitalists, anglophiles, and intellectuals, who believe that their future, and the future of mankind, depend upon the domination of the British Empire. Add to these the Communistic groups who were opposed to intervention until a few weeks ago, and I believe I have named the major war agitators in this country." He distinguished between the "war agitators," on the one hand, and the "sincere but misguided men and women who, confused by misinformation and frightened by propaganda, follow the lead of the war agitators." He emphasized that the "war agitators comprise only a small minority of our people; but they control a tremendous influence." He discussed in some detail

**161**

each of the three major groups and concluded that "If any one of these groups—the British, the Jewish, or the Administration—stops agitating for war" there would "be little danger of our involvement." He did "not believe that any two of them are powerful enough to carry this country without the support of the third." He charged that the three groups "planned, first, to prepare the United States for foreign war under the guise of American defense; second, to involve us in the war step by step, without our realization; third, to create a series of incidents which would force us into the actual conflict." The plans were, he charged, "covered and assisted by the full power of their propaganda." He berated their "smear campaign" against the noninterventionists. Lindbergh concluded that the only thing keeping the United States out of the war was "the rising opposition of the American people." Though America was "on the verge of war," he said, it was "not *yet* too late to stay out." In his view, "the last stronghold of democracy and representative government in this country is in our House of Representatives and our Senate." He urged his listeners to make their wishes known and expressed the hope that if they did so, "independence and freedom will continue to live among us, and there will be no foreign war." Lindbergh's address won enthusiastic applause from most of his audience, and he got standing cheers with his reference to "the British, the Jewish, and the Roosevelt Administration."[10]

Nevertheless, no speech by Charles Lindbergh or by any other noninterventionist speaker before Pearl Harbor provoked such widespread controversy and criticism. In most newspapers President Roosevelt's "shoot-on-sight" address won the headlines, but Lindbergh's speech got ample publicity without them. The *Des Moines Register* editorialized that "it may have been courageous for Colonel Lindbergh to say what was in his mind, but it was so lacking in appreciation of consequences—putting the best interpretation on it—that it disqualifies him for any pretensions of leadership of this republic in policy-making." Scores of newspapers and hundreds of speakers all over the United States echoed that reaction or more extreme variations of it.[11]

## "Who Are the War Agitators?"

In his references to the three groups of "war agitators," Lindbergh's tone was most sympathetic and understanding of the Jewish; he was most critical in his references to the Roosevelt administration. The responses to his address, however, gave a radically different proportion to his remarks than he had given. His references to the British and the Roosevelt administration were largely ignored by his critics; the uproar centered almost exclusively on his reference to the Jews.

Undoubtedly much of the uproar was due to genuine disapproval of Lindbergh's key statement regarding the Jews. Many may have denounced the speech publicly to protect themselves from any possible charges of anti-Semitism. But there can be no doubt that interventionists exploited the incident in their attempts to discredit Lindbergh and weaken the campaign against intervention in the European war. Whatever one concludes about the sincerity, accuracy, or wisdom of Lindbergh's statements, his Des Moines speech was an extremely serious political blunder. It dealt America First and the noninterventionist movement a staggering blow. It gave the interventionists their best opportunity to discredit Lindbergh and America First. The deluge of criticism that the Des Moines speech precipitated was so all-encompassing that it dwarfed all succeeding noninterventionist efforts in the few weeks remaining before Pearl Harbor. To examine the matter in depth, it will be well to analyze Lindbergh's views and the reactions from each of the three groups of "war agitators."

# 20/Capitalists, Intellectuals, and the British

LINDBERGH included the British, capitalists, and intellectuals among the greater or lesser "war agitators." By the last half of 1941, however, he was devoting comparatively less attention to the British than he had earlier. And the capitalists and intellectuals never loomed large in his public statements. They were, however, among the adversaries in his battle against intervention.

His father's active opposition to American entry into World War I a quarter of a century earlier had been aimed particularly against eastern capitalists and financiers—against the Money Trust. The Minnesota Congressman had charged them with involving the United States needlessly in wars and imperialism abroad to advance their selfish economic interests. Many agrarian progressives continued to use such analyses in later opposing entry into World War II. Senators William E. Borah of Idaho, Hiram Johnson of California, Burton K. Wheeler of Montana, and Gerald P. Nye of North Dakota were among the progressives whose agrarian economic analyses were fundamental to their noninterventionism.[1]

A year before his Des Moines speech, in the early rough drafts of his "A Letter to Americans," Colonel Lindbergh had listed "capitalists" first among those to whom he considered directing his message. And in his Des Moines speech he included capitalists among the war agitators "of lesser importance." Occasionally he mentioned economic interests and profit seeking in his other analyses of war and intervention. In October, 1939, when the arms embargo and cash-and-carry were being debated, he said he did "not believe that the material welfare of this country needs, or that our spiritual welfare could withstand," a policy of making profits by capitalizing "on the destruction and death of war." If American industry depended "upon a commerce of arms for its strength, then our industrial system should be changed." In defending cash-and-carry, he thought the "extension of credit to a belligerent country" was "a long step toward war." He found it "unfortunate but true that there are interests in America who would rather lose American lives than their own dollars." In his *Reader's Digest* article of November, 1939, Lindbergh worried about the "spiritual decline which seems invariably to accompany an industrial life." In a tone that agrarian radicals would have approved, Lindbergh asked: "How long can men thrive between walls of brick, walking on asphalt pavements, breathing the fumes of coal and of oil, growing, working, dying, with hardly a thought of wind, and sky, and fields of grain, seeing only machine made beauty, the mineral-like quality of life?" He thought that was "our modern danger." His father would have approved when, in his broadcast on June 15, 1940, Lindbergh said that "our capitalists as well as our soldiers should be willing to serve without personal profit."[2] Most of his friends in eastern financial circles sharply disagreed with his positions on foreign affairs.

Nevertheless, Colonel Lindbergh did not attach great weight to economic bases for war and involvement abroad. For the most part, his opposition to American entry into World War II emerged from a substantially different analysis than that on which his father's opposition to entry into World War I many years before had been based.

Lindbergh focused even less attention on intellectuals and idealists, though he saw them, too, as among the "lesser" war agitators. He was uncertain whether to include intellectuals in his early rough drafts of "A Letter to Americans." In the final version, published in March, 1941, the Colonel complained that "politicians and idealists harangue" Americans about defending freedom and democracy by destroying Hitler's Nazi regime, but that they offered "not one feasible plan" for successfully invading Europe. He told an America First audience in St. Louis early in May, 1941, that in England, France, and the United States he had "listened to politicians and idealists calling upon the people for war, with hardly a thought of how that war is to be fought or won." A few days later, he recalled for his audience in Minneapolis that before the United States entered World War I "Idealists called on us to fight. Hysteria, hatred and intolerance arose. Even college presidents and their faculties joined in the cry." He reminded his listeners that when his father opposed war "his meetings were broken up, his patriotism was questioned, and the plates of his book were destroyed by government agents." He contended that after World War I "we left the future of the world in the hands of our college presidents and our idealists," but that "the idealists themselves seem to be about all we fought for in the last war that remains intact." He charged that in 1941 "Our college presidents are shouting for war, just as they did before." But he pointed out that there were "many people in the nation who have ideals of another kind." He was one of them: "There are many of us who believe that the place to save democracy is right here in America. We do not accept the claim that Christianity will thrive on famine, or that our way of life can be spread around the world by force. We believe that it is possible for a man or a nation to be self reliant, to be practical, to be successful, even to be tolerant, and still have ideals of the highest type." After the beginning of the Russo-German war, Lindbergh charged that "the idealists who have been shouting against the horrors of Nazi Germany" were then ready to ally with the Soviet Union, "whose record of cruelty, bloodshed, and barbarism, is without parallel in modern history." Rather than follow their lead, Lindbergh urged his compatriots to "build an impregnable defense for America, and keep this hemisphere at peace."[3]

The capitalists and intellectuals might have been war agitators "of lesser importance," but in his Des Moines speech Lindbergh listed the British first among the three groups he thought most important in pressing the United States toward war. In elaborating on the British influence, he conceded that it was "perfectly understandable that Great Britain wants the United States in the war on her side." As he had said many times before, however, Lindbergh insisted that England could not win the war against Germany by itself, even with American material aid. "Even if America entered the war it is improbable that the Allied armies could invade Europe and overcome the Axis powers." (He was speaking during the period before Soviet forces checked Germany's advance into the Soviet Union.) He believed that if the British had not been hopeful of making the United States "responsible for the war financially, as well as militarily," they "would have negotiated a peace in Europe many months ago, and be better off for doing so." He charged that "England has devoted and will continue to devote every effort to get us into the war." He conceded that "If we were Englishmen we would do the same." But he insisted that "our interest is first in America; and, as Americans, it is essential for us to realize the effort that British interests are making to draw us into their war."[4]

He had, of course, warned against British propaganda before and would do so again. In "A Letter to Americans," published in March, 1941, Colonel Lindbergh wrote that "British propaganda in the United States attempts to persuade us that Great Britain will win the war, providing she receives somewhat more help than we have, up to that moment, given her." He also charged the British with trying to convince Americans "that a British victory is essential to American security."[5]

British leaders had long been aware of the distrust with which Americans viewed foreign propaganda in general, and British propaganda in particular. They tried to avoid playing into the hands of isolationists by any obvious attempts to propagandize the American people. They correctly recognized that American public opinion in the years 1939–1941 was overwhelmingly sympathetic to the British in their struggle against Nazi Germany but was opposed to entering the European war. British leaders were persuaded that Americans were most likely to be moved by emotional and ideological themes. They were confident of President Roosevelt's sympathy for their cause and of his determination to lead the United States in internationalist and interventionist directions as rapidly as public opinion would permit. They saw their role as tactfully encouraging and quietly assisting the Roosevelt administration and its interventionist supporters in those efforts as much as they could without making it appear that they were doing so. British diplomats in the United States encouraged those methods, and Prime Minister Winston Churchill's personal and official dealings with President Roosevelt skillfully followed such a pattern.[6]

In June, 1940, for example, Lord Lothian, the Ambassador to the United States, advised the British government in dealing with the United States "to stress the gravity of the [British] position, the fearful consequences for civilization which would follow a Nazi victory, the determination of the Allies to fight on in order to maintain the freedom of civilization and their confidence that if enough people show enough resolution in that cause it is bound to prevail." He thought it "a profound mistake for anybody in Europe to make appeals to the United States to intervene." In Lord Lothian's opinion, "The case for the British is already being very well made over here by influential Americans." Prime Minister Churchill instructed Lothian to make it clear in speaking with President Roosevelt that "If we go down Hitler has a very good chance of conquering the world."[7]

Late in 1940, T. North Whitehead of the American Department in the British Foreign Office prepared a long document on "Policy for Publicity in the United States." He defined the British objective as obtaining "the utmost assistance from the United States as quickly as possible, not excluding direct participation in the war." The British task was "to help in the process both of educating and also of sensitising American public opinion to the need for assisting us more vigorously as a means of saving themselves." He recommended that Britain constantly "flood America with the relevant facts so presented as to make them fit into the general picture of our strategic problem." He urged the British to "avoid even the implication of advising Americans what they should do in their own interests. Any such advice would be at once regarded by Americans as 'propaganda,' and would be hotly resented." Besides, he thought such propaganda "quite unnecessary" because "literally hundreds of American press and radio commentators are performing this service for us daily." He believed it was "always more effective for information to reach Americans by an American rather than a British medium." Whitehead urged that "full advantage should be taken of the American press correspondents in London and of Mr. Child's organization in New York for supplying information to the press writers in the United States."[8] That was essentially the approach the British government used.

Harold Nicolson, Parliamentary Secretary to the British Ministry of Information, had been a friend of the Lindberghs for some years, both in America and in England. He first met them while preparing a biography of Anne's father, Dwight W. Morrow. He and his wife befriended Anne and Charles when they fled to England in 1935. But he and Lindbergh differed sharply on foreign affairs, and in 1939 Nicolson struck hard and personally at the Colonel in public print.[9]

The British Library of Information in New York provided English leaders with impressively full and accurate information on the state of American public and press opinion. Anne Lindbergh's younger sister, Constance, was married to Aubrey Neil Morgan of the British Information Service in New York. It actively helped American interventionists, including the Fight for Freedom Committee, in efforts to move public opinion in the direction of aid and involvement on the side of Great Britain's struggle against the Axis Powers.[10]

Similarly, William S. Stephenson and his British Security Co-Ordination in New York quietly and effectively helped Fight for Freedom and other interventionist groups. Stephenson's organization also worked to discredit Lindbergh, the America First Committee, and other isolationists. Those efforts helped defeat the noninterventionist movement in the United States. Once Stephenson's efforts to down Lindbergh accidentally backfired.

## "War Agitators" and American Democracy

Before Lindbergh's final America First address, in New York's Madison Square Garden on October 30, 1941, Stephenson had duplicate tickets printed and distributed to pro-British organizations. He hoped the holders of those tickets would cause trouble at the rally. But, as he remembered it later, the attendance at the rally was smaller than expected, and his counterfeit tickets apparently provided Lindbergh with a somewhat larger audience for his last noninterventionist address than he would otherwise have had. Nonetheless, one study concluded that Stephenson's efforts against the America First Committee in 1941 "did considerably reduce its usefulness" and "the way was paved for the great disrepute into which it [and Lindbergh] shortly fell."[11]

Lindbergh's reference to the British as "war agitators" did not greatly increase attacks upon him, and only rarely was he charged with being an Anglophobe. In striking contrast, however, his reference in the same breath to the Jewish as "war agitators" brought a torrent of charges that he was anti-Semitic.

# 21/The Jewish Interventionists

CHARLES A. LINDBERGH's speech in Des Moines, Iowa, on September 11, 1941, was the only public address in which he mentioned the Jews. In that speech he listed the Jewish along with the British and the Roosevelt administration as the three most important groups pressing the United States into war. Though he opposed the interventionist efforts of all, the one out of the three groups that he expressed greatest sympathy for was the Jewish. But he was most vehemently denounced for listing the Jews.

In elaborating on the Jewish group in his address, Lindbergh said: "It is not difficult to understand why Jewish people desire the overthrow of Nazi Germany. The persecution they suffered in Germany would be sufficient to make bitter enemies of any race. No person with a sense of the dignity of mankind can condone the persecution of the Jewish race in Germany. But no person of honesty and vision can look on their pro-war policy here today without seeing the dangers involved in such a policy, both for us and for them.

"Instead of agitating for war, the Jewish groups in this country should be opposing it in every possible way, for they will be among the first to feel its consequences. Tolerance is a virtue that depends upon peace and strength. History shows that it cannot survive war and devastation. A few far-sighted Jewish people realize this, and stand opposed to intervention. But the majority still do not. Their greatest danger to this country lies in their large ownership and influence in our motion pictures, our press, our radio, and our Government.

"I am not attacking either the Jewish or the British people. Both races, I admire. But I am saying that the leaders of both the British and the Jewish races, for reasons which are as understandable from their viewpoint as they are inadvisable from ours, for reasons which are not American, wish to involve us in the war. We cannot blame them for looking out for what they believe to be their own interests, but we also must look out for ours. We cannot allow the natural passions and prejudices of other peoples to lead our country to destruction."[1]

Those three paragraphs constitute, in full, Lindbergh's only public reference to the Jews. So far as one can determine from his private journal, personal correspondence, and reports by others of conversations with him, Lindbergh's privately expressed views on the subject were essentially the same as those he voiced publicly in his Des Moines speech. For example, after the violence against the Jews in Nazi Germany in November, 1938, Lindbergh wrote in his diary: "I do not understand these riots on the part of the Germans. It seems so contrary to their sense of order and their intelligence in other ways. They have undoubtedly had a difficult Jewish problem, but why is it necessary to handle it so unreasonably? My admiration for the Germans is constantly being dashed against some rock such as this." In June, 1939, after a conversation with Senator Harry Byrd of Virginia, Lindbergh wrote in his diary: "We are both anxious to avoid having this country pushed into a European war by British and Jewish propaganda, of which there is already too much. I can understand the feeling of both the British and the Jews, but there is far too much at stake for us to rush into a European war without the most careful and cool consideration." After a dinner conversation with William R. Castle and Fulton Lewis, Jr., in August, 1939, he wrote in his journal: "We are disturbed about the effect of the Jewish influence in our press, radio, and motion pictures. It may become very serious. Lewis told us of one instance where the Jewish advertising firms threatened to remove all their advertising from the Mutual system if a certain feature were permitted to go on the air. The threat was powerful enough to have the feature removed. I do not blame the Jews so much for their attitude, although I think it unwise from their own standpoint." On May 1, 1941, there is this diary entry: "Most of the Jewish interests in the country are behind war, and they control a huge part of our press and radio and most of our motion pictures."[2] In his references to the Jews, he explained their foreign policy positions in terms of their conceptions of their own self-interest. He did not embrace a "conspiracy theory"; he agreed with his wife in rejecting what she called "hidden-hands" conceptions of public affairs.

Lindbergh fully expected his references to the Jews in his Des Moines speech to cause an uproar and to bring charges of anti-Semitism down upon him. In his handwritten first draft of the speech he had scribbled: "I realize that in speaking this frankly I am entering in where Angels fear to tread. I realize that tomorrow morning's headlines will say 'Lindbergh attacks Jews.' The ugly cry of Anti-Semitism will be eagerly joyfully pounded upon and waved about my name. It is so much simpler to brand someone with a bad label than to take the trouble to read what he says. I call you people before me tonight to witness that I am not anti-Semitic nor have I attacked the Jews."[3] In the speech's final form Lindbergh omitted that part of his first draft, but he was completely correct in his expectations. Rarely has any public address in American history caused more of an uproar, or brought more criticism on any speaker, than did Lindbergh's Des Moines speech.

Denunciations were most concentrated in New York, but they came from all across the United States. They came from Jews, but also from Protestants and Catholics. They came from interventionists, but also from noninterventionists. They came from Democrats, but also from Republicans and Communists. They came from high government leaders, but also from grass-roots America. They charged Lindbergh with anti-Semitism, Nazism, and sympathy for Hitler. They called on the America First Committee to repudiate him. They urged a congressional investigation. And individual letter writers wanted to send him back to Germany.

Newspapers across the land joined in editorial attacks on

Lindbergh and his speech. The *Des Moines Register* called it "the worst speech he has made so far." The *New York Herald Tribune* flailed the speech's anti-Semitism and called it an appeal to "dark forces of prejudice and intolerance." The *Philadelphia Record* charged that "Lindbergh hates what Hitler hates." The *Kansas City Journal* concluded that "Lindbergh's interest in Hitlerism is now thinly concealed." The *San Francisco Chronicle* concluded that "The voice is the voice of Lindbergh, but the words are the words of Hitler." The passionately interventionist *PM* in New York sent telegrams to members of the America First national committee urging them to disavow Lindbergh.[4]

Understandably, Jews and Jewish organizations criticized the speech, urged America First to repudiate Lindbergh, and called for an investigation of America First. But non-Jews were equally critical. The Christian theologian and interventionist Reinhold Niebuhr urged America First to "divorce itself from the stand taken by Lindbergh and clean its ranks of those who would incite to racial and religious strife in this country." *Commonweal,* a liberal Catholic magazine, was noninterventionist but thought it "a bad speech." It also pointed out that Jews probably controlled less than their share of the daily newspapers and magazines.[5]

Organized interventionist groups eagerly seized on the Des Moines speech as a club with which to beat Lindbergh, America First, and the whole noninterventionist movement. The Committee to Defend America and the Fight for Freedom Committee denounced the speech and called on America First to repudiate Lindbergh. The national executive secretary of Fight for Freedom pointed out that though interventionist sentiment was strongest in the South, that section had the smallest Jewish population. Fight for Freedom also distributed a thirty-six-page pamphlet entitled *America's Answer to Lindbergh* that quoted editorials and articles from newspapers, writers, and spokesmen all over the country attacking Lindbergh and his speech.[6]

Communist publications, now thoroughly interventionist, joined in the cries against Lindbergh. The *Daily Worker* charged that his speeches and activities were "entering the realm of treason and outright violations of the laws of the land" and demanded "the practical attention of the Federal government." It called Lindbergh a fascist, Nazi, traitor, and an "Open Hitler Ally." *New Masses* called him "a racist and fascist" and urged a congressional investigation of America First.[7]

But criticism emanated from high political levels in the United States as well. President Roosevelt made no public comment, but his secretary, Stephen T. Early, said there was "a striking similarity" between Lindbergh's statement and "the outpourings of Berlin in the last few days." The Republican Party's 1940 presidential nominee, Wendell Willkie, called it "the most un-American talk made in my time by any person of national reputation." Governor Thomas E. Dewey of New York, who was to be the Republican presidential nominee in 1944 and 1948, called Lindbergh's speech "an inexcusable abuse of the right of freedom of speech." Assistant Secretary of State Adolf A. Berle, Jr., in an address at Harvard, said that Lindbergh was "following the exact line which had been laid down in Berlin for the use of Nazi propagandists in the United States."[8]

Critical responses were not limited to words. Vandals broke windows in the Manhattan offices of America First. The Board of Education in Sioux City, Iowa, refused permission for an America First rally in a school auditorium unless the Committee guaranteed there would be "no un-American utterances." The lower house of the Texas legislature adopted a resolution advising Lindbergh he was not welcome on any speaking tour he might plan in that state.[9]

The Des Moines speech provided a field day for interventionist critics of Lindbergh, America First, and the noninterventionist movement. But it caused dismay and consternation within the America First Committee as well, and in noninterventionist ranks in general. Responses by noninterventionists ranged all the way from angry resignations from America First, at one extreme, to enthusiastic praise from anti-Semites, who were delighted that Lindbergh had spoken out publicly on "the real issue," with every imaginable response between the extremes. Most noninterventionists, however, generally supported Lindbergh, thought he had spoken the truth, and opposed any repudiation of him.

Some wrote to America First resigning in protest. Some of those were Jews, but others were not.[10] Still others lavishly praised Lindbergh and his speech. One woman in Illinois wrote Lindbergh: "I have never so respected and deeply admired any man as I do you! Your wonderful fight against involvement in this war was climaxed by your truthful and courageous speech last night at Des Moines. I thank God that we have men like you of indomitable courage and undying faith in the American tradition! Mr. Lindbergh, you would make a great AMERICAN President." Countless others responded with similar enthusiasm.[11]

Though most such responses gave no evidence of anti-Semitism, some wrote in such extreme anti-Semitic terms that the America First staff stamped their letters "CRANK – IGNORE." One Chicagoan who praised Lindbergh's speech wrote: "History shows, that whenever the Jews get hold of a nation, this very nation is doomed to destruction from within and without." Another, from Long Beach, California, wrote that as long as Lindbergh spoke on flying he did not "bother the war mongers so very much," but when he put his "finger upon the trickery of the Administration, and the double-cross of the Jewish profiteers, there and then you really became a great orator." A woman from Los Angeles insisted that "we need thousands of fearless men and women to rid this country of the JEWS, who have already taken it over." She wrote that Roosevelt was a Jew. A man from Blythe, California, wrote that he hated "a Jew worse than poison" and insisted that "If we dont curb him in the USA very shortly we are going to be working as his slaves."[12] Individuals and organizations publicly identified with the far right or with anti-Semitism cheered Lindbergh's speech. Merwin K. Hart, Father Charles E. Coughlin's *Social Justice* magazine, Gerald L. K. Smith and his Committee of 1,000,000, and

*Scribner's Commentator,* for example, all praised the speech.[13]

Noninterventionists in exposed positions with responsibilities separate from America First often ran for cover. That seemed particularly true for newsmen. The publisher Frank E. Gannett informed General Robert E. Wood that because of Lindbergh's speech he could not "run the risk of being identified with the Committee." The Hearst newspapers opposed American entry into World War II, but they attacked Lindbergh's "intemperate and intolerant address in Des Moines." The noninterventionist commentator Boake Carter wrote that Lindbergh "performed a disservice to himself and to the nation" in his speech and "was unjust to the Jews as a people." Even Colonel Robert R. McCormick's *Chicago Tribune* refused to go along with its hero. Its headline the day after the speech told of Lindbergh's attack on the Roosevelt administration, but a careful examination of the news columns was necessary to learn of his reference to the Jews. On September 13, the *Tribune* carried an editorial designed to explain that the newspaper was not anti-Semitic. A feature page with pictures of some of Lindbergh's medals had already been printed for the September 21 issue. On September 20, the *Tribune* carried an editorial that denounced the "impropriety" of Lindbergh's reference to the Jews and hoped that none of its readers would "assume that the publication of this page at this time is to be regarded as in any sense an evidence of approval of the Des Moines speech." President Henry Noble MacCracken of Vassar College and Norman Thomas of the Socialist Party were both noninterventionists, but in their efforts to disassociate themselves from Lindbergh's reference to the Jews both declined to speak at any more America First meetings.[14]

Norman Thomas's reaction was significant. A Socialist and a pacifist, he held many views on public issues that differed sharply from Lindbergh's. But the two men liked and respected each other; they had appeared together on the programs of America First rallies. Two years earlier, in a book urging the United States to stay out of war, Thomas had advised American Jews in words much like those that Lindbergh used in his Des

Moines speech. He believed Lindbergh was not anti-Semitic and that what he had said "was mostly true, but by no means all the truth." He thought much of the criticism was "quite insincere and hypocritical." Nevertheless, Thomas contended that the speech "did great harm," and he said so "publicly for the sake, not only of the cause of keeping out of war, but of preserving some tolerance in America." He thought Lindbergh oversimplified, "exaggerated the solidarity of the Jews in this matter and their power, and overlooked the power of other groups." He believed that even if the Jews or the British stopped their propaganda, the President might still get the United States into the war. In a letter to General Wood, Thomas said he thought it "an enormous pity that our friend the Colonel will not take the advice on public relations which he would expect an amateur in aviation to take from an expert." The national executive committee of the Socialist Party denounced Lindbergh's speech as a "serious blow to democracy and to the movement to keep America out of war."[15]

The executive director of the Keep America Out of War Congress (composed of pacifist noninterventionist organizations) wrote that the speech had "done more to fan the flames of Anti-Semitism and push 'on-the-fence' Jews into the war camp than Mr. Lindbergh can possibly imagine." The governing committee of the Keep America Out of War Congress announced its "deep disagreement" with Lindbergh's "implication that the American citizens of Jewish extraction or religion are a separate group, apart from the rest of the American people, or that they react as a separate group, or that they are unanimously for our entrance into the European war." Nevertheless, that statement also criticized interventionists for concealing Lindbergh's "denunciation of the treatment of the Jews in Germany" in his speech. All of the twenty-five persons at the meeting that authorized the statement, including four Jews, agreed that the speech was not anti-Semitic.[16]

Lindbergh's speech sparked a vendetta between Oswald Garrison Villard and the Council Against Intolerance in America under George Gordon Battle. Villard had devoted his long life to active crusades for peace, humanitarian causes, and civil liberties. He was a member of the Council Against Intolerance; he was also a noninterventionist. After the Des Moines speech, Battle wired prominent Americans seeking statements "to counteract Charles Lindbergh's injection of race and religious issue into American life." The statements he obtained subsequently were published by the Council as a fifteen-page pamphlet, *America Answers Lindbergh!* And in a Council mailing sent out by the thousands in October, Battle charged Lindbergh and Senator Nye with "seeking to destroy liberty through bigotry." Villard's name was on the letterhead of the official Council stationery that Battle used for his mailing, but Villard was angered by the Council's attacks on Lindbergh and Nye. He wrote to Battle contending that Lindbergh had not really "injected the race and religious issue." He insisted that Lindbergh had "made a truthful statement," though Villard thought it "would have been better" if he had not mentioned the Jews. Villard did not "want to play into the hands of Colonel Lindbergh's enemies, who have seized upon this mistaken judgment of his to distort or misrepresent what he said." Battle did not answer the letter. Subsequently, Villard, "outraged by the attacks being made by the Council Against Intolerance in America upon Colonel Lindbergh," resigned from the Council. He criticized it for being "so intolerant" as to brand Lindbergh and Nye "with faithlessness to America because they say things that the Council doesn't like."[17] President Robert M. Hutchins of the University of Chicago and Senator Bennett Champ Clark of Missouri also resigned from the Council Against Intolerance in protest against the intolerance it had directed against Lindbergh. Alf M. Landon, the Republican presidential nominee in 1936, was not an isolationist, and he publicly regretted "the tragedy of raising racial, class, and religious issues." But he thought Lindbergh had "suffered from unjust and fearful slanderous attacks on his Americanism," and he refused to provide a statement joining in the Council's "proposal to stone him."[18]

Most politicians either criticized Lindbergh's speech or avoided comment. Senator Gerald P. Nye of North Dakota, however, publicly defended the aviator. Nye had recently spent an afternoon with him and concluded that there was "not a shred of anti-Semitism in a single fibre of the being of this courageous American." Nye agreed with Lindbergh that "the Jewish people are a large factor in our movement toward war." Senator Robert A. Taft of Ohio in a private letter wrote that he disapproved "entirely of Colonel Lindbergh's speech, and particularly that part attacking the Jews." He pointed out that Lindbergh "referred to the Jews as if they were a foreign race, and not Americans at all, a grossly unjust attitude." But Taft did "not propose to criticize Colonel Lindbergh for intolerance when his intolerance is more than matched by the intolerance of the Fight for Freedom Committee and others toward him and his views."[19]

Within the America First Committee there were wide differences of opinion. Many members disapproved of the speech. The chairman of the Indianapolis chapter and the Oklahoma state chairman, for example, both criticized it. John T. Flynn, chairman of the New York chapter and a member of the national committee, was particularly upset. He complained to America First national headquarters that Lindbergh could not play "a lone hand" and drag the Committee "out into the no man's land of this debate on any issue that he chooses to adopt." Flynn pointed out that in the East he was right "on the firing line"; the speech complicated his earnest efforts to bar unsavory elements from his chapter, and it inundated the chapter with assaults from its adversaries. Flynn saw the problem as "one of clearing the America First Committee of this taint without at the same time breaking it up or weakening its influence to keep us out of war."[20]

In a personal letter to Lindbergh, Flynn wrote that his first reaction to the speech was "one of utter distress." He contended that anti-Semites in his chapter were "uproariously delighted" with the speech, while those who had been afraid of the issue were "depressed." He conceded that Lindbergh was "completely without anti-Semitism," but that the charge would stick and America First would be "tagged with the anti-Jewish label."

Flynn agreed "that the Jewish population of New York" was "practically unanimously for war," but he insisted that no one could publicly denounce them as war makers "without incurring the guilt of religious and racial intolerance and that character is poison in a community like ours."[21]

Lindbergh found it difficult to understand Flynn's view. After the two men had discussed the matter in conversation for an hour, Lindbergh wrote in his journal: "He feels as strongly as I do that the Jews are among the major influences pushing this country toward war. He has said so frequently, and he says so now. He is perfectly willing to talk about it among a small group of people in private. But apparently he would rather see us get into the war than mention in public what the Jews are doing, no matter how tolerantly and moderately it is done."[22]

Most America First leaders and members, however, gave Lindbergh at least qualified support. Eighty-five to 90 per cent of the letters received by national headquarters supported him. Most did not believe Lindbergh was anti-Semitic. They believed the references to the Jews might have been phrased more tactfully and accurately or, better still, not have been voiced at all. Most Committee members believed Lindbergh's statements concerning the Jews were largely correct, and the overwhelming majority opposed repudiating him. Most of them, however, hoped America First would make a clear statement that it was not anti-Semitic.[23]

Gregory Mason, chairman of the Stamford-Greenwich-Norwalk America First chapter in Connecticut and later a national committee member, turned the charge of anti-Semitism back on the interventionists. Professor Mason wrote: "A great deal of hypocrisy has been evidenced by smug citizens in our midst who sounded off to condemn Lindbergh on the basis of a hasty reading of two or three sentences lifted from his Des Moines address. Many such citizens *practice* anti-Semitism every day of their lives. Many of the individual supporters of the Committee to Defend America by Aiding the Allies and of the Fight for Freedom Committee and of other interventionist organizations belong to exclusive social clubs from which Jews are strictly barred. . . . the Greenwich Real Estate Board opposes renting or selling houses to Jews in the 'exclusive' part of Greenwich from which was subscribed in a few weeks enough money to buy England six ambulances . . . and from which comes the loudest local denunciation of Lindbergh." Mason concluded his letter by challenging the chairman of the Greenwich chapter of the Committee to Defend America to a public debate on the subject "Resolved, That the Committee to Defend America by Aiding the Allies is riddled with Anti-Semitism."[24] His challenge was not accepted.

America First national headquarters could not ignore the massive criticism of the Des Moines speech without serious consequences for the Committee. It urged local chapters to withhold comment on the speech until after the national committee met on September 18, a week after the Des Moines rally. Lindbergh went to Chicago and discussed the matter at length with General Wood, R. Douglas Stuart, Jr., Flynn, and staff members before the meeting. General Wood suggested adjourning America First, on grounds that the President had already involved the United States in war through executive action; Lindbergh and Stuart both opposed that course. Lindbergh would not repudiate or modify his Des Moines speech. He was willing, if the Committee wished, to issue a statement saying that the speech represented only his personal opinions and not America First policy, though he thought such a statement would be unwise. Since the discussions would focus on him and his speech, he did not attend the first part of the national committee meeting held in Janet Ayer Fairbank's home that Thursday afternoon.[25]

With General Wood presiding, the committee members discussed the matter at length. Members pointed out that Lindbergh had sacrificed much for America First. Most of them believed that what Lindbergh had said was true. Consequently the national committee decided not to repudiate Lindbergh or his speech. A letter by Amos R. E. Pinchot, a national committee member present at the meeting, throws light on the view taken in the discussion. Pinchot wrote: "We did not consider

the Lindbergh speech anti-Semitic. . . . It did not criticize
. . . the Jewish people on the ground of race or religion. It did,
however, state plainly what I think you will agree is true,
namely that, as a group, the Jews of America are for intervention, and that they constitute one of the main forces for intervention. . . . I think the Lindbergh statement was true. And
so far I have met no Jewish man or woman who doesn't admit
it's true. . . . Needless to say I'm thoroughly opposed to anti-
Semitism in any form. . . . I am personally grateful to Colonel
Lindbergh for helping to keep America patriotic and sane."
With Flynn in the minority, the national committee decided not
to ask Lindbergh to issue a separate statement.[26]

Only eleven members of the national committee (including
Lindbergh) attended the meeting on September 18. That was
less than half, so General Wood had the absent members polled
before the statement approved at that meeting was issued.
Several (both those attending the meeting and those consulted
later) thought the statement weak or deficient in one way or
another. For example, Chester Bowles thought it did not answer
the issue raised in the Des Moines speech. He had "the greatest
admiration" for Lindbergh and did not think him anti-Semitic.
He believed the Des Moines speech "was simply poorly worded,
tactless and in bad judgment." But Bowles thought Lindbergh's
"remarks sounded definitely anti-Semitic," and he wanted the
Committee to take the stand that it could not be responsible for
every individual statement its members or representatives made.
William R. Castle initially had thought Lindbergh's references
to the Jews "were the exact truth," but he wished "the statement had never been made because it clouds the issue and pins
on us, however unfairly, the anti-Semitic label." He wondered if
there were any chance "that Lindbergh would let somebody
censor his speeches." He approved the national committee
statement but was not terribly impressed by it. Despite reservations, however, ten members in addition to those at the meeting
voted to approve the statement, and the Committee made it
public on September 24.[27]

In that statement the national committee charged the interventionists with trying "to hide the real issue by flinging false charges at the America First Committee and at every leader who has spoken out against our entry into the European conflict." It declared: "Colonel Lindbergh and his fellow members of the America First Committee are not anti-Semitic. We deplore the injection of the race issue into the discussion of war or peace. It is the interventionists who have done this. America First, on the other hand, has invited men and women of every race, religion and national origin to join this committee, provided only that they are patriotic citizens who put the interests of their country ahead of those of any other nation. We repeat that invitation. . . . There is but one real issue—the issue of war. From this issue we will not be diverted." At the same time Stuart sent a letter to all chapter chairmen admonishing them to redouble their efforts "to keep our membership rolls clear of those who seek to promote racial and religious intolerance."[28]

A few days later America First released a letter from Dr. Hyman Lischner, a physician and former president of B'nai B'rith in San Diego. In his letter, Dr. Lischner, a Russian-born Jew, defended Lindbergh and insisted that there was no race prejudice in any of Lindbergh's talks. He agreed that the Jewish group was one of the most important of those pressing America toward war.[29]

The Des Moines speech was the only major foreign policy address by Lindbergh in which he specifically mentioned the Jews. Without explicitly referring to that speech or to Jews, however, he did attempt to defend himself at an America First rally in Fort Wayne, Indiana, on October 3. He maintained that his statements had been distorted and his motives and meanings "falsely ascribed." He said he did not "speak out of hate for any individuals or any people."[30] Many years later, Lindbergh said that if he had been a Jew he "might have been for war" before Pearl Harbor. He said some Jews had been aboveboard in advocating war but others had not. Lindbergh had found it frustrating not to be able to talk about the subject publicly. As he had seen it, most Jews (though not all) were pushing for war before Pearl Harbor, and he thought "You should not hide reality."[31]

## The Jewish Interventionists

As he intended, Lindbergh in his Des Moines speech publicly placed on the record his conviction that Jews were one of the most important groups pressing the United States into war, along with the British and the Roosevelt administration. Other than that, however, his reference to the Jews in that address was largely counterproductive so far as the noninterventionist movement was concerned. It did not reduce Jewish support for intervention, and it did not win Jews to the noninterventionist cause. It encouraged anti-Semites to be more boldly outspoken. It strengthened the interventionists and gave them their best opportunity to go on the offensive against the isolationists. It greatly increased the ferocity and effectiveness of the attacks on Lindbergh and America First. It divided and weakened the noninterventionist movement and placed it on the defensive. Because of the repercussions from that speech, the Committee canceled its plans for a major Lindbergh rally in Washington, D.C., later in September.[32] The organization director for America First in the East found it necessary to set aside projects he had under way for forming new chapters.[33] And the repercussions of the Des Moines speech diverted attention from Lindbergh's continuing criticisms of President Roosevelt's tactics in leading the United States toward war.

# 22/"Government by Subterfuge"

IN his treatment of the three major groups of "war agitators," Charles A. Lindbergh was most critical, least sympathetic, and most persistent in his criticisms of the Roosevelt administration. Unlike his references to the British, which he made with decreasing frequency, and unlike his reference to the Jews, which he made publicly only once, Lindbergh's criticisms of the Roosevelt administration grew increasingly frequent, bold, and strident during 1941. He did not mention Franklin D. Roosevelt by name in any of his speeches during 1939 and 1940. A year before the Des Moines speech, in his rough drafts for "A Letter to Americans," he directed his attention to "the Politician" generally, rather than to the Roosevelt administration specifically. His early allusions to politicians and the administration focused on their relation to the war and intervention. Increasingly during 1941, however, he voiced alarm about the President's role in undermining democratic processes and representative government. He called for "new leadership," and he berated "government by subterfuge." He saw President Roosevelt as using dishonest methods to take the United States into war, contrary to the wishes of 80 per cent of the American people. And he feared those methods were creating for the United States the dictatorship that the President professed to be opposing abroad. Lindbergh urged open discussion, more legislative authority in foreign affairs, and limitations on the President's war-making powers. He used arguments in attacking

Roosevelt in 1941 that were almost identical to those that liberal internationalists would use in attacking President Richard M. Nixon thirty years later.

In August, 1940, in a rough draft of his "A Letter to Americans," Lindbergh wrote that history would "attach the greatest blame for the debacle of this period" on the politician. In his Des Moines speech on September 11, 1941, he charged the Roosevelt administration with using "the war to justify the restriction of congressional power, and the assumption of dictatorial procedures." In his opinion, the *"danger* of the Roosevelt administration" lay in "its subterfuge." He insisted that the administration had "promised us peace" but had led the United States toward war, "heedless of the platform" upon which it was elected.[1]

Lindbergh's attacks on President Roosevelt's "government by subterfuge" coincided with efforts by the America First Committee to move the foreign policy debate away from the issue of "aid-short-of-war" and place it on the simple issue of whether the United States should or should not declare war. The majority of the American people had approved each major proposal advanced by the administration to aid Britain short of war. By the middle of 1940, a clear majority believed it was more important to aid Britain in its efforts to defeat Germany than it was for the United States to keep out of the war. At the same time, however, public opinion polls indicated that approximately 80 per cent of the American people opposed entry into the war. At no time before Pearl Harbor did a majority favor a declaration of war on the Axis. Those seemingly conflicting desires of the American people enabled both interventionists and noninterventionists to contend that they spoke for a majority of Americans.[2]

America First Committee leaders feared, however, that, despite public opposition to a declaration of war, the administration steps short of war would make intervention inevitable. They feared that lend-lease, the Atlantic patrols, the "shoot-on-sight" policy, and allowing armed American merchant ships to enter the war zones would lead to incidents that would plunge

the United States into the European conflagration. And, increasingly, America First leaders became convinced that the
administration and the interventionists actually *hoped* steps short
of war would lead to intervention. During the last half of 1941,
America First spokesmen, including Lindbergh, repeatedly denounced the "subterfuge" by which interventionists and the
Roosevelt administration were leading the United States to war
while professing to be working for peace.

In June, 1941, the America First executive committee formally approved a new Committee principle advocating a national
advisory referendum on the issue of peace or war. It was not to
be in the form of a constitutional amendment, nor was it to bind
the hands of Congress or the President. America First proposed
that Congress pass a concurrent resolution authorizing a purely
advisory vote by the people on the issue of war or peace. There
was no real expectation that the measure would pass or even be
voted on in Congress. The Committee approved the policy as a
basis around which to conduct a positive campaign on the issue
of war or peace. It also hoped that agitation for the referendum
might put the administration on the defensive. It might put
interventionists in the embarrassing position of opposing a
democratic procedure. In addition to proposing the national
referendum, the America First Committee financed war-peace
referendums in specific areas—each showing that approximately 80 per cent of those polled opposed a declaration of
war.[3]

In the fall of 1941, the America First Committee tried to
have the issue of war or peace submitted for a definite vote in
Congress. On October 20, the America First national committee voted to send an open letter to President Roosevelt urging
him to submit a war resolution to Congress. General Wood sent
such a letter to the President two days later. In it he made clear
that America First would vigorously oppose the war resolution
but would honor it if Congress voted for war. At the same time,
General Wood insisted that if Congress voted against a declaration of war "the Administration must respect that decision and
take no further step toward our involvement." Secretary of War
Henry L. Stimson and others had been urging the President to

follow just such a course. Roosevelt was convinced, however, that he would be defeated in such a vote. He did not ask Congress to declare a state of war until after the Japanese attacked Pearl Harbor. The America First Committee was never able to focus public attention exclusively on the simple issue of war or peace. Despite its efforts, the foreign policy debate in 1941 was conducted primarily upon grounds chosen by the President.[4]

Lindbergh's attacks on the Roosevelt administration bore his own individual stamp, but they were consistent with those of the America First Committee in general. In an address in Minneapolis on May 10, he complained that the President asked Americans to fight for the "Four Freedoms," but then he denied them "the freedom to vote on vital issues" and also denied them "freedom of information—the right of a free people to know where they are being led by their government." On May 23, he told the America First audience in Madison Square Garden that in the 1940 presidential campaign Americans were given "just about as much chance" to express their foreign policy views "as the Germans would have been given if Hitler had run against Goering."[5]

In a controversial address in Philadelphia on May 29, Lindbergh called for "new leadership" in the United States. That was the first speech in which he referred to Roosevelt by name. He ridiculed the President's assertion that the safety of America depended upon control of the Cape Verde Islands off the coast of Africa: "Even Hitler never made a statement like that." Lindbergh said: "If we say that our frontier lies on the Rhine, they can say that theirs lies on the Mississippi." He charged that "Mr. Roosevelt claims that Hitler desires to dominate the world. But it is Mr. Roosevelt himself who advocates world domination when he says that it is our business to control the wars of Europe and Asia, and that we in America must dominate islands lying off the African coast." In his speech he asked: "Is it not time for us to turn to new policies and to a new leadership?" He urged his listeners to join with the America First Committee to "create a leadership for our nation that places America first."[6]

Critics promptly charged that in calling for "new leadership"

Lindbergh was attempting to become the catalyst, "the man on horseback," for a violent fascist overthrow of the American government. For the only time in his noninterventionist speaking career, Lindbergh issued a clarifying statement after that address. In a telegram to the *Baltimore Sun,* he explained: "Neither I nor anyone else on the America First Committee advocate proceeding by anything but constitutional methods. It is our opposition who endanger the American Constitution when they object to our freedom of speech and expression. Under the Constitution we have every right to advocate a leadership for this country which is non-interventionist and which places the interests of America first."[7] Many who opposed Lindbergh felt no hesitation, earlier and later, in urging new leadership when a President they disliked was in office. But, in the emotional atmosphere before Pearl Harbor, they were prepared to put the worst interpretation on anything Lindbergh said.

On August 9, in Cleveland, Lindbergh spoke on "Government by Representation or Subterfuge." His speech was a direct attack on Roosevelt's tactics. He charged that "our President consults our representatives in Congress with less and less frequency." In a key statement, he said: "The hypocrisy and subterfuge that surrounds us comes out in every statement of the war party. When we demand that our Government listen to the 80% of the people who oppose war, they shout that we are causing disunity. The same groups who call on us to defend democracy and freedom abroad, demand that we kill democracy and freedom at home by forcing four-fifths of our people into war against their will. The one-fifth who are for war call the four-fifths who are against war the 'fifth column.' " He charged that the interventionists "know that the people of this country will not vote for war, and they therefore plan on involving us through subterfuge." He contended that the interventionists and the administration "plan on creating incidents and situations" to force the United States into war. He insisted that the issue in America was "even greater than the issue of war or peace." He saw it as "the issue of whether or not we still have a representative government; whether or not we in the United States of America are still a free people, with the right to decide the fundamental policies of our nation."[8]

Thus by the time Lindbergh singled out the Roosevelt administration as one of the major "war agitators" in his Des Moines speech on September 11, he had already been emphasizing that theme vigorously for some months. He would continue to do so until the Japanese attack on Pearl Harbor. And he never changed his opinion of Roosevelt and his tactics.

In Fort Wayne, Indiana, on October 3, in his first address after the Des Moines rally, Lindbergh worried that he might be giving his "last address." He warned "that an Administration which can throw this country into undeclared naval war against the will of our people, and without asking the consent of Congress, can by similar methods prevent freedom of speech among us." Consequently, he spoke to his audience as though he were giving his last speech (he did give only one more before Pearl Harbor silenced him). He charged that "Not one step the Administration has taken in these last two years was placed honestly before our people as a step toward war." He contended that the administration had "been treating our Congress more and more as the German Reichstag has been treated under the Nazi regime. Congress, like the Reichstag, is not consulted. The issue of war or peace has never been put up to the people nor to its duly elected representatives in Congress because the President and his Administration know that the people would not accept it."[9]

Less than six weeks before Pearl Harbor, in New York's Madison Square Garden, Lindbergh delivered what proved to be his final America First address. In that speech, he reviewed Europe's path to war, his long battle against intervention, and the administration's steps toward involvement. He charged that President Roosevelt and his administration "preach about preserving Democracy and freedom abroad, while they practice Dictatorship and subterfuge at home." In his view, "They used the phrase 'Steps Short of War' to *lead* us to foreign war." He insisted that "The most fundamental issue today is not one of war or peace, but one of integrity. . . . There is no danger to this nation from without. The only danger lies from within." In the last sentence of what was to be his last noninterventionist speech, Lindbergh said: "I appeal to all Americans, no matter what their viewpoint on the war may be, to unite behind the demand for a leadership in Washington that stands squarely upon American traditions—a leadership of integrity instead of subterfuge, of openness instead of secrecy; a leadership that demonstrates its Americanism by taking the American people into its confidence."[10]

Prior to the Japanese attack on Pearl Harbor on December 7, Lindbergh had agreed to address an America First rally in Boston on December 12. With the coming of war, America First canceled the rally. But Lindbergh had already drafted his speech for that meeting. Though he never delivered it, it provides a final expression of his views before Pearl Harbor. He had intended to speak on "What do we mean by Democracy and Freedom?" He had planned to say "that *democracy* is gone from a nation when its people are no longer informed of the fundamental policies and intentions of their government," and that *"freedom* is a travesty among men who have been forced into war by a President they elected because he promised peace." He wrote that *"Freedom* and *Democracy* cannot long exist without a third quality, a quality called *Integrity*. It is a quality whose absence is alarming in our government today. Without integrity, freedom and democracy will become only politicians' nicknames for an American totalitarian state." In his opinion, the word that best described the "danger in America" was not invasion, intervention, Germany, Russia, or Japan; "that word is subterfuge." He insisted that "Subterfuge marked every step we made 'short of war,' and it now marks every step we are making 'short of' a dictatorial system in America. Our nation has been led to war with promises of peace. It is now being led toward dictatorship with promises of democracy." He suggested that before America crusaded "for freedom and democracy abroad, let us decide how these terms are to be applied to the negro population in our southern states."[11]

## "Government by Subterfuge"

In its final desperate efforts to keep the United States out of the war, the America First Committee announced on December 1, 1941, that it would play an active role in the 1942 congressional elections. That announcement followed careful planning within the Committee and consultations with noninterventionist Senators and Congressmen. It had the endorsement of America First chapter leaders and the national committee. America First did not intend to form a third party. Instead, it hoped to provide nonpartisan political support for noninterventionist candidates in both parties and to oppose interventionist candidates.[12]

Charles A. Lindbergh had often been urged to run for political office—perhaps for the position of United States Senator from Minnesota or for President. His noninterventionist activities and his opposition to President Roosevelt revived such ideas on the part of his admirers. He had been urged to run for elective office as early as 1927, after his solo flight to Paris. The suggestion was repeated many times later.

After Colonel Lindbergh's testimony against lend-lease before the Senate Foreign Relations Committee in February, 1941, Senator Gerald P. Nye and others publicly urged him to run for Congress. By July, Chester Bowles (a member of the America First national committee) and Senator Burton K. Wheeler believed that a new political party would have to be developed in the postwar period to provide a democratic alternative to the twin threats of communism and fascism in the United States. Bowles privately believed that "Lindbergh may, when the war is over, loom as the logical spokesman for such a group." He thought that if the United States entered the war "a great deal of bitterness will follow the peace." And if the United States stayed out of war, there would be "a vast disillusionment when the public becomes aware of the vicious methods that have been used by the interventionists during the last year or two in their efforts to trick us into this mess in Europe." Bowles and Wheeler were "most enthusiastic" about the possible leadership role that Lindbergh could play for "millions upon millions of Americans who are determined to bring about the right kind of economic and social system through traditional American, democratic methods." Bowles suggested that Lindbergh run for the Senate in Minnesota in 1942 so that he might be in an important position for the future. In September, 1941, the press carried rumors that Lindbergh might run for office in Minnesota. Early in 1942, he was still being urged to run for the Senate there, by Senator Henrik Shipstead and others.[13]

At various times Lindbergh had given thought to running for public office. But he always decided against it. As a boy he had observed his father's experiences and learned to dislike politics. When Senator William E. Borah suggested to him in 1939 that he would make a good presidential candidate, Lindbergh recorded in his journal that he preferred "intellectual and personal freedom to the honors and accomplishments of political office—even that of President." In May, 1941, when friends told him he could not avoid eventually running for office, that he would be pushed into it, he recorded in his diary that he could avoid it "by making one address, or by writing one article in which I discuss truthfully and openly the fundamental issues which face this country today." If he wrote and spoke exactly what he believed, he "need have little fear of being pushed into politics—even by his friends." After his Des Moines speech, former President Herbert Hoover told him the speech had been a mistake and that in politics one "learned not to say things just because they are true." Lindbergh's response was that that was one of the reasons he did not wish to be a politician. He would rather say what he believed than "measure every statement" he made "by its probable popularity." In January, 1942, he wrote in his journal that politics would cut him off from the things he valued most in life, including the "freedom to move and think and act" as he thought best.[14]

It is impossible to determine just what effect the America First Committee might have had on the election campaigns of 1942 if the United States had stayed out of the war until then. According to a Gallup poll in the fall of 1941, 16 per cent of American voters would have supported candidates of a hypothetical "keep-out-of-war party" led by Lindbergh, Wheeler, Nye, and others. That would have been a larger vote than any third party had won since 1924. But America First did not intend to form a third party. Since it proposed to give nonpartisan support to noninterventionist candidates of the two established political parties, America First strength might have been sufficient to swing some close elections.[15]

Whatever the results might have been, the Japanese attack on Pearl Harbor on December 7, 1941, took the decision of war or peace out of American hands. By the time of the 1942 congressional elections the United States was engaged in an all-out war against the Axis. The America First Committee had long since dissolved. Prewar isolationists did better than expected in the elections of 1942. But Lindbergh's reputation was by then so scarred that he might have had difficulty winning election to public office had he sought it. In any event, he neither sought nor accepted it. And insofar as he had contested politically with Franklin D. Roosevelt in the "Great Debate" before Pearl Harbor, the President emerged the decisive victor. Lindbergh was to depart the arena "bloodied but unbowed."

# 23/The End Is Near

NEITHER Charles A. Lindbergh nor the America First Committee slackened their efforts in the battle against intervention during the short time remaining before Pearl Harbor. In October and November, 1941, the Committee vigorously fought against repeal of the vital provisions of the Neutrality Act. It mobilized its maximum strength and used every proved method to make that strength felt in the nation's capital. That dramatic effort was the most efficiently organized in the Committee's history. The interventionists once again triumphed in the contest, and consequently armed American merchant ships were permitted to carry cargoes in the war zones. The vote against the administration in both houses of Congress, however, was greater than it had been a few months earlier on lend-lease. A shift of ten votes in the House of Representatives would have defeated the measure. Those Congressmen who voted against the Roosevelt administration represented approximately 50 per cent of the American voters. Among the House members from twenty states, a majority of those voting cast their votes against the President's proposal. The administration even lost the votes of a few southern Congressmen. The margin of Roosevelt's victory was much too narrow to encourage any move for a declaration of war. And public opinion polls continued to indicate that the overwhelming majority of Americans opposed a declaration of war. The noninterventionists never gave up, and their strength remained formidable in and out of Congress.[1]

## The End Is Near

Nevertheless, Lindbergh, General Robert E. Wood, R. Douglas Stuart, Jr., and other noninterventionists could not avoid asking themselves whether continued activity would be worth the effort, whether they had any real chance for success in their attempts to keep the United States out of the war, whether they were fighting a hopelessly lost cause. Both President Roosevelt's "shoot-on-sight" speech, proclaiming an undeclared naval war against Nazi Germany in the Atlantic, and the traumatic repercussions of Lindbergh's Des Moines speech on the same night encouraged their self-doubts and stocktaking. Lindbergh, Wood, Stuart, and other America First leaders were not politicians. Each had other responsibilities that required his attention and other interests he ordinarily would have preferred to pursue. And though all had plenty of courage, none was so tough-skinned or insensitive as to be unaffected by the increasingly vicious smears and abuse to which they were subjected.

Young Stuart confessed to a "beaten down" feeling in mid-August. After taking only one day off in over a year, he had slipped away for a few days' relaxation in the West. He seriously considered returning to law school at Yale in the fall, urged in that direction by his father. He finally decided, instead, to stay on with America First, but his momentary indecision was shared by others as they examined their separate roles in the battle against intervention.[2]

On September 20, Hanford MacNider, national vice-chairman of America First, wrote to General Wood that the Committee had "come to the end of the road" so far as keeping the United States out of war was concerned. MacNider thought the President's "shoot-on-sight" speech was, in effect, an illegal declaration of war that would "bring about the necessary incidents" to make war a reality. He wrote that Roosevelt had "short circuited the Constitution, violated the Neutrality Act, showed his contempt for Congress by not even bothering to consult them. Congress could stop it, but there are no signs whatsoever that it intends to do so. Hitler still has his choice. The President has left us none." MacNider saw "no good reason" for America First "to continue being dragged along with our heels dug in, stirring up dust, but accomplishing little else in our present hopeless cause." He thought America First should not continue its "present procedure a single additional day." The Iowa manufacturer concluded that if the Committee determined to press on, he would "have no choice but to jump off and swim home" as best he could.[3]

Even before he received MacNider's letter, General Wood had independently reached much the same conclusion. With his heavy responsibilities as chairman of the board of Sears Roebuck and his duties as national chairman of America First, General Wood had been under tremendous pressures for months. He was as opposed to intervention and as dedicated to the America First cause as ever, but he had wanted to step down from the chairmanship of the Committee from the beginning. Three days before MacNider wrote his letter, Wood suggested to Lindbergh, Stuart, and two America First staff members that in October the Committee adjourn until the congressional election campaigns of 1942. He thought that Roosevelt had already involved the United States so deeply in the war that for the time being the Committee could accomplish little by continued activity. At the national committee meeting on September 18, he said the Committee should either adjourn or disband. He wrote MacNider that he would have favored "stopping right now were it not for the fact that if we did so now, the matter would be linked up with the Lindbergh speech at Des Moines and taken as a repudiation of Lindbergh." He did not want to do that. But, to bolster his plea for an October adjournment, he sent copies of MacNider's letter to Lindbergh and several other members of the national committee. He also consulted non-interventionist Congressmen and Senators in Washington on the matter.[4]

Despite MacNider's agreement with General Wood, other Committee leaders strongly disagreed. Stuart and Lindbergh both felt a warm affection and great respect for the General, but both opposed his proposal and did their influential best to dissuade him. When Wood first advanced his suggestion to Lindbergh, Stuart, and the others, the day before the national committee meeting, they all opposed it, believing the Committee should continue until Congress declared war or until it was obvious that the Commitee could not succeed. Lindbergh discussed the matter further that night at General Wood's home. Lindbergh preferred "to go down fighting for what we believe in, if we must go down at all." Similarly, at the national committee meeting the next day those present disagreed with the General's suggestion. But Wood hoped to win them over. Stuart urged him not to let his idea become public, "because nothing would encourage the opposition more than knowing this; nothing would put more pressure on the Committee than if it were known there was a possibility of this."[5]

On September 24, Lindbergh wrote to Wood expressing the fear that "an adjournment at this time would be misunderstood by our supporters, and used to great advantage by the Interventionists." He thought the Committee had played a major role in keeping the country out of the war so far and pointed out that polls continued to show strong opposition to war. Lindbergh insisted that the Committee "should continue its activities unless (1.) Congress declares war or (2.) conditions become such that continued activity is ineffective." He feared that if it stopped before one or the other of those conditions was met, noninterventionists would feel that the Committee had let them down, and it "would also be a go signal to our opposition." He worried that it "might even be the element which decides the issue of peace or war this coming winter, and all that this issue involves both in America and the rest of the world." To adjourn until the next congressional elections might be risky, Lindbergh said, as he was not entirely confident that under Roosevelt those elections would even be conducted in 1942.[6]

On October 4, the day after the Fort Wayne rally, Lindbergh conferred with Wood, Stuart, and others in Chicago on the matter. General Wood had been working much too hard, was discouraged, and looked tired. Lindbergh again advised against adjournment. Committee members "would feel we were showing weakness at the very moment we should be fighting the hardest." General Wood insisted that he "must soon choose between giving up his work with Sears, Roebuck and giving up such active participation in the affairs of the America First Committee." He said he could not "continue to carry on both."[7]

Nonetheless, the combined efforts of Lindbergh, Stuart, and others prevailed. General Wood laid aside his proposal for adjournment. By the latter part of October he was back "in a fighting mood."[8] He continued as America First national chairman. He led the Committee's opposition to repeal of the vital provisions of the Neutrality Act. Under his guidance, the Committee announced its plans for bipartisan support of noninterventionist candidates in the election campaigns of 1942. The America First Committee, with General Wood at its helm and Lindbergh as its most sought-after speaker, continued its battle against intervention until Congress declared war.

Though Lindbergh helped persuade General Wood to continue the fight, and though he shared in that effort, he, too, began to rethink his role and his future. The aviator had spent more than two years in the battle against intervention. That "semipolitical activity" was "not leading to the type of life" he wanted to live. He wanted to press ahead with the writing of what was to become his prize-winning book, *The Spirit of St. Louis*. And since he had "no intention of going into politics permanently," he thought it time for him "to begin building toward the future of a different type of life." He still loved to travel, but he wanted to build a permanent home in the country for his family. "I want one; Anne deserves one; and the children need one." Nevertheless, he thought his time was "well spent in opposing our participation in this war." He "simply could not stand idly by" and watch the United States "follow a leadership" that he believed was "so dishonest, so incompetent, and so wrong."[9]

On October 27, three days before his final America First address and just over a month before the Committee announced its plans for activity in the 1942 elections, Lindbergh wrote a long, careful letter to General Wood outlining his tentative plans. He thought he was not suited, "either by temperament or desire, to the field of active politics." He did not regret the time he had devoted to America First and would continue those efforts in the future. But he found himself "headed toward a position" he did not wish to hold and one that he thought "would be inadvisable from the standpoint of the Committee itself." He believed the Committee should "avoid building up any one man to a position of too great importance in the organization." The Committee was made up of too many conflicting views "to permit its membership to be satisfied with any single leader"; the reactions to his Des Moines address illustrated his point. Also, he felt "written out" on speeches. He did not want to speak unless he had something he believed "worth saying." He was, he believed, "speaking much too often." And each meeting he addressed increased the problem. "Instead of building up new speakers," it made America First members depend on him even more for their rallies.[10]

Consequently, he informed General Wood that he intended "to withdraw gradually from participation in these rallies." That work should, he believed, be turned over to others who had "a natural aptitude for politics and speaking." He wanted to help America First as much as he could "from the standpoint of a supporter, rather than from the standpoint of a Committee leader." He worried that many Committee members felt responsible for his personal views on matters outside the war-peace issue. "Their primary interest often lies in popularity and effect, whereas I think my primary interest lies in belief and fact. We frequently disagree on the compromise that is to be made between these elements."[11]

He wanted both his plans and those of America First kept flexible, however, to allow for unknown developments of the war. "The collapse of the Russian armies may easily bring the demand in England for negotiation. If so, I think we should be ready to support that demand over here, and that I shall hold myself in readiness to assist in doing." But if America First entered "the field of domestic politics," he thought it best for him to become less prominent in the Committee. He promised General Wood that he would "continue opposing American intervention as strongly as ever, and in whatever way I think will be most effective." The course he outlined did not require any "immediate decisions," and he realized it was "quite possible that war developments will sweep these problems entirely out of our control."[12] He was correct. But those "war developments" did not entail the collapse of the Russian armies or British moves for a negotiated peace. Instead, they came in the form of a surprise attack by Japan that abruptly ended the foreign policy debate and projected the United States into the war.

As he proposed in his letter to Wood, Lindbergh spoke less frequently in the fall of 1941 than he had earlier in the year. His address at Fort Wayne came three weeks after the Des Moines speech, and nearly four weeks then elapsed before his Madison Square Garden speech in New York. He did not address any rallies in November, and if war had not intervened there would have been an interval of more than six weeks before his next planned America First rally, in Boston on December 12.

Furthermore, Lindbergh's last four addresses increasingly took on summing-up and for-the-record tones. At Fort Wayne he said: "In making these addresses, I have no motive in mind other than the welfare of my country and my civilization. This is not a life that I enjoy. Speaking is not my vocation, and political life is not my ambition. For the past several years, I have given up my normal life and interests; first, to study the conditions in Europe which brought on this war, and, second, to oppose American intervention. I have done this because I believe my country is in mortal danger, and because I could not stand by and see her going to destruction without pitting everything I had against that trend. I am moved by no personal interest or animosity. I do not speak out of hate for any individuals or any people. But neither have I tried to avoid facts in order to have my speeches politically popular. I have tried, and I shall continue to try, as long as it is possible, to give you the truth without prejudice and without passion."[13]

In Madison Square Garden on October 30, he surveyed his experiences and thinking from the beginning of his stay in

Europe onward. He explained why he had opposed war before it erupted in Europe. He described his motives for opposing American intervention in the war. He pointed out that he and other noninterventionists had, "from the beginning, encountered an insidious opposition. . . . an opposition that has made constant use of under cover methods; an opposition that has fought in personalities and smearing campaigns, and not on issues; an opposition that has discarded one American tradition after another, while it claims to be upholding the American way of life." He described the steps short of war that he saw as moving the United States ever closer to war. "These steps to war were taken in a way that was cunningly calculated to disarm opposition. They were taken under cover of false promises and implications." He described in alarming terms the possible consequences for the United States if it entered the war. He thought it clear "that it would be disastrous for us to enter this war abroad." But he insisted that "even more disastrous" would be "a continuation of the subterfuge, the confusion, and the irresponsibility, with which we have been led along the road to war."[14] Even as he spoke, Japanese warships, military airplanes, and personnel were readying for their attack on American military installations in Hawaii and the Philippines.

# V

## Aftermath

# 24/Pearl Harbor

JUST before eight o'clock on Sunday morning, December 7, 1941, the quiet of that lovely day at Pearl Harbor was shattered by the roar of Japanese dive bombers flying low with their deadly cargoes. Within one hour and forty-five minutes, two big waves of Japanese planes had destroyed much of America's sea and air power in Hawaii. Some 3,500 Americans were dead, dying, or wounded. With incredible surprise and tactical success, Japan had brought war to the United States in the Pacific. And with equal decisiveness, the Japanese attack abruptly ended Charles A. Lindbergh's battle against intervention in World War II.

Few adult Americans who lived then would ever forget the moment they first heard the startling news that Sunday afternoon in the States. When the news arrived, Senator Gerald P. Nye was addressing an America First rally in Pittsburgh, Pennsylvania. It was the Committee's last public meeting. Lindbergh was spending a quiet day with his family on the island of Martha's Vineyard, off Cape Cod in Massachusetts. They had moved there from Long Island in August to gain greater privacy.

Like that of Senator Nye, Lindbergh's initial response to the news of the attack included a touch of disbelief. Was it really a major attack or just an exaggerated story by radio commentators? In his journal he wrote that he was "not surprised that the Japs attacked," believing the United States had "been

**207**

prodding them into war for weeks." He had expected an attack in the Philippines. He was surprised that the Japanese also struck Pearl Harbor, however, and he was surprised by the size of the attack and by America's heavy losses. He wondered if the United States had sent so many of its planes and ships to the Atlantic that the Japanese thought they could successfully attack Pearl Harbor.[1]

In the "Great Debate" on American foreign policies, both the interventionists and the noninterventionists had focused their attention largely on the war in Europe and in the Atlantic. They had given much less attention to the war in Asia and the Pacific. On August 11, 1941, the America First executive committee had adopted a formal resolution opposing war with Japan except in case of attack. But the Committee had never mounted a major campaign to prevent war with Japan.[2]

Anne and Charles Lindbergh had visited Japan in 1931 during their flight to the Orient. But, like America First, Lindbergh had looked primarily to Europe and spent little time discussing policies toward Japan. He did not think Orientals had the natural talents for aviation and air power that Americans and Europeans had. In his *Atlantic Monthly* article of March, 1940, Lindbergh wrote that "Asia alone is no threat to the powerful mechanized armies of the West." He believed it was "only when western nations turned inward toward war among themselves that Asiatic armies stir from their contemplation and feel the smothering strength of their myriad numbers." In his speech at Yale University on October 30, 1940, he said: "If we intend to fight a war in the Orient, it is long past time for us to begin the construction of bases in the Pacific, and to stop our wavering policy in the Philippines—we should either fortify these islands adequately, or get out of them entirely." He believed that an adequately prepared United States "could probably wage a successful war in the Orient—provided Europe remained neutral, or was on our side." But he criticized the "blundering diplomacy" of the United States that "forced Japan to turn toward Germany for assistance." He insisted that if the United States intended "to attack Europe, then we have no forces to spare for an Oriental war." In April, 1941, just before Lindbergh's initial America First rally, William R. Castle wrote him a long letter on Japanese-American relations. He urged the Colonel to make a speech opposing American involvement in a war to block Japanese expansion.[3] But Lindbergh did not make the major appeal that Castle urged.

On Sunday evening, December 7, America First national headquarters issued a statement urging its followers to support America's war effort against Japan. The Committee ceased its noninterventionist activity, advised chapters to postpone scheduled rallies, and stopped its distribution of noninterventionist literature. But the Committee statement deliberately left the door open for possible continued opposition to participation in the European war.[4]

On the Monday morning after the Japanese attack, Lindbergh telephoned Stuart at America First headquarters to urge that his scheduled rally in Boston be canceled. He also called General Wood. Wood's first words to Lindbergh on the telephone were: "Well, he got us in through the back door." Lindbergh prepared a statement for immediate release to the press through the America First Committee. In his statement he wrote: "We have been stepping closer to war for many months. Now it has come and we must meet it as united Americans regardless of our attitude in the past toward the policy our government has followed. Whether or not that policy has been wise, our country has been attacked by force of arms, and by force of arms we must retaliate. Our own defenses and our own military position have already been neglected too long. We must now turn every effort to building the greatest and most efficient Army, Navy, and Air Force in the world. When American soldiers go to war, it must be with the best equipment that modern skill can design and that modern industry can build."[5]

At noon that same day, December 8, he listened to President Roosevelt's broadcast speech calling for a declaration of war on Japan. Lindbergh was convinced that if the President had asked for a declaration at any time before the Japanese attack, Congress would have refused. He thought America had brought that attack on itself, but he could see no alternative for the United States under the circumstances "except to fight." In his journal he wrote that if he had been in Congress he "certainly would have voted for a declaration of war." In actual practice, only one person in either house (Congresswoman Jeanette Rankin of Montana) voted against war with Japan.[6]

On December 11, 1941, Germany and Italy declared war on the United States, and Congress promptly and unanimously voted for war against those Axis Powers in Europe. The United States was formally and fully a belligerent in World War II. As Lindbergh wrote in his journal: "Now, all that I feared would happen has happened. We are at war all over the world, and we are unprepared for it from either a spiritual or a material standpoint. Fortunately, in spite of all that has been said, the oceans are still difficult to cross; and we have the time to adjust and prepare, which France lacked and which England has had only in part since aviation has spanned the barrier of her Channel." But he feared that to defeat the Axis Powers "probably means the bloodiest and most devastating war of all history."[7]

Lindbergh did not attend the America First national committee meeting in Chicago on December 11. Before it met he wired his preference for adjourning the Committee rather than dissolving it; such a course "would be burning no bridges." The majority at the meeting, however, voted to dissolve and disband America First. And when he learned of the decision later, Lindbergh was persuaded that the decision to dissolve was correct. America's war had been extended to Europe as well as to Asia, most national committee members preferred dissolution, and he was concerned about "the hysteria and intolerance which seem to be rising rapidly in the country." He believed history would show that the America First Committee's principles had been wise and that its activities were "among the constructive efforts of the pre-war period."[8]

At its meeting the America First national committee approved a final public statement: "Our principles were right. Had they been followed, war could have been avoided. No good purpose can now be served by considering what might have been, had our objectives been attained." It urged the protection of the rights of American citizens during the war and spoke for the powers of "the people through Congress" to shape America's "long range aims and policies." But it concluded that the "period of democratic debate on the issue of entering the war is over; the time for military action is here." It urged its followers "to give their full support to the war effort of the nation, until peace is attained."[9]

The next day, General Wood wrote to Lindbergh explaining the Committee's action and warmly praising him: "I have never met a man anywhere whom I admired or respected more—your character, your courage and your patriotism." Wood felt "no regrets" about his and Lindbergh's noninterventionist efforts. They had stood for what they believed was right, and he was sure that history would vindicate them. He thought Lindbergh had "a destiny" in America and advised him to bide his time; the country would need and call him.[10]

On December 14, Lindbergh prepared a letter to the members of America First. In it he expressed the conviction that they had been correct in their stand. "The final judgment of our policies must be left to the future and to more objective times; but in this final judgment, I have complete confidence." For the present, however, he maintained that there was nothing to be gained "by arguing about who was right and who was wrong." He urged a concentration on "prosecuting this war in the most constructive and intelligent manner. We have contributed the best we could give to our country in time of peace. Now, we must contribute the best we can give in time of war."[11]

But Lindbergh was to learn that, so far as prewar isolationist leaders were concerned, America's wartime President could be unforgiving. The administration blocked Lindbergh's efforts to serve in the United States armed forces. Only with much difficulty did he eventually find ways to put his knowledge and ability to use. Nevertheless, as a civilian aviator Lindbergh shared in waging America's war against the Axis Powers from 1942 to 1945.

# 25/Rebuffed by FDR

CHARLES A. LINDBERGH was nearly forty years old, married, and the father of three living children when the United States entered World War II. Most men in comparable circumstances made their contributions to the war effort as civilians, generally without departing drastically from their peacetime routines. That was not the course Lindbergh preferred for himself.

Trained as a military pilot in the mid-1920's and commissioned as an officer, Lindbergh had been a Colonel in the Air Corps Reserve until his resignation in April, 1941. Proud of his commission, his technical knowledge, and his flying skills, and devoted to his country, Lindbergh earnestly wanted to serve the United States in the war. And he did so—even in combat. But President Roosevelt and the more fervent interventionists in his Cabinet blocked his attempts to regain his Air Force commission and prevented him from serving as a member of America's armed forces during World War II.

Initially Lindbergh considered writing directly to the President to offer his services, without repudiating his prewar convictions. But he did not trust Roosevelt. He feared the President might be vindictive, that he might use the offer for "politics and publicity" and then assign him to some "out of the way" position where he could not be effective. Lindbergh considered making his contribution through the aviation industry. But he really wanted to be back in the Air Force, so much so that he almost regretted his resignation. In any event, Lindbergh determined that he must take some active part in the war effort.[1]

To that end he telephoned seeking an appointment with General H. H. Arnold of the Army Air Force. When there was no response to his call, he wrote to the General on December 20 offering his services to the Air Force. Newsmen called Arnold on December 29 to ask if Lindbergh had offered his services and what the response had been. The General said that "if Lindbergh did volunteer his services to the War Department it indicated that he had changed from a noninterventionist status to one in which he desired to participate in activities for which his years of experience had best qualified him." Though he had not changed his views, Lindbergh felt encouraged that Arnold's statement to the press meant his offer might be accepted.[2]

Rumors circulated, and the press and others gave the Air Force and the White House conflicting advice on whether to accept the offer or not. Though some urged "forgive and forget," others vehemently objected to allowing a man they called "a traitor" and "Nazi" to serve in America's armed forces. One couple wrote: "Our son is in the service and we want no Quislings behind his back." The *New York Times,* however, believed Lindbergh's offer should and would be accepted.[3]

Several in Roosevelt's Cabinet had strong feelings on the matter. As usual, Secretary of the Interior Harold L. Ickes was in the vanguard. On December 30, he wrote the President vigorously opposing acceptance of Lindbergh's services. Ickes charged that Lindbergh was "a ruthless and conscious fascist, motivated by a hatred for you personally and a contempt for democracy in general." He insisted that Lindbergh's speeches showed "an astonishing identity with those of Berlin" and that the similarity was "not accidental." He charged that Lindbergh's actions were "coldly calculated with a view to attaining ultimate power for himself" and that "a military service record" was part of that effort. Citing examples from history, Ickes warned that it would be "a tragic disservice to American democracy to give one of its bitterest and most ruthless enemies

**213**

a chance to gain a military record." He urged that Lindbergh "be buried in merciful oblivion." Roosevelt's response was prompt and unequivocal: "What you say about Lindbergh and the potential danger of the man, I agree with wholeheartedly." Without identifying its author, the President sent copies of Ickes's letter to Secretary of War Henry L. Stimson and Secretary of the Navy Frank Knox.[4]

Secretary Knox's response was equally blunt. He wrote the President, on January 1, that if it were a Navy matter he "would offer Lindberg an opportunity to enlist as an air cadet, like anybody else would have to do. He has had no training as an officer and ought to earn his commission." Knox's facts were wrong, but his attitude was clear. President Roosevelt endorsed the view, and on January 12 he forwarded Knox's memo to Secretary of War Stimson. He suggested: "For the time being the matter can be possibly maintained 'under consideration.' "[5]

If Stimson's own predilections and the advices of the President, Knox, and Ickes were not sufficient, others were eager to help. For example, James P. Warburg in New York sent John J. McCloy, Assistant Secretary of War, a report on a private meeting of America Firsters in the home of Edwin S. Webster, Jr., an America First national committee member. The Reverend Leon M. Birkhead of Friends of Democracy had provided the report. It contended that Lindbergh attended the gathering in Webster's home on the evening of December 17 and spoke for an hour. According to the report, Lindbergh had said that the only danger in the world was "the yellow danger" and that Germany, in control of Poland and the Soviet Union, should have formed, in collaboration with Britain, "a block against the yellow people and bolshevism." Instead, "the British and the fools in Washington had to interfere." The report quoted him as saying that Britain was "the real cause of all the trouble in the world today." He was supposed to have urged America First to "keep on the alert" and become "a political force again" later. McCloy telephoned Arthur Sulzberger of the *New York Times* to check on the report. Sulzberger had sent a reporter to interview Webster. The reporter was able to confirm that there had been a meeting and that Lindbergh had spoken informally. Webster denied that Lindbergh had said much of what the report contended. Unable to confirm the report adequately, the *New York Times* decided it was inadvisable to print it.[6] The *New York Post, PM,* the *New York World-Telegram,* and other newspapers, however, felt no such inhibitions. They carried stories on the report, sometimes with editorial embroidery. One copy of the report was sent to Mrs. Eleanor Roosevelt, who passed it on to her husband, who then forwarded it for Secretary Stimson and General Arnold to see.[7]

Lindbergh's personal account of the gathering differed substantially from the one originating with Birkhead. Lindbergh's journal put the episode on December 16 rather than 17. Webster's party was a combination of an engagement dinner with his fiancée and a farewell dinner for former "street speakers" for America First. In Lindbergh's opinion, the group of about forty had included some of "the more radical" who had not wanted America First to dissolve. Lindbergh had not known about the dinner until he telephoned Webster the same morning. Webster invited him to attend and promised he would not have to speak. On that condition, he came to "a sort of last get-together and farewell party." Lindbergh did speak for five or ten minutes. According to his recollections ten weeks later, he said nothing about the "yellow race," or about England and Germany getting together. Instead, as he recalled, he said that since the United States had been attacked, it must fight, that America First was correct in dissolving, that the Committee had been right in urging strong defenses for America, and that all Americans should concentrate on conducting the war successfully. In the privacy of his journal, Lindbergh conceded that he believed a protracted war would benefit Russia and Japan, that he hoped the war would end "before all Western nations are too worn out to resist the nations of the East," and that he thought "A Russian-dominated Europe would . . . be far worse than a German-dominated Europe." But he insisted that he had said none of those things at the dinner because he thought it inopportune when the United States was in the war. Lindbergh conceded, however, that he may have said that "it was a tragedy for us to fight among ourselves while we gave Japan a free hand in the Orient."[8]

Regardless of what Lindbergh may or may not have said at that private gathering in December, the Birkhead report of the meeting reached the President, the War Department, and the press. It reinforced the course that Stimson undoubtedly would have pursued anyway in dealing with Lindbergh's efforts to serve in the Army Air Force.

After making various preliminary inquiries, Lindbergh took the night train to Washington and spent ten days there, from January 8 through 17, 1942, trying to determine how he might best serve the nation's war effort. It was a discouraging sojourn. Through his second cousin, Rear Admiral Emory S. Land, he met on January 8 with Colonel William J. Donovan, who headed the secret Office of Strategic Services throughout World War II. Donovan said he would be glad to have the airman in his organization if the President did not object, but he was not sure just where Lindbergh's expertise might fit in. Nothing came of that initiative, and the flyer preferred to serve in the Air Force, anyway, if possible.[9]

On Saturday, January 10, he telephoned General Arnold's office seeking an appointment. The General's aide, however, advised him to make an appointment directly with the Secretary of War. Believing that such a course had been prearranged, Lindbergh telephoned the War Department and got an appointment with Secretary Stimson for Monday afternoon, January 12. Stimson received him courteously, in his office in the Munitions Building, just after four-thirty in the afternoon. The two men talked for half an hour. Lindbergh told Stimson that he wanted to be of service in the war effort. He was considering taking some sort of position in the aviation industry, but first he wanted to see if he could help in the Air Force, where he really preferred to serve. Stimson said he welcomed ideas and suggestions, but because of Lindbergh's prewar views he would be extremely hesitant about placing him in any position of command. Lindbergh confirmed that he still held the opinions he had expressed before Pearl Harbor, but now that the United States was at war he wanted to help in whatever way he might be most effective. Because of Lindbergh's views (Lindbergh thought Stimson held mistaken impressions about them), the Secretary of War doubted that Lindbergh would feel the necessary aggressiveness in a "position of command."

Stimson then called in Assistant Secretary of War for Air Robert A. Lovett. Lindbergh felt uncomfortable as Stimson explained to Lovett, in his presence, that because of his "political views" and consequent "lack of aggressiveness" it was inadvisable to place him in a "position of command." Lovett arranged for Lindbergh to meet with him and General Arnold the next day, and the session ended on a friendly tone.[10]

Early Tuesday afternoon, Lindbergh met for a half hour with Lovett and General Arnold. Again the discussion was friendly and courteous, but the differences proved irreconcilable. Lovett and Arnold thought Lindbergh might not be able to serve "loyally" under the President without, in effect, repudiating his prewar beliefs. Lindbergh was willing to issue additional statements, but he would not retract his earlier views. He said he had "very little confidence in the President" and would like to see the administration changed, but if he returned to the Air Force he "would follow the President of the United States as Commander-in-Chief of the Army." That was not sufficient for Lovett and Arnold. Consequently Lindbergh concluded that, under the circumstances, it would be a mistake for him to return to the Air Force, and that it would be better for him to make his contribution to the war effort through the aviation industry. In answer to Lindbergh's inquiry, Lovett said he did not think the War Department would object to his working for a commercial aviation company. Lindbergh got the impression that Lovett and Arnold were operating under restraints from higher political authority and found their assignment a bit awkward. Lindbergh regretted not being in the Air Force during the war, but he was "convinced" that the stand he "took on the war was right" and that that would "be realized eventually."[11]

The Roosevelt administration not only blocked Lindbergh's

efforts to serve as an Air Force officer during World War II, it also prevented him from serving as a civilian with various aviation businesses that had government contracts. Lindbergh had many friends in the aviation industry. Among those through whom he sought positions were Juan Trippe and Harold M. Bixby of Pan American Airways, Eugene E. Wilson and Lauren D. Lyman of United Aircraft Corporation, and Guy Vaughan of Curtiss-Wright. In each instance, the corporation would have welcomed Lindbergh's services; in each instance, the executives checked with the War Department and the White House to determine if there would be any objections; in each instance, there were objections that made it inexpedient for the corporation to employ Lindbergh. So far as Pan American and Curtiss-Wright were concerned, the obstacle was the White House. In the case of United Aircraft, the difficulty apparently came from the Senate. That company had sold equipment to Japan and Germany before the war. Lindbergh had had no connection with those developments, but under the circumstances it seemed best for him not to make a connection with the company. None of those businesses felt free to use Lindbergh in their war work in 1942, and he did not wish to endanger those companies, or his friends in them, by working for them against the wishes of the wartime government.[12]

It seemed that in whatever direction he turned, Lindbergh came up against a wall. His failures and frustrations produced one of the rare instances when he allowed his spirits to flag and his discouragement to show. On February 25, 1942, he wrote in his personal journal: "I am beginning to wonder whether I will be blocked in every attempt I make to take part in this war. I have always stood for what I thought would be to the best interest of this country, and now we are at war I want to take my part in fighting for it, foolish and disastrous as I think the war will prove to be. Our decision has been made, and now we must fight to preserve our national honor and our national future. I have always believed in the past that every American citizen had the right and the duty to state his opinion in peace and to fight for his country in war. But the Roosevelt Administration seems to think otherwise."[13]

## Rebuffed by FDR

Not until nearly four months after Pearl Harbor was Charles A. Lindbergh able to secure a position that would let him use his knowledge and skills for the nation's war effort. It was old Henry Ford who provided that opportunity.

# 26/A War to Fight

DESPITE the unwillingness of the Roosevelt administration to use his knowledge and talents in the war effort, Charles A. Lindbergh found opportunities to serve. Through the Ford Motor Company and the United Aircraft Corporation, he aided in the development, production, and testing of American bombers and fighter planes. As a civilian he tested fighters in combat in the South Pacific, shooting down a Japanese plane in the process. He went to Europe just after V-E Day to study German jet and rocket propulsion. He used his technical skills and talents constructively for America's war against the Axis during World War II. And he did so without ever repudiating the stands he had taken on American foreign policies before Pearl Harbor.

Henry Ford provided an excellent entree for Lindbergh. A prewar noninterventionist himself, Ford was independent, unconventional, and powerful. He was no more impressed or awed by Roosevelt than was Lindbergh. Ford used his company's talents and production facilities for America's war effort, but, like Lindbergh, he did not abandon his personal independence and private convictions in the process. Lindbergh had known Ford since 1927, and had given him a ride in the *Spirit of St. Louis* (Ford's first airplane ride). Though the industrialist was nearly forty years older than the aviator, the two men had developed a warm affection and respect for each other. Both had emerged from rural backgrounds and simpler times in the

Middle West, and each retained some of the values rooted in those backgrounds. In their tenacious independence they were kindred spirits; each felt responsibilities toward others, but neither was prepared to sell his genius for the mess of pottage of personal popularity. Both tenaciously resisted attempts to beat them into conformist molds.[1]

As early as May, 1940, newspapers reported Henry Ford as saying that with the counsel of men like Lindbergh and Edward Rickenbacker he could soon turn out a thousand airplanes a day if red tape did not interfere. Late in 1940, the government contracted for the Ford Company to begin producing Pratt & Whitney aircraft engines at its River Rouge plant. In 1941, the War Department arranged for Ford to produce Consolidated B-24 Liberator four-engine bombers. The company built the huge Willow Run plant for that purpose. But the initial production schedules were beyond the capacities of even that huge industrial installation, and it did not begin mass-producing the heavy bombers until the fall of 1942.[2]

In March, 1942, Ford approached Lindbergh about helping at the Willow Run factory. The airman responded immediately and met with Ford and his top executives in Detroit. The War Department had no objections, and that time the White House did not block the arrangement. Ford paid the Lindberghs' moving expenses to Michigan, but the airman did not draw any salary or retainer for his work for the Ford Company during the war.[3] Lindbergh preferred to fly single-engine planes, and he had more knowledge of and experience with fighters than with bombers. Nevertheless, he had flown multiengine aircraft (including the old Ford Tri-motor plane), and he soon familiarized himself with the heavy bomber. His experience with the design and production of airplanes had begun in 1927 or before, had been enriched by his prewar inspections of aircraft factories in Europe, and had been updated by his service with the Air Corps and NACA in 1939. He quickly put his technical expertise to work on problems in design, production, and testing.

He located a house for his family in Bloomfield Hills, near Detroit, and Anne and the children moved there in July. Their son Scott was born in August (making a family of three sons and a daughter). Charles tried to spend Sundays and extra hours with his family whenever possible, but his work often kept him away from home from daybreak until after dark, and it involved much travel. He avoided public comment on the war and foreign affairs. As he wrote in personal letters to friends from prewar days, he had "purposely entered technical fields" in which he could give his "utmost support" to America's war effort "without taking part in the responsibility for policies" that he thought were "badly conceived" and with which he strongly disagreed. When President Roosevelt visited Willow Run in September, 1942, Lindbergh quietly absented himself.[4]

In the course of his work, he made high-altitude flights in a P-47 Thunderbolt fighter, to test the ignition system used on the aircraft engines that the Ford Company manufactured. That led him to make some experimental flights to determine the effects, on both pilot and plane, of very high altitudes (over 40,000 feet, well above effective combat altitudes at that time). In 1943, Henry Ford's production of Pratt & Whitney engines, along with Lindbergh's own personal friendships, brought him into consulting and flight-testing projects for the United Aircraft Corporation in Connecticut, in addition to his continuing work for Ford. In that capacity he helped improve the Navy Marine Corsair F4U fighter, which used a Pratt & Whitney engine.[5]

Other America First leaders also actively served the war effort. Robert E. Wood, a retired Brigadier General, volunteered and served with Army Ordnance in Chicago. From 1943 to 1944, at the request of General H. H. Arnold, he went on extended missions for the Air Force in combat areas. Because of administration opposition, however, Wood (like Lindbergh) did not have his commission restored, and he served as a civilian. Hanford MacNider, the national vice-chairman of America First, had been in combat during World War I. He volunteered again after Pearl Harbor and had a distinguished combat record in the South Pacific. He rose to Brigadier General, and added a second Purple Heart and other medals to those he had been awarded in World War I. R. Douglas Stuart, Jr., had an ROTC commission, and he volunteered for active duty after Pearl Harbor. As an Army Major he served in General Dwight D. Eisenhower's SHAEF headquarters in England and landed in Europe shortly after D-Day. Lindbergh's friend Colonel Truman Smith had been retired for health reasons in 1941, but General George C. Marshall called him back to active duty as a G-2 intelligence officer after Pearl Harbor. Marshall made certain that Colonel Smith was decorated for his work, but because of White House attitudes he concluded that he could not get Lindbergh's friend promoted to general-officer rank.[6]

In April, 1944, Lindbergh went to the Pacific, as a technical representative for United Aircraft, to study fighters under combat conditions. He was then forty-two years old—middle-aged by usual standards and little less than ancient for a fighter pilot. The purpose of his trip was to get information to help in planning the design of future fighter airplanes, including data on the relative advantages of single-engine and twin-engine fighters. To that end, during a period of nearly five months from April to September, Lindbergh, a civilian, flew fifty combat missions against the Japanese in the South Pacific. Half of those missions were in Army Air Force twin-engine Lockheed P-38 Lightning fighters, and half were in Marine Corps Vought Corsair single-engine fighters. They included patrol, escort, reconnaissance, strafing, and dive-bombing missions. Lindbergh was not under fire on all of the missions, but on some he came under heavy fire from the Japanese. And on July 28, 1944, in a thrilling encounter in which he narrowly missed a head-on crash with his adversary, Lindbergh shot down a Japanese plane while he was flying a P-38.[7]

Less spectacular, but important for the war effort, while he was in the South Pacific he improved the combat effectiveness of the P-38 by greatly increasing its range. He demonstrated that fuel consumption could be reduced by flying the plane at low revolutions-per-minute, high manifold pressure, and auto-lean mixture-control setting. The procedure did not damage the aircraft engine, and it substantially increased the effective range of the P-38. He gave lectures on fuel economy for P-38's and P-47's to various fighter pilot units.[8]

Lindbergh also experimented with carrying heavier bomb loads in Corsairs. Some Marine Corps pilots were uneasy about carrying thousand-pound loads. He not only flew with such a load, he gradually increased the load his plane carried until it was four times that weight—the heaviest bomb load ever carried on a Corsair. That had little military effect at the time, but it may have improved the confidence and morale of the less experienced pilots flying with thousand-pound loads.[9]

Lindbergh enjoyed the flying, the adventure, and the challenge of combat, and he recognized the necessity for killing to defeat the enemy in war. But he was saddened by the ugly devastation and death that he and his fellow airmen wrought. He never became callous or insensitive to the tragedy of war. The fact that in bombing and strafing the combat pilot could not see or even know what death or agony he was causing did not ease his concern. "I don't like this bombing and machine-gunning of unknown targets," he wrote in his journal. In another entry he wrote: "That's the trouble with this air war. You don't know what you're shooting at. The hut may be empty. It may be full of Japanese soldiers. It may be a cover for machine guns. It may hold a mother and a child. . . . Inside may be emptiness or writhing agony. You never know. Holes in a dirt floor; a machine gun out of action; a family wiped out; you go on as you were before."[10]

He was troubled by the impact of the war and of Western civilization on the island peoples: "The natives have lost their natural habits and resourcefulness without gaining enough from Western civilization to make up. Their wild, barbaric freedom has been taken away from them and replaced with a form of civilized slavery which leaves neither them nor us better off. The white man has brought them a religion they do not understand, diseases they are unable to combat, standards of life which leave them poverty stricken, a war which has devastated their homes and taken their families away; and they are still supposed to be grateful to us for giving them the benefits of Christianity and civilization."[11] These wartime thoughts merged with his interest in and activity on behalf of primitive peoples in later years.

Lindbergh was also shocked by the atrocities committed by some Americans against captured Japanese soldiers. He personally saw the nauseating physical evidences of such episodes. He conceded that the Japanese were guilty of atrocities, but he insisted that that was no justification for the American actions. In his journal he wrote: "It was freely admitted that some of our soldiers tortured Jap prisoners and were as cruel and barbaric at times as the Japs themselves. Our men think nothing of shooting a Japanese prisoner or a soldier attempting to surrender. They treat the Jap with less respect than they would give to an animal, and these acts are condoned by almost everyone. We claim to be fighting for civilization, but the more I see of this war in the Pacific the less right I think we have to claim to be civilized. In fact, I am not sure that our record in this respect stands so very much higher than the Japs'." On another occasion he wrote: "It is not the willingness to kill on the part of our soldiers which most concerns me. That is an inherent part of war. It is our lack of respect for even the admirable characteristics of our enemy—for courage, for suffering, for death, for his willingness to die for his beliefs, for his companies and squadrons which go forth, one after another, to annihilation against our superior training and equipment. What is courage for us is fanaticism for him. We hold his examples of atrocity screamingly to the heavens while we cover up our own and condone them as just retribution for his acts."[12]

Because of his love for the beauties of nature, Lindbergh would actively serve the causes of conservation and ecology in later years. That same kind of concern made him sensitive to the ugly devastation that modern man and war were bringing to the South Pacific. "War is like a flame. Where it sweeps, life disappears, the birds and the trees with the Japanese." He wondered: "The gashes modern man has cut in the jungle—how long will they show?"[13]

Though he performed superbly, both the Army and the Navy

were uneasy about having a civilian, particularly one so famous and controversial, flying in combat. If he were downed and captured, they assumed, he would be executed immediately. They also feared an adverse public uproar back in the States. Twice Lindbergh was called to Brisbane, Australia, and had meetings with General Douglas MacArthur and others there. MacArthur knew of his combat flying and welcomed his help in extending the effective range of the P-38. Both Army and Marine commanders managed to "look the other way" most of the time with regard to his combat flying. But their uneasiness increased, especially when he went on notably risky missions. In mid-August, General George C. Kenney, commander of the Air Force in the South Pacific, finally ordered that he do no more combat flying. That did not prevent him from going on more missions with the Marine Corsair units, but he was already beginning to plan his return to the United States. By the middle of September he was back on the American mainland. And on September 20, 1944, Anne welcomed him home to the house she had rented for the family in Connecticut.[14]

His combat was over, but Lindbergh continued to serve America's war effort through United Aircraft and Ford. And in May, 1945, he again traveled abroad. That time he went to Europe as a United Aircraft representative with a Naval Technical Mission sent to Germany at the close of World War II to study advanced German military airplanes. He was particularly interested in German jet and rocket propulsion. It was his first visit since he left Europe more than six years before, in the spring of 1939. He stopped in Paris a few days, where he inquired about the fate of his old friend Dr. Alexis Carrel. Dr. Carrel had returned to his native France from the United States early in the war and had died there in 1944.[15]

On May 17, 1945, just ten days after the German surrender, Lindbergh flew to Munich, Germany. The ravages of war were everywhere—particularly in the cities. "When you looked at the cities, you felt it would take a century for the Germans to rebuild and reorganize. When you looked at the farms and villages, you felt it would not take long. It is interesting to contemplate the fact that the city, which has produced these devices of sciences and warfare, has reaped the whirlwind they caused. In the country lie the seeds of new strength and the soil for new growth." The center of Munich was "a mass of rubble." It was "a city destroyed." He found "Mile after mile of bombed and ruined buildings, high piles of rubble where God knows how many people died or how many bodies still lie buried." With time out for a brief return to Paris, Lindbergh traveled more than 2,000 miles by jeep during some three weeks in the American-occupied areas of Germany and Austria. Everywhere he found hunger, suffering, destruction, vandalism, and devastation. He felt deep compassion for the hungry German people and the displaced persons, and he sharply disapproved of the vandalism and looting by American GI's as well as by troops from other countries. And he feared the Soviet danger there.[16]

In the performance of his duties for the Technical Mission, Lindbergh talked with top German aeronautical scientists and engineers, including Willy Messerschmitt, the aircraft designer; Dr. Helmut Schelp, head of German jet and rocket development; Adolf Baeumker, head of the German Experimental Institute for Aviation; Dr. Heinz Schmitt, director of jet development for Junkers; and many others. He inspected Me-262 jet fighters and Me-163 rocket fighters. He and others on the Technical Mission obtained detailed plans of jet engines, helped arrange for shipment of engines to the United States for tests, and aided some Junkers technical experts to move with their families from the Soviet to the American zone.[17]

On June 11, in the course of inspecting the underground factory at Nordhausen that had produced the V-1 and V-2 weapons, Lindbergh came on Camp Dora, a Nazi extermination camp. Skeletonlike, starved, and dying ex-prisoners were still there, as were the cremation furnaces that had consumed 25,000 bodies in a year and a half. The smell of death was everywhere. He described the scene and his reactions in his private journal: "Here was a place where men and life and death had reached the lowest form of degradation. How could any reward in national progress even faintly justify the establishment and operation of such a place?" It was a horrifying scene. He thought those responsible for the atrocities "should be found and punished according to civilized standards of justice." It reminded Lindbergh of the smells and scenes of death and American atrocities against Japanese that he had seen in the South Pacific. "We, who claimed that the German was defiling humanity in his treatment of the Jew, were doing the same thing in our treatment of the Jap." He recalled the Biblical admonition: "And why beholdest thou the mote that is in thy brother's eye but considerest not the beam that is in thine own eye?" As a long list of atrocity incidents against Japanese in the Pacific passed before his mind's eye, and as he looked down into the pit of ashes from the furnaces at Camp Dora, he concluded that such atrocities were "not a thing confined to any nation or to any people. What the German has done to the Jew in Europe, we are doing to the Jap in the Pacific." In his view, "What is barbaric on one side of the earth is still barbaric on the other. 'Judge not that ye be not judged.' It is not the Germans alone, or the Japs, but the men of all nations to whom this war has brought shame and degradation."[18] As he flew back to the United States later, Lindbergh felt no cause to regret his opposition to the beginning of the war, nor his opposition to American entry into that war.

By the time the American B-29 fire bombings of Tokyo and the atomic bombings of Hiroshima and Nagasaki brought the final surrender of Japan on V-J Day, September 2, 1945, some 300,000 Americans had died in World War II. They had given all that man has to give. Another 700,000 had been wounded, some horribly. There were still other Americans who had contributed more to the task of defeating the Axis and winning World War II than Charles A. Lindbergh had. But most had not.

# 27/New Horizons

T HE leading isolationists paid high prices for their opposition to the war. Voters turned most of those in elective positions out of office. Senators Gerald P. Nye of North Dakota and Bennett Champ Clark of Missouri, as well as Congressman Hamilton Fish of New York, lost their bids for re-election in 1944. Two years later Senators Burton K. Wheeler of Montana and Henrik Shipstead of Minnesota suffered defeat. Others also fell by the wayside. In most cases, their opponents got money and help from internationalists outside their states who wanted to make certain that isolationism did not revive after World War II as it had after World War I. Robert A. Taft served on in the Senate and made major bids for the Republican presidential nomination in 1948 and 1952. But his isolationist past hurt him politically; he did not get the nominaton. Chester Bowles, Philip C. Jessup, and Senator Arthur H. Vandenberg managed to escape their "shady" noninterventionist pasts and gained respectability in internationalist circles—but they were exceptions. To have been prominently identified with opposition to American entry into World War II was to be forever suspect and stigmatized; generally the stain would not rub out. To make matters worse, most prominent prewar noninterventionists refused to confess error and wear sackcloth and ashes; they continued to believe they had been right in opposing American entry. Even Senator Vandenberg and Chester Bowles did not disavow the stands they had taken on foreign affairs before Pearl Harbor.[1]

**229**

In many respects, Charles A. Lindbergh, too, was made to suffer for opposing American entry into World War II. The Roosevelt administration had prevented him from regaining his commission and from serving as a member of the armed forces during the war. No isolationist was more vilified than Lindbergh for his prewar views and activities. In August, 1942, he honored a subpoena to testify for the defense in the sedition trial of William Dudley Pelley, head of the fascistic Silver Shirts. Lindbergh had not known Pelley personally and was on the stand only twelve minutes. But the episode further identified him in the public mind with unsavory and seditious elements in America.[2]

During and after the war, the sensational book *Under Cover,* by John Roy Carlson (pseudonym for Avedis Derounian), was sold and distributed by the tens of thousands throughout the country. It claimed to reveal, according to its subtitle, *How Axis Agents and Our Enemies Within Are Now Plotting to Destroy the United States.* It made most leading isolationists (including Lindbergh) seem little better than Nazis.[3] At best the liberal-internationalists saw Lindbergh as a naïve dupe of the Nazis; at worst they saw him as a conscious fascist determined to destroy democracy and build a Nazi dictatorship in America. Those images and stereotypes even affected some who had shared Lindbergh's views before Pearl Harbor. More than thirty years later, many who prided themselves on their scholarly precision and tolerance were still prepared to see Lindbergh as the epitome of anti-Semitism, racism, and fascism in America.[4]

During and after the war, Lindbergh kept in touch with noninterventionist friends from prewar days, most notably with General Robert E. Wood. He occasionally had lunch with some of those friends. They speculated on the future and on what they might do to give life to their cause. But, so far as Lindbergh was concerned, little came of such speculations. Since he was close to Henry Ford, some approached him concerning the prospect of getting Ford's financial aid for projects related to the prewar noninterventionist movement. For example, General

Wood consulted Lindbergh for support for the historian Harry Elmer Barnes in writing a revisionist history of the causes for World War II. Partly through Lindbergh's intercession, the Ford Company helped Barnes.[5]

Lindbergh, Wood, and other leading prewar noninterventionists hoped for and expected ultimate historical vindication of the positions they had taken on foreign affairs before Pearl Harbor. But the revisionist interpretations of American entry into World War II did not gain the dominant position among historians after the war. And the generally critical reception that Lindbergh's own *Wartime Journals* got from reviewers when published in 1970 suggested that the time for vindication or even for a sympathetic hearing had not yet arrived. Lindbergh was disappointed by the tardy recognition from Clio.

Nevertheless, the aftermath of his noninterventionist activities damaged Lindbergh less than many others. And some of the consequences were beneficial to him personally. By taking him out of the limelight, they left him more free than he had been earlier. They did not prevent him from moving on to new interests and new challenges. He held no elective position and had no political ambitions, so he could not be put out of office, as isolationist legislators were. His inner strength and self-reliance made him less dependent on popular approval than most might have been. In conversations many years later, General Lindbergh minimized the viciousness of the attacks on him. He said that one had to expect such things in public life, and that if an individual could not take it he should stay out of public controversies. He pointed out, correctly, that the pre-Pearl Harbor foreign policy debate had been almost completely free of physical violence, in contrast to the controversies over Vietnam later. The attacks on him had been less vicious and damaging than those against his father in World War I.[6]

As the years passed, newspapers paid little attention to him. Young people knew and cared less about him than their elders had. Though he continued to look younger than he was, over the decades nature gradually provided a partial disguise as his hair slowly thinned and greyed. He and Anne could travel in public without being identified, without being besieged by newsmen and photographers. They enjoyed trips together, including safaris in Africa. They took pride as their three sons and two daughters grew into adults, began careers, married, and reared families of their own. During the decades after World War II, Lindbergh inconspicuously channeled his energies and talents into Air Force affairs, Pan American Airways, writing, helping Anne with her books, and activities relating to conservation and ecology.

For several years after World War II he served on various Air Force and Defense Department committees, including those dealing with Army ordnance and weapons research, reorganization of the Strategic Air Command, selection of the site for the new Air Force Academy, and ballistic missiles.[7] Confronted with Soviet developments in hydrogen bombs, planes, and missiles, in 1954 Lindbergh wrote an article for the *Saturday Evening Post* urging the United States to maintain "a method of delivering our bombs in the event a surprise attack is made upon this country, and after we have absorbed the first terrific blow." American defense, in his judgment, required modern aircraft scattered over hundreds of bases, "research, development and industrial-decentralization programs," and "development of the human element in our military forces." He urged the United States, in the interests of national security, to maintain "the indestructible power to destroy." His article was widely distributed in Air Force circles, and its ideas were incorporated officially into Air Force policy. When the Republicans regained the White House, President Dwight D. Eisenhower and Congress in 1954 restored his commission in the Air Force Reserve and promoted him to Brigadier General. He wore the wings of an Air Force command pilot.[8]

In the 1950's he resumed his prewar position as consultant for Pan American World Airways, and he later became a director of Pan American. He devoted much time to travel all over the world on airline matters.[9]

Lindbergh also returned to writing. In 1948, Scribner's published his thoughtful little book, *Of Flight and Life*. Drawing on his wartime experiences, he developed the theme that "To live modern man needs both science and religion." He concluded: "Our salvation, and our only salvation, lies in controlling the arm of western science by the mind of a western Philosophy guided by the eternal truths of God. It lies in the balanced qualities of spirit, mind, and body of our people. Without this control, without this balance, our military victories can bring no lasting peace, our laws no lasting justice, our science no lasting progress."[10]

In 1953, Scribner's published his autobiographical *The Spirit of St. Louis*. Young Lindbergh had written *We* during less than three weeks of concentrated effort in 1927. He began writing *The Spirit of St. Louis* in Paris in 1938, revised it many times during his travels to remote parts of the world, and did not complete the final manuscript until fourteen years later.[11] It was a best seller and won a Pulitzer Prize. The movie based on it starred James Stewart, but it was not a box-office success. (Anne and Charles took three of their children with them to see the movie. About halfway through the film, as the tiny airplane struggled through storms over the vast Atlantic, their eleven-year-old daughter, Reeve, turned to her mother and asked, "He is going to get there, isn't he?") In 1970, Harcourt Brace Jovanovich published the personal wartime journals that Lindbergh had kept from 1938 to 1945. He assisted his wife in preparing her diaries and letters for publication in the 1970s. And he wrote various articles for *Life* and *Reader's Digest,* concentrating particularly on ecology and conservation topics.[12]

Lindbergh's love of nature—the land, water, skies, and wildlife—extended back to his childhood days in rural Minnesota. His early flying had kept him close to the elements. He and Anne found beauty and tranquility in the skies and on seashores. He worried about the deteriorating impact of urbanization, of brick and concrete, on human character and on Western civilization. He was saddened as he saw science, industry, and urbanization destroying the natural environment and the wildlife dependent on that environment. Consequently, long before it was fashionable, Lindbergh became active in conservation projects and in efforts to save endangered species. He was a member of the Citizens Advisory Committee on Environmental Quality and of the International Union for the Conservation of Nature. He was a director of the World Wildlife Fund. He played important roles in efforts to save the humpback whale and the blue whale. In the Philippines, he helped preserve the tamarau and the monkey-eating eagle from extinction. He helped raise funds for national wildlife parks in East Africa. Deeply interested in primitive peoples, he was a member of the board of trustees of the Panamin Foundation of the Philippines, designed to protect and assist national minorities.[13]

So far as Lindbergh's public role in American foreign policy was concerned, it essentially ended with Pearl Harbor. The United States had rejected the course he had urged in foreign affairs; the interventionists had triumphed. There was no turning back. Foreign affairs were now the responsibility of those who had downed him. After World War II he seldom made speeches. The few he did make generally focused on either aviation or conservation. Only rarely did he comment on foreign affairs, and then without any real expectation of influencing policy decisions.[14]

During World War II, Lindbergh thought America's "unconditional surrender" policy was unwise; he would have preferred a negotiated peace.[15] In July, 1945, after his return from Europe, he permitted a press release through the *Chicago Tribune*. In it he contended that "the seeds of a third world war" were "already being sown." He "attributed the collapse of the German Luftwaffe to the fighting qualities of our own airmen, to our ability to mass produce aircraft, to the switch of communist Russia from the side of the Axis to the side of the Allies, and to the incompetence of the Nazi form of government." He saw the performance of that government as an example "of the weakness which results from the suppression of criticism and opposition." Lindbergh complained that many of the so-called "liberated" countries of Europe had "simply exchanged the Nazi form of dictatorship for the Communist form." He believed the United States should help relieve the terrible "suffering of Europe, to feed her starving, and to help in her reconstruction, and that for the time being we should maintain sufficient forces abroad to make this possible." But he thought neither military victories, political systems, nor the United Nations would "be enough unless based on a dynamic strength of character and the power of Christian ethics." In his judgment, "No peace will last which is not based on Christian principles, on justice, on compassion allied with strength, and on a sense of the dignity of man."[16]

In an address before the Aero Club of Washington in December, 1945, to mark the forty-second anniversary of the Wright brothers' flight, Lindbergh expressed regret that airplanes were being used to bring death and destruction. "What peaceful men take a thousand years to build, fools can now destroy in a few seconds." Reconsidering circumstances in the new atomic age, he said: "The oceans . . . which proved effective barriers to bombing aircraft of World War II, will not protect this country from atomic rockets of World War III, if such a war begins." He pointed out that "aircraft and the atomic bomb have brought us to a time when we will either live in an organized world or in constant insecurity." But he opposed any world organization based on the extremes of either "the arbitrary power of a Roman State" or "on the complete equality of man." In the latter case, he feared that the United States would have less influence than the more populous states of China, India, and the Soviet Union. He insisted that whatever compromise was made between the "extremes of Roman state and mass control, it must contain an element of power to be effective." He was skeptical of the adequacy of the United Nations after World War II. At the same time he was "fearful of the use of power" and urged "strong military forces only because," he believed, "the alternative is worse." "Power, to be ultimately successful, must be backed by morality, just as morality, must be backed by power. A world organization, to have permanent influence, must wield a power that is guided not by the desire for revenge, not by the intent to exploit or enslave, but by the qualities represented in Christian ideals." Speaking in 1945, he called for "charity, humility and compassion" in the postwar world; he complained that those qualities were lacking "in the complacency with which we greeted the inverted hanging of Mussolini's body" and "in the court trials of our conquered enemies."[17]

Two years later, in April, 1947, Lindbergh touched on foreign affairs in a short talk. In it he said that though the United States had been victorious, it had emerged from World War II "with western civilization greatly weakened in a world full of famine, hatred, and despair. We have destroyed Nazi Germany only to find that in doing so we have strengthened Communist Russia, behind whose 'iron curtain' lies a record of bloodshed and oppression never equalled." He thought World War II had "resulted in one of the greatest of human tragedies," but that it would "do little good to argue the wisdom of the past." What had been done could not be changed. Now that the United States was involved in Europe, it must carry through what it had started. Speaking just after the beginning of Truman Doctrine aid to Greece and Turkey and just before the beginning of Marshall Plan aid to Europe, Lindbergh said: "We must help to rebuild western civilization. We must reestablish and protect the ideals we believe in. This will require our extending financial assistance. It may require the use of military force." He said that "in a rocket-atomic age, the welfare of other nations is more than important, it is vital to us." He concluded that American security depended "on the cooperation of peoples who believe in the freedom and dignity of man, and in a way of life that is basically similar to our own. Wherever these peoples need help, we must assist them. There is no better way, probably there is no other way to attain security, peace, and the progress of our civilization."[18]

In later years, commenting on the McCarthy era of the early 1950's, Lindbergh said he disliked both the "radical right" and the "radical left." But he favored activity by the one to balance the other—providing neither got too strong. So far as Senator Joseph McCarthy was concerned, Lindbergh was "never impressed" by him. He did not like McCarthy's tactics, but he did not think the Wisconsin Senator had enough ability to be a great danger.[19]

Lindbergh was "unhappy" about America's roles in both the Korean War of 1950–1953 and the Vietnam War. But since he was not in a position to be closely informed on the circumstances in either war, he was not prepared to urge alternative policies. Consequently he supported the Administration policies both in Korea and in Vietnam. He thought it unfortunate that the United States got into the fighting in Vietnam, but he did not see any easy way out. He voted for Democrat Adlai Stevenson against Dwight D. Eisenhower for President in 1952, in the midst of the Korean War, but he voted for Eisenhower four years later. He opposed John F. Kennedy at the polls in 1960, but he voted for Lyndon B. Johnson in 1964 against Republican Barry Goldwater (despite his friendship with Goldwater). He cast his ballot for Richard M. Nixon for President in 1960 and again in 1972 (in 1968 he had been out of the country and returned too late to vote). Nevertheless, he was shocked by the Watergate episode. Generally he supported the Johnson-Nixon policies in Vietnam. But those were personal views, and he took no public positions on them. In private correspondence he expressed the fear that "if we are not careful, the means we use to insure our survival today and tomorrow will lead to our destruction the day after." He had in mind "Nuclear weapons, overemphasis of science and technology, neglect of man himself."[20]

Late in 1969, thirty years after he began his battle against intervention in World War II, Lindbergh wrote: "We won the war in a military sense; but in a broader sense it seems to me we lost it, for our Western civilization is less respected and secure than it was before.

"In order to defeat Germany and Japan we supported the still greater menaces of Russia and China—which now confront us in a nuclear-weapon era. Poland was not saved. The British Empire has broken down with great suffering, bloodshed, and confusion. England is an economy-constricted secondary power. France had to give up her major colonies and turn to a mild dictatorship herself. Much of our Western culture was destroyed. We lost the genetic heredity formed through aeons in many million lives. Meanwhile, the Soviets have dropped their iron curtain to screen off Eastern Europe, and an antagonistic Chinese government threatens us in Asia.

"More than a generation after the war's end, our occupying armies still must occupy, and the world has not been made safe for democracy and freedom. On the contrary, our own system of democratic government is being challenged by that greatest of dangers to any government: internal dissatisfaction and unrest.

"It is alarmingly possible that World War II marks the beginning of our Western civilization's breakdown, as it already marks the breakdown of the greatest empire ever built by man. Certainly our civilization's survival depends on meeting the challenges that tower before us with unprecedented magnitude in almost every field of modern life. Most of these challenges were, at least, intensified through the waging of World War II." He hoped that his wartime journals, published in 1970, would "help clarify issues and conditions of the past and thereby contribute to understanding issues and conditions of the present and the future."[21]

By 1974, the seventy-two-year-old, grey-haired General Lindbergh was still slender, quick, alert, and active. He supported his government in its conduct of foreign affairs. But he focused most of his energies on airline matters and on conservation and ecology. And he still believed that he and his fellow noninterventionists had been right before Pearl Harbor.

Americans have been quick to judge Lindbergh, and most of America's opinion-forming elite has concluded that he was wrong. Any judgment in depth, however, must wrestle with difficult questions about the consequences of alternative policies in the years before and during World War II. For the most part one can only guess at the possible consequences of alternative courses of action—those proposed either by Lindbergh or by others. But even intelligent guesses cannot properly be made without facing the following questions directly and squarely:

Would Hitler and his Nazis have triumphed in Germany if Britain, France, and the United States had followed either more generous or more severe policies in dealing with Germany after World War I? Would earlier and more effective military and air preparations by Britain, France, the United States, and the Soviet Union have limited or moderated Nazi Germany's course in foreign affairs in the 1930's? Once Hitler built up Germany's military might, would it have been possible to work out a durable negotiated settlement of differences with his government without war in the west? Would Britain and France have gone to war in 1939 if the United States had made it clear that they could not expect American aid or intervention? If Britain and France had not declared war on Germany when Hitler attacked Poland in September, 1939, would he have stopped after driving to the east in Europe, or would Nazi Germany have turned west to strike at France and England sooner or later? If Hitler's Germany had driven east against the Soviet Union without war in the west, would he have triumphed over Stalin's Russia, would he have been defeated, or would there have been a stalemate in the east? And would the result then have been a stronger and more dangerous Nazi Germany, a stronger and more dangerous Communist Russia, a devastated Europe in a condition little better than anarchy, or a balanced Europe with both Germany and the Soviet Union checked by that balance?

If the United States had not extended aid-short-of-war to Britain, would Britain have fallen? If it had not encouraged Britain to hope for growing support from the United States, would Britain have concluded a negotiated peace with Germany? What would have been the long-term consequences of such a settlement for England, Germany, the United States, and the world? If Hitler and Nazi Germany had triumphed everywhere in Europe and Africa, and if Japan had triumphed in Asia, could the United States have successfully guarded its security, its freedom, its economy, and its survival in the Western Hemisphere? Would the alternative courses of action urged by Colonel Charles A. Lindbergh from 1937 through 1941 have provided a more or less secure, free, and stable world for Americans and others than they find today? To what extent did the "Great Debate" and the tactics by both the isolationists and the interventionists enhance or undermine democracy, freedom, peace, and security for the United States? To what extent did American involvement in World War II enhance or undermine a moral order in the United States and the world? These and others are difficult questions to answer with any certainty, even a generation after the war. Any evaluation of Charles A. Lindbergh's battle against intervention that goes beyond mere passion and prejudice, moreover, must face up to thoughtful responses to such questions. They were not to be taken lightly when he helped to raise them before Pearl Harbor; they are not to be treated superficially when one attempts fairly to evaluate his role a generation and more later.

# Notes

# Notes

## 1/The Great Debate

1. Earl C. Jeffrey to Richard A. Moore, June 24, 1941, John L. Wheeler to Robert E. Wood, June 26, 1941, Wheeler to Katrina McCormick, July 31, 1941, Moore to Fred Allhoff, August 23, 1941, America First Committee Papers, Hoover Institution on War, Revolution and Peace, Stanford, California; *The Wartime Journals of Charles A. Lindbergh* (New York: Harcourt Brace Jovanovich, Inc., 1970), pp. 503–6.

2. *Chicago Tribune,* June 21, 1941, p. 1.

3. Hadley Cantril (ed.) and Mildred Strunk, *Public Opinion, 1935–1946* (Princeton: Princeton University Press, 1951), pp. 966–78.

4. For examples of definitions of the terms, see Albert K. Weinberg, "The Historical Meaning of the American Doctrine of Isolation," *American Political Science Review,* XXXIV (June, 1940), pp. 539–47; Selig Adler, *The Isolationist Impulse: Its Twentieth-Century Reaction* (London and New York: Abelard-Schuman Limited, 1957), pp. 26–29; Wayne S. Cole, *America First: The Battle Against Intervention, 1940–1941* (Madison: University of Wisconsin Press, 1953), p. 6; Wayne S. Cole, *Senator Gerald P. Nye and American Foreign Relations* (Minneapolis: University of Minnesota Press, 1962), pp. 4–5; and Manfred Jonas, *Isolationism in America, 1935–1941* (Ithaca: Cornell University Press, 1966), pp. 22–31.

5. Final draft of address that Charles A. Lindbergh read at America First Committee meeting, Los Angeles, June 20, 1941, Charles A. Lindbergh Papers, Sterling Memorial Library, Yale University, New Haven, Connecticut. Lindbergh's speeches

were widely printed in newspapers and magazines at the time, sometimes inaccurately. Throughout this volume the quotations and citations refer to the final drafts of the typed speeches that he read at the broadcasts or meetings.

6. Wayne S. Cole, "America First and the South, 1940–1941," *Journal of Southern History,* XXII (February, 1956), pp. 36–47; Harry C. Schnibbe to R. T. Small, September 24, 1941, America First Papers.

7. *Chicago Tribune,* August 27, 1941, p. 1.

8. *Ibid.,* August 27, 1941, p. 1, August 28, 1941, p. 1, August 29, 1941, p. 4; Jeffrey to Wood, September 5, 1941, America First Papers.

9. *Wartime Journals,* pp. 529–32; Jeffrey to Wood, September 5, 1941, America First Papers.

10. Final draft of Lindbergh speech on "Air Power" read at America First Committee meeting in Oklahoma City, August 29, 1941, Lindbergh Papers. See also *Chicago Tribune,* August 30, 1941, p. 1.

11. Jeffrey to Wood, September 5, 1941, Wood to Arthur Geisler, September 6, 1941, Moore to Mr. Camphausen, August 27, 1941, August 28, 1941, America First Papers; *Wartime Journals,* p. 532.

### 2/The Making of a Hero

1. For descriptions of Lindbergh's personality and character by individuals who knew him well, see C. B. Allen, "The Facts About Lindbergh," *Saturday Evening Post,* 213 (December 28, 1940), pp. 12–13, 51–53; Donald E. Keyhoe, *Flying with Lindbergh* (New York: Grosset & Dunlap, 1928), pp. 205–61, 279–95; Lauren D. Lyman, "The Lindbergh I Know," *Saturday Evening Post,* 225 (April 4, 1953), pp. 22–23, 84–88; Nigel Nicolson (ed.), *Harold Nicolson: Diaries and Letters, 1930–1939* (New York: Atheneum, 1966), pp. 131–32, 180–85; and a printed leaflet containing remarks of Thomas W. Lamont at a dinner commemorating the tenth anniversary of Lindbergh's Atlantic flight, New York City, May 20, 1937, in Lindbergh Papers. Also, the present author had numerous conversations with General Lindbergh in Connecticut and in Washington, D.C., in 1972 and 1973.

2. For an excellent biography of Lindbergh's father, see Bruce L.

Larson, *Lindbergh of Minnesota: A Political Biography* (New York: Harcourt Brace Jovanovich, Inc., 1973).

3. For Lindbergh's own account of his boyhood in Minnesota, see Charles A. Lindbergh, *Boyhood on the Upper Mississippi: A Reminiscent Letter* (St. Paul: Minnesota Historical Society, 1972).

4. Interviews with General Lindbergh, Washington, D.C., June 7, 1972, and May 17, 1973.

5. Larson, *Lindbergh of Minnesota*, pp. 33, 37, 286; and telephone conversation with General Lindbergh, June 14, 1973. For a similar influence by his maternal grandfather, see Charles A. Lindbergh, *The Spirit of St. Louis* (New York: Charles Scribner's Sons, 1953), pp. 318–20.

6. Lindbergh, *Boyhood on the Upper Mississippi*, pp. 32–46; Lindbergh, *Spirit of St. Louis*, pp. 380–84.

7. Lindbergh, *Spirit of St. Louis*, pp, 247, 384–85, 403–4; Charles A. Lindbergh, *We* (New York: G. P. Putnam's Sons, 1927), pp. 22–25.

8. Lindbergh, *We*, pp. 25–197; Lindbergh, *Spirit of St. Louis*, pp. 3–50, 231, 244–68, 272–89, 314, 405, 417–22, 436–50.

9. Lindbergh, *Spirit of St. Louis, passim;* Lindbergh, *We, passim.*

10. Lindbergh, *We*, pp. 231–318; Lindbergh, *Spirit of St. Louis*, pp. 517–30.

11. For an account of his flying tour of America by one who accompanied him in a second airplane, see Keyhoe, *Flying with Lindbergh*. His visit to Mexico is treated in *Bring Me a Unicorn: Diaries and Letters of Anne Morrow Lindbergh, 1922–1928* (New York: Harcourt Brace Jovanovich, Inc., 1972). The log of the *Spirit of St. Louis* detailing its every flight is in Lindbergh, *Spirit of St. Louis*, pp. 503–16.

12. For their meeting and courtship, see *Bring Me A Unicorn, passim.* For their marriage and early married life, see *Hour of Gold, Hour of Lead: Diaries and Letters of Anne Morrow Lindbergh, 1929–1932* (New York: Harcourt Brace Jovanovich, 1973), pp. 3–207.

13. Anne Morrow Lindbergh, *North to the Orient* (New York: Harcourt Brace and Company, 1935).

14. Anne Morrow Lindbergh, *Listen! the Wind* (New York: Harcourt, Brace and Company, 1938).

15. *Hour of Gold, Hour of Lead, passim; The Wartime Journals of*

*Charles A. Lindbergh* (New York: Harcourt Brace Jovanovich, Inc., 1970), p. 349.

16. For Mrs. Lindbergh's account, see *Hour of Gold, Hour of Lead,* pp. 211–325. For the morgue episode, see *Wartime Journals,* p. 187.

### 3/ The English, the French, and the Russians

1. Lindbergh to Harold M. Bixby, February 29, 1936, Harold M. Bixby Papers, Library of Congress, Washington, D.C.; Lindbergh to Colonel H. Norman Schwarzkopf, January 27, 1937, Lindbergh Papers; Clinton Rossiter and James Lare (eds.), *The Essential Lippmann: A Political Philosophy for Liberal Democracy* (New York: Random House, 1963), pp. 406–7.

2. J. P. Morgan to Lindbergh, January 27, 1936, Lindbergh Papers; Lindbergh to Bixby, February 29, 1936, Bixby Papers; General Lindbergh to author, March 19, 1973.

3. Lindbergh to Bixby, February 29, 1936, March 9, 1937, Bixby Papers; Lindbergh to Schwarzkopf, January 27, 1937, Lindbergh to Buster [Keaton], March 13, 1937, Lindbergh Papers; Nigel Nicolson (ed.), *Harold Nicolson: Diaries and Letters, 1930–1939* (New York: Atheneum, 1966), pp. 247, 255, 263, 283; General Lindbergh to author, March 19, 1973.

4. Lindbergh to Alexis Carrel, January 16, 1937, Lindbergh to Juan Trippe, March 9, 1937, Lindbergh to Keaton, March 13, 1937, Lindbergh Papers; *The Wartime Journals of Charles A. Lindbergh* (New York: Harcourt Brace Jovanovich, Inc., 1970), pp. 11, 161, 163.

5. Lindbergh to William C. Bullitt, October 26, 1938, Lindbergh Papers; *Wartime Journals,* pp. 11, 22.

6. Lindbergh to Arthur Train, Jr., May 12, 1938, Lindbergh Papers; Arthur Train, Jr., "More Will Live," *Saturday Evening Post,* 211 (July 25, 1938), pp. 5–7, 67–70.

7. Interview with General Lindbergh, Washington, D.C., June 7, 1972.

8. *Wartime Journals,* pp. 8–10.

9. Lindbergh to Henry Breckinridge, June 30, 1936, Lindbergh Papers; interview with General Lindbergh, June 7, 1972.

10. Charles A. Lindbergh, "A Letter to Americans," *Collier's* (March 29, 1941), pp. 14, 76; interview with General Lindbergh, June 7, 1972.

11. Lindbergh to Raymond Lee, September 13, 1938, Lindbergh to Bixby, November 3, 1938, Lindbergh Papers; *Wartime Journals,* pp. 48–65; Pierrepont Moffat to Sumner Welles and Adolph A. Berle, October 11, 1938, and enclosed G-2 Report by Raymond E. Lee, September 19, 1938, File No. 861.248/105, Department of State Records, National Archives, Washington, D.C.

12. *The Week* (London), October 5, 1938, p. 4; *New York Herald Tribune,* October 11, 1938, p. 3; Lee to Truman Smith, October 10, 1938, Lindbergh to Philip R. Faymonville, October 15, 1938, December 7, 1938, Lindbergh Papers; telegram [Alexander] Kirk to Secretary of State, October 10, 1938, and attached memorandum, October 11, 1938, and unidentified clipping, File No. 861.248/104, Department of State Records.

### 4/Air Power and Nazi Germany

1. Colonel Truman Smith, "Air Intelligence Activities: Office of the Military Attache, American Embassy, Berlin, Germany, August 1935–April 1939 With Special Reference to the Services of Colonel Charles A. Lindbergh, Air Corps (Res.)," 1956, unpublished manuscript in Sterling Memorial Library, Yale University, New Haven, Connecticut, pp. 1–2, 4–5.

2. *Ibid.,* pp. 18–21.

3. Truman Smith to Lindbergh, May 25, 1936, Lindbergh to Smith, June 5, 1936, Lindbergh Papers.

4. Address by Lindbergh, Berlin, Germany, July 23, 1936, Lindbergh Papers.

5. Smith, "Air Intelligence Activities," pp. 30–50.

6. *Ibid.,* pp. 27, 47–49; radiogram Henbreck to Lindbergh, July 20, 1936, Smith to Lindbergh, August 12, 1936, Lindbergh Papers.

7. Lindbergh to Smith, August 6, 1936, Lindbergh to Henry Breckinridge, September 23, 1936, Lindbergh Papers.

8. Lindbergh to Harry Davison, January 23, 1937, Lindbergh Papers.

9. Lindbergh to Breckinridge, September 23, 1936, Lindbergh Papers.

10. Lindbergh to Davison, January 23, 1937, Lindbergh Papers.

11. *Ibid.,* Lindbergh to Breckinridge, September 23, 1936, Lindbergh Papers.

12. Lindbergh to H. Norman Schwarzkopf, January 27, 1937, Lindbergh to Alexis Carrel, January 13, 1937, April 17, 1937, Lindbergh Papers; Lindbergh to author, February 5, 1973, March 19, 1973. The trip to India included stops in Italy and Egypt; the return flight included brief stops in Yugoslavia and Germany.
13. Smith, "Air Intelligence Activities," pp. 58–65.
14. *Ibid.,* pp. 66–73.
15. *Ibid.,* pp. 73–75.
16. Franklin D. Roosevelt to Chief of Staff and Chief of Naval Operations, February 10, 1938, undated memo Joseph P. Kennedy to Roosevelt and enclosed excerpt from Lindbergh letter, William D. Leahy to Roosevelt, February 14, 1938, Malin Craig to Colonel Edwin M. Watson, February 11, 1938, President's Secretary's File, Navy 1938 folder, Franklin D. Roosevelt Papers, Franklin D. Roosevelt Library, Hyde Park, New York.
17. Lindbergh to Davison, October 28, 1937, Lindbergh Papers.
18. *Ibid.,* Lindbergh to Smith, May 9, 1938, Lindbergh Papers.
19. Lindbergh to Smith, May 9, 1938, Lindbergh Papers; *The Wartime Journals of Charles A. Lindbergh* (New York: Harcourt Brace Jovanovich, Inc., 1970), pp. xiii, 3–45.
20. *Wartime Journals,* pp. 48–69.
21. Smith, "Air Intelligence Activities," pp. 91–110; Lindbergh to General Ernst Udet, November 7, 1938, Lindbergh Papers.

### 5/That German Medal

1. This account is based on the records of three of the participants: Wilson, Smith, and Lindbergh. Truman Smith, "Air Intelligence Activities," pp. 99–104; *The Wartime Journals of Charles A. Lindbergh* (New York: Harcourt Brace Jovanovich, Inc., 1970), pp. 101–3; Lindbergh to John T. Flynn, May 2, 1941, Lindbergh to Bennett Champ Clarke, May 3, 1941, Lindbergh to Wilson, July 31, 1941, Wilson to Lindbergh, August 4, 1941, Lindbergh Papers; Hugh R. Wilson Diary, October 18, 1938, Hugh R. Wilson Papers, Herbert Hoover Presidential Library, West Branch, Iowa; Wilson to Secretary of State, October 31, 1938, Files No. 123 W 693/565 and 093.622/45, Department of State Records, National Archives, Washington, D.C.
2. Smith, "Air Intelligence Activities," pp. 102–3.

3. *The Secret Diary of Harold L. Ickes: The Inside Struggle, 1936–1939* (New York: Simon and Schuster, 1954), pp. 532–34; *The Secret Diary of Harold L. Ickes: The Lowering Clouds, 1939–1941* (New York: Simon and Schuster, 1954), pp. 581–82; Confidential Print Mr. Mallet to Viscount Halifax, December 23, 1938, F.O. 414/276, p. 1, British Foreign Office Records, Public Record Office, London, England.
4. Lindbergh to Franklin D. Roosevelt, July 16, 1941, President's Personal File 1080, Roosevelt Papers.
5. Lindbergh to Flynn, May 2, 1941, Lindbergh to Clark, May 3, 1941, Lindbergh to Wilson, July 31, 1941, Lindbergh Papers.
6. Smith, "Air Intelligence Activities," pp. 103–4.
7. *Wartime Journals,* pp. 110–11; Lindbergh to Smith, May 9, 1938, Lindbergh Papers; Wilson Diary, October 25, 1938, Wilson Papers.
8. Wilson Diary, November 5, 1938, Wilson Papers; Smith to Lindbergh, November 17, 1938, Alexis Carrel to Lindbergh, November 18, 1938, November 30, 1938, and enclosed clipping from *The New Yorker,* November 26, 1938, p. 11, Lindbergh Papers.
9. Lindbergh to Carrel, November 28, 1938, Lindbergh Papers.
10. Lindbergh to Carrel, December 10, 1938, Lindbergh Papers.

### 6/Munich

1. Charles A. Lindbergh, "A Letter to Americans," *Collier's* (March 29, 1941), pp. 14, 76; Lindbergh to Jean Monnet, October 7, 1938, Lindbergh to William R. Castle, February 7, 1939, Lindbergh Papers.
2. Lindbergh to Monnet, October 7, 1938, Lindbergh to William C. Bullitt, October 26, 1938, Lindbergh to Truman Smith, March 25, 1939, Lindbergh to Arthur H. Vanaman, April 6, 1939, Lindbergh Papers; *The Wartime Journals of Charles A. Lindbergh* (New York: Harcourt Brace Jovanovich, Inc., 1970), p. 159.
3. Lindbergh to Joseph P. Kennedy, September 22, 1938, Lindbergh to Monnet, October 7, 1938, Lindbergh to Henry Breckinridge, December 15, 1938, Lindbergh to Alexis Carrel, February 7, 1939, Lindbergh Papers.
4. *Wartime Journals,* pp. 115–16, 163, 172; interview with General Lindbergh, Washington, D.C., June 7, 1972.

5. *Wartime Journals,* pp. 279–81; Nigel Nicolson (ed.), *Harold Nicolson: Diaries and Letters, 1930–1939* (New York: Atheneum, 1966), pp. 255, 263.
6. *Wartime Journals,* pp. 25–32; Nicolson, *Harold Nicolson,* p. 343; Lindbergh, "Letter to Americans," *Collier's,* pp. 14, 76.
7. Reference copy of Lindbergh address read before America First rally, St. Louis Arena, May 3, 1941, Lindbergh Papers.
8. *Wartime Journals,* pp. 35–36.
9. *Ibid.,* pp. 69–70.
10. E. L. Woodward and Rohan Butler (eds.), *Documents on British Foreign Policy, 1919–1939,* Third Series (London: Her Majesty's Stationery Office, 1949), II, pp. 310–12, 452–54, 473–74.
11. *Wartime Journals,* pp. 71–73; Lindbergh to Kennedy, September 22, 1938, telegram Kennedy to Secretary of State, September 22, 1938, Lindbergh Papers; *The Memoirs of Cordell Hull,* 2 vols. (New York: Macmillan Company, 1948), Vol. I, p. 590; Truman Smith, "Air Intelligence Activities," pp. 139–44. The material in the last two sentences quoted was in Lindbergh's letter to Kennedy but not in Kennedy's telegram to Hull. See also U.S. Department of State, *Foreign Relations of the United States: Diplomatic Papers, 1938* (Washington: Government Printing Office, 1955), Vol. I, pp. 72–73.
12. *Wartime Journals,* pp. 73–74; Sir John Slessor, *The Central Blue: Recollections and Reflections* (London: Cassell and Company, Ltd., 1957), pp. 218–22.
13. *Wartime Journals,* pp. 73–79.
14. *Ibid.,* pp. 77–78.
15. *Ibid.*
16. *Ibid.,* p. 79.

### 7/French Failures

1. *The Wartime Journals of Charles A. Lindbergh* (New York: Harcourt Brace Jovanovich, Inc., 1970), pp. 79–91; Orville H. Bullitt (ed.), *For the President, Personal and Secret: Correspondence Between Franklin D. Roosevelt and William C. Bullitt* (Boston: Houghton Mifflin Company, 1972), pp. 296–300.
2. [Charles A. Lindbergh], "Canadian Plan," October 7, 1938, Lindbergh to Jean Monnet, October 7, 1938, Lindbergh Papers.
3. Interview with General Lindbergh, June 13, 1972; *Wartime Journals,* pp. 92, 116.

4. Lindbergh to General H. H. Arnold, November 2, 1938, Arnold to Lindbergh, November 17, 1938, Lindbergh to Arnold, November 29, 1938, Lindbergh Papers.

5. *Wartime Journals,* pp. 84–87, 112, 120, 125–32; Truman Smith, "Air Intelligence Activities," pp. 111–15.

6. Smith, "Air Intelligence Activities," pp. 115–16, 139–43; Bullitt, *For the President,* pp. 312–15.

7. Lindbergh to Arthur Vanaman, April 6, 1939, Lindbergh Papers.

### 8/Home Again

1. *The Wartime Journals of Charles A. Lindbergh* (New York: Harcourt Brace Jovanovich, Inc., 1970), pp. 166–69, 173–78.

2. *Ibid.,* pp. 182–83, 191–93.

3. *Ibid.,* pp. 181–84; H. H. Arnold, *Global Mission* (New York: Harper & Brothers, 1949), pp. 188–89; radiogram Arnold to Lindbergh, April 13, 1939, Lindbergh Papers.

4. Arnold to Lindbergh, April 18, 1939, Lindbergh Papers; Arnold, *Global Mission,* p. 189; Wesley Frank Craven and James Lea Cate (eds.), *The Army Air Forces in World War II: Men and Planes* (Chicago: University of Chicago Press, 1955), pp. 178–79; *Wartime Journals,* pp. 184–85, 198, 254.

5. *Wartime Journals,* pp. 186–87; E. M. W. [Watson] to the President, April 17, 1939, President's Personal File 1080, Roosevelt Papers; interview with General Lindbergh, June 7, 1972.

6. Statement of Colonel Lindbergh, Wednesday, May 17, 1939, Lindbergh Papers; *Wartime Journals,* pp. 202–3.

7. *Wartime Journals,* pp. 181, 214–15, 217, 254–57; Edwin P. Hartman, *Adventures in Research: A History of the Ames Research Center, 1940–1965* (Washington: National Aeronautics and Space Administration, 1970), pp. 16–22.

### 9/The Battle Begins

1. William R. Castle to Lindbergh, January 19, 1939, Lindbergh to Castle, February 7, 1939, Castle to Lindbergh, April 12, 1939, Lindbergh Papers; *The Wartime Journals of Charles A. Lindbergh* (New York: Harcourt Brace Jovanovich, Inc., 1970), p. 245n; interview with General Lindbergh, June 7, 1972.

2. Castle to Lindbergh, [July, 1939], telegram Lindbergh to Castle, July 16, 1939, Lindbergh Papers.

3. *Wartime Journals,* p. 245; undated "America First" memorandum, William Allen White Papers, Library of Congress, Washington, D.C.; Castle to Carl W. Ackerman, September 20, [1939], Carl W. Ackerman Papers, Library of Congress, Washington, D.C.; interview with General Lindbergh, June 7, 1972.
4. *Wartime Journals,* pp. 243–48.
5. *Ibid.,* pp. 249–50.
6. *Ibid.,* pp. 252–56.
7. *Ibid.,* pp. 254–55; *The Secret Diary of Harold L. Ickes: The Lowering Clouds, 1939–1941* (New York: Simon and Schuster, 1954), pp. 11–12.
8. *Wartime Journals,* pp. 256–58; interview with General Lindbergh, June 7, 1972; C. B. Allen, "The Facts About Lindbergh," *Saturday Evening Post,* 213 (December 28, 1940), p. 12; C. B. Allen, "The Day F. D. R. Tried to Bribe Lindbergh," *Pathway* (November, 1970), pp. 7–8.
9. Castle to Lindbergh, September 1, 1939, Lindbergh Papers; interview with General Lindbergh, June 7, 1972; Lindbergh to author, March 19, 1973.
10. Lindbergh to author, March 19, 1973; *Wartime Journals,* p. 258.
11. Memorandum H. H. Arnold to Lindbergh, September 18, 1939, Lindbergh Papers.
12. Herbert Hoover to Lindbergh, September 20, 1939, Castle to Lindbergh, September 22, 1939, September 25, 1939, Lindbergh Papers; *Wartime Journals,* pp. 260–75.
13. *Wartime Journals,* pp. 273–75.
14. Copies of the final drafts and earlier rough drafts of all Lindbergh's speeches and articles are in the Lindbergh Papers. The complete texts or excerpts were widely printed in newspapers and elsewhere, but sometimes in incomplete or inaccurate forms.

### 10/The European War and Western Civilization

1. Quotations from his speeches in this and subsequent chapters are from copies of the final drafts in the Lindbergh Papers unless otherwise indicated. Lindbergh, "Neutrality and War," October 13, 1939, Lindbergh Papers.
2. Charles A. Lindbergh, "What Substitute for War?," *Atlantic Monthly* (March, 1940), pp. 305–7.
3. Final draft of Lindbergh address read at Chicago rally, August 4, 1940, Lindbergh Papers.

4. Lindbergh, "America and European Wars," September 15, 1939, Lindbergh Papers.
5. Charles A. Lindbergh, "Aviation, Geography, and Race," *Reader's Digest*, XXXV (November, 1939), pp. 64–67; Lindbergh, "What Substitute for War?," *Atlantic Monthly*, pp. 307–8; Lindbergh, "Neutrality and War," October 13, 1939, Lindbergh Papers.
6. Lindbergh to author, June 21, 1973, and October 19, 1972.
7. Lindbergh, "America and European Wars," September 15, 1939, Lindbergh Papers.
8. Final draft of Lindbergh address read at Yale University, October 30, 1940, Lindbergh Papers.
9. Lindbergh to General Robert E. Wood, October 13, 1940, November 12, 1940, Lindbergh Papers; Lindbergh to author, March 19, 1973.
10. Lindbergh statement read before the House Committee on Foreign Affairs, January 23, 1941, Lindbergh Papers.
11. For examples of his several statements of these views, see Lindbergh statement read before Senate Committee on Foreign Relations, February 6, 1941, Lindbergh address at America First rally in Chicago, April 17, 1941, Lindbergh address at America First rally in New York, April 23, 1941, and Lindbergh address at America First rally in Los Angeles, June 20, 1941, Lindbergh Papers.

### 11/Air Power and American Defense

1. Lindbergh, "America and European Wars," September 15, 1939, Lindbergh Papers; Charles A. Lindbergh, "What Substitute for War?," *Atlantic Monthly* (March, 1940), pp. 307–8.
2. Lindbergh, "A Plea for American Independence," October 14, 1940, Lindbergh address on April 23, 1941, Lindbergh address on May 23, 1941, Lindbergh Papers.
3. Lindbergh, "America and European Wars," September 15, 1939, Lindbergh address on October 30, 1940, Lindbergh Papers.
4. Lindbergh, "The Air Defense of America," May 19, 1940, Lindbergh Papers.
5. Reference copy of Lindbergh statement read before the House Committee on Foreign Affairs, January 23, 1941, Lindbergh address on "Air Power," August 29, 1941, Lindbergh address on

October 30, 1940, Lindbergh address on "Facing the Record and the Facts," October 30, 1941, and Lindbergh address on "A Plea for American Independence," October 14, 1940, Lindbergh Papers.

6. Lindbergh statement before House Committee, January 23, 1941, Lindbergh address on "Air Power," August 29, 1941, Lindbergh Papers.

7. Lindbergh address on "Air Power," August 29, 1941, Lindbergh, "The Air Defense of America," May 19, 1940, Lindbergh statement before House Committee, January 23, 1941, Lindbergh Papers.

8. Lindbergh statement before House Committee, January 23, 1941, Lindbergh Papers.

9. Lindbergh, "The Air Defense of America," May 19, 1940, Lindbergh, "Air Power," August 29, 1941, Lindbergh Papers.

10. Lindbergh, "Neutrality and War," October 13, 1939, Lindbergh Papers.

11. *Hearings before the Committee on Foreign Affairs, House of Representatives,* on H.R. 1776, 77th Congress, 1st session, 1941, pp. 371–435; *Hearings before the Committee on Foreign Relations, United States Senate,* on S. 275, 77th Congress, 1st session, 1941, pp. 490–550.

12. Lindbergh, "Air Power," August 29, 1941, Lindbergh Papers.

### 12/The Russo-German War

1. Lindbergh to Henry Breckinridge, September 23, 1936, Lindbergh to Harry Davison, January 23, 1937, Lindbergh Papers; Truman Smith, "Air Intelligence Activities," p. 152; General Lindbergh to author, February 5, 1973.

2. Final draft of Lindbergh address read at meeting in San Francisco, California, July 1, 1941, Lindbergh Papers.

3. *Ibid.*

4. *Ibid.*

5. *Ibid.*

6. Lindbergh, "Facing the Record and the Facts," read at meeting in Madison Square Garden, New York, October 30, 1941, Lindbergh Papers.

7. For example, see Wayne S. Cole, *America First: The Battle Against Intervention, 1940–1941* (Madison: University of Wisconsin Press, 1953), pp. 85–87.

8. Hadley Cantril (ed.) and Mildred Strunk, *Public Opinion,*

*1935–1946* (Princeton: Princeton University Press, 1951), p. 961; William L. Langer and S. Everett Gleason, *The Undeclared War, 1940–1941* (New York: Harper & Brothers, 1953), pp. 537–47.

### 13/Veterans and Legionnaires

1. *The Wartime Journals of Charles A. Lindbergh* (New York: Harcourt Brace Jovanovich, Inc., 1970), pp. 271–72, 332–33, 339, 351–53, 365, 390–92; William R. Castle to Lindbergh, September 25, 1939, O. K. Armstrong to Lindbergh, December 11, 1939, Lindbergh to Alan Valentine, December 20, 1939, Lawrence Dennis to Lindbergh, February 6, 1940, Lindbergh Papers; interview with General Lindbergh, June 7, 1972. Critics have called Dennis "the intellectual leader of American Fascism." After first meeting Dennis, Lindbergh wrote in his diary: "I must get to know Dennis better. He has a brilliant and original mind—determined to the point of aggressiveness. I like his strength of character, but I am not yet sure how far I agree with him." *Wartime Journals,* p. 391. In a memorandum that Lindbergh wrote on August 21, 1969, he commented: "I met Lawrence Dennis on only a few occasions, and read only parts of his book. I was interested in his philosophy, but doubtful about its wisdom and practicability. His influence on my thought and action was negligable." Memorandum by Lindbergh, August 21, 1969, Lindbergh Papers.
2. Telephone conversation with General Lindbergh, March 6, 1973.
3. *Wartime Journals,* pp. 353–58.
4. *Ibid.,* pp. 360–62; telegram Bennett Champ Clark to Lindbergh, June 24, 1940, William J. Grace to Lindbergh, July 1, 1940, R. O. Sargent to Frank Campsall, June 26, 1940, Lindbergh Papers.
5. Grace to Lindbergh, July 1, 1940, Lindbergh Papers.
6. Lindbergh to Armstrong, July 19, 1940, Lindbergh Papers.
7. Final draft of address Lindbergh read at Chicago rally, August 4, 1940, Lindbergh to Armstrong, August 9, 1940, Lindbergh Papers; *Wartime Journals,* pp. 374–75; *Chicago Tribune,* August 3, 4, 5, 1940.
8. *Wartime Journals,* pp. 374–76; R. Douglas Stuart, Jr., to Lindbergh, August 5, 1940, September 30, 1940, Lindbergh Papers; Stuart to Oswald Garrison Villard, October 5, 1940,

Oswald Garrison Villard Papers, Houghton Library, Harvard University, Cambridge, Massachusetts.

9. *Wartime Journals,* pp. 353–58; interview with General Lindbergh, June 7, 1972; telephone conversation with General Lindbergh, March 6, 1973.

10. Mimeographed letter from Armstrong to "Dear Friend," September 4, 1940, Gerald P. Nye Papers, Herbert Hoover Presidential Library, West Branch, Iowa; mimeographed letter Armstrong to "Dear Friend," September 14, 1940, Lindbergh Papers; Roscoe Baker, *The American Legion and American Foreign Policy* (New York: Bookman Associates, 1954), pp. 159–86.

11. *Wartime Journals,* pp. 410–11; final draft of address Lindbergh read at Yale University, October 30, 1940, Samuel Flagg Bemis to Lindbergh, October 31, 1940, Edwin Borchard to Lindbergh, October 31, 1940, Lindbergh Papers.

### 14/No Foreign War Committee

1. Mimeographed letter from O. K. Armstrong to "Dear Friend," October 7, 1940, and attached list of persons, presumably those who had been invited to the meeting, Lindbergh Papers.

2. Handwritten draft of Lindbergh's remarks at the Emergency Peace Conference, October 21, 1940, Lindbergh Papers.

3. Armstrong to "Dear Friend," October 29, 1940, Herbert Hoover Post-Presidential Individual File, Herbert Hoover Presidential Library, West Branch, Iowa.

4. Interview with Verne Marshall, Cedar Rapids, Iowa, December 19, 1948; biographical note in finding aid for Verne Marshall Papers, Marshall to Senator B. B. Hickenlooper, December 16, 1945, Marshall to Representative Karl E. Mundt, December 23, 1948, Marshall to Charles C. Tansill, April 11, 1951, Verne Marshall Papers, Herbert Hoover Presidential Library, West Branch, Iowa.

5. R. Douglas Stuart, Jr., to Lindbergh, October 28, 1940, Stuart to Robert E. Wood, November 28, 1940, Stuart to John T. Flynn, December 2, 1940, Stuart to Wood, December 8, 1940, Stuart to William R. Castle, December 18, 1940, Castle to Wood, December 18, 1940, America First Papers.

6. Marshall to Castle, November 9, 1940, Marshall to Stuart, November 25, 1940, Marshall Papers; Castle to Wood, Novem-

ber 24, 1940, America First Papers; Stuart to Hoover, December 3, 1940, Hoover Post-Presidential Subject File.

7. Lindbergh to Stuart, November 13, 1940, Lindbergh Papers.

8. Frederick J. Libby to Lindbergh, December 2, 1940, Stuart to Lindbergh, December 9, 1940, Libby to Mrs. Mildred S. Olmstead, December 28, 1940, Lindbergh Papers; Sidney Hertzberg to Stuart, December 2, 1940, Stuart to Flynn, December 2, 1940, Stuart to Wood, December 8, 1940, Wood to Castle, December 14, 1940, America First Papers.

9. *The Wartime Journals of Charles A. Lindbergh* (New York: Harcourt Brace Jovanovich, Inc., 1970), pp. 426–31.

10. *Ibid.;* Marshall to D. M. Linnard, January 21, 1941, Marshall Papers; interview with Marshall, December 19, 1948; telephone conversation with General Lindbergh, March 6, 1973.

11. *Wartime Journals,* p. 421; Lindbergh to Armstrong, January 6, 1941, Lindbergh to Thomas Dysart, January 6, 1941, Lindbergh Papers.

12. Castle to Wood, January 7, 1941, minutes of America First National Committee Meeting, January 14, 1941, America First Papers; Armstrong to Lindbergh, January 13, 1941, and enclosed press release, Lindbergh Papers.

13. Telegram Lindbergh to United Press, International News Service, and Associated Press, January 16, 1941, Lindbergh Papers; *Wartime Journals,* p. 440.

14. Marshall to Linnard, January 21, 1941, Marshall Papers; Stuart to Lansing Hoyt, January 24, 1941, America First Papers; interview with Marshall, December 19, 1948.

15. Telegram Armstrong to Stuart, May 5, 1941, Libby to Stuart, May 5, 1941, Armstrong to Stuart, May 6, 1941, Armstrong to Stuart, undated, [Stuart] to Page Hufty, Richard A. Moore, and Mr. Camphausen, undated, Stuart to Lindbergh, June 13, 1941, Stuart to Wood, June 20, 1941, Stuart to Armstrong, June 20, 1941, telegram Wood to Armstrong, July 10, 1941, Armstrong to Stuart, July 11, 1941, Stuart to Wood, Lindbergh, and all staff members, July 14, 1941, America First Papers.

### 15/America First

1. For a detailed history of the America First Committee, see Wayne S. Cole, *America First: The Battle Against Intervention, 1940–1941* (Madison: University of Wisconsin Press, 1953), *passim*. That book was reprinted by Octagon Books in 1971.

2. "General Robert E. Wood, President," *Fortune,* XVII (May, 1948), pp. 104–8; *Current Biography,* II (May, 1941), pp. 88–90; *St. Louis Post-Dispatch,* October 27, 1940.
3. *Future: The Magazine for Young Men* (March, 1941), p. 6.
4. Cole, *America First, passim.*
5. Daniel V. McNamee, Jr., Potter Stewart, R. Douglas Stuart, Jr., Windham Gary, Millard Brown, and Sargent Shriver to Lindbergh, November 1, 1939, O. K. Armstrong to Eugene Locke, July 11, 1940, Armstrong to Lindbergh, July 12, 1940, Stuart to Lindbergh, August 5, 1940, Lindbergh Papers; Stuart to Potter Stewart, August 6, 1940, America First Papers; Stuart to Oswald Garrison Villard, October 5, 1940, Villard Papers; interview with R. Douglas Stuart, Jr., San Francisco, California, April 6, 1949.
6. Stuart to Lindbergh, September 30, 1940, Armstrong to "Dear Friend," October 7, 1940, and enclosed list, Stuart to Lindbergh, October 28, 1941, Lindbergh Papers; Stuart to Kingman Brewster, Jr., October 25, 1940, America First Papers; *The Wartime Journals of Charles A. Lindbergh* (New York: Harcourt Brace Jovanovich Inc., 1970), pp. 408–31.
7. *Wartime Journals,* pp. 387–89; Lindbergh to Stuart, November 13, 1940, Lindbergh to Robert E. Wood, October 13, 1940, Christine L. Gawne to Stuart, February 5, 1941, Lindbergh to William L. Chenery, April 7, 1941, Lindbergh Papers; Janet Ayer Fairbank to Illinois Chapter Chairmen, February 25, 1941, S. Euphemia Aicken to Louie Fife, March 18, 1941, Hugh W. Fisher to Mrs. Eunice B. Armstrong, April 12, 1941, America First Papers.
8. *Wartime Journals,* pp. 387–89, 426–27; interview with General Lindbergh, June 7, 1972; Wood to Lindbergh, October 8, 1940, Lindbergh to Wood, October 13, 1940, Wood to Lindbergh, November 1, 1940, Lindbergh to Wood, November 12, 1940, telegram Wood to Lindbergh, January 22, 1941, and many other letters between the two men in Lindbergh Papers.
9. Minutes of Meeting of Board of Directors of the America First Committee, Chicago, Illinois, March 28, 1941, America First Papers; Wood to Lindbergh, March 29, 1941, Lindbergh Papers; *Wartime Journals,* pp. 472–73.
10. Lindbergh to Wood, April 8, 1941, Lindbergh Papers.
11. Minutes of Meeting of Board of Directors, Chicago, April 10,

1941, America First Papers; Wood to Lindbergh, April 11, 1941, Lindbergh Papers.

12. Wood to Lindbergh, April 11, 1941, Lindbergh Papers; Stuart to Hanford MacNider, April 10, 1941, Stuart to Page Hufty, April 18, 1941, America First Papers.

13. William J. Grace to Lindbergh, April 11, 1941, Lindbergh to Grace, April 14, 1941, Lindbergh Papers.

14. Wood to Lindbergh, May 23, 1941, Lindbergh to Wood, June 4, 1941, Lindbergh Papers.

15. *Wartime Journals,* pp. 474–75; *Chicago Tribune,* April 18, 1941, pp. 1, 6; *New York Times,* April 18, 1941, p. 8; final draft of address Lindbergh read in Chicago, April 17, 1941, Lindbergh Papers.

16. The final drafts of all those speeches are in the Lindbergh Papers, and the meetings were reported in major newspapers at the time. For a convenient summary account of some of the Lindbergh rallies, see Richard A. Moore to Fred Allhoff, August 23, 1941, America First Papers.

17. Mrs. Barbara McDonald to Robert Orr Baker, May 8, 1941, McDonald to Ray F. Moseley, May 9, 1941, America First Papers; Lindbergh to Wood, October 13, 1940, Lindbergh to Stuart, September 16, 1941, Robert L. Bliss to Lindbergh, November 26, 1941, Lindbergh Papers.

18. Stuart to Lindbergh, July 14, 1941, Millard C. Dorntge to Hufty, September 3, 1941, and many items in Lindbergh folder of Speakers Bureau file, America First Papers.

### 16/The Roosevelt Administration

1. Telegram Franklin D. Roosevelt to Colonel and Mrs. Charles A. Lindbergh, December 16, 1933, telegram Anne and Charles Lindbergh to Roosevelt, December 17, 1933, President's Personal File 1080, Roosevelt Papers.

2. Telegram Lindbergh to Roosevelt, February 11, 1934, telegram Lindbergh to George H. Dern, March 14, March 15, 1934, Lindbergh Papers; William Phillips Diary, February 13, March 16, 1934, Houghton Library, Harvard University, Cambridge, Massachusetts.

3. Interview with General Lindbergh, June 7, 1972.

4. Eleanor Roosevelt to Anne Lindbergh, September 26, 1939, Anne Lindbergh to Mrs. Roosevelt, October 12, 1939, Vannevar

Bush to Lindbergh, February 7, 1940, Lindbergh Papers; *The Wartime Journals of Charles A. Lindbergh* (New York: Harcourt Brace Jovanovich, Inc., 1970), pp. 32, 186–87, 257–58; interview with General Lindbergh, June 7, 1972.

5. Roosevelt to William Allen White, December 14, 1939, White to Roosevelt, December 22, 1939, PPF 1196, and materials dated April 15, 1941, and May 1, 1941, Official File 4230, Roosevelt Papers; Walter Johnson, *The Battle Against Isolation* (Chicago: University of Chicago Press, 1944), pp. 59–223.

6. Henry Morgenthau, Jr., Presidential Diaries, May 20, 1940, p. 563, Franklin D. Roosevelt Library, Hyde Park, New York; Roosevelt to Henry L. Stimson, May 21, 1940, Henry L. Stimson Papers, Sterling Memorial Library, Yale University, New Haven, Connecticut.

7. Confidential memorandum Roosevelt to Attorney General, May 21, 1940, President's Secretary's File, Justice Department–Robert Jackson folder, unsigned memorandum, May 31, 1940, Official File 463–C, file memo, May 6, 1941, Official File 4193, Roosevelt Papers; Elliott Roosevelt (ed.), *F. D. R.: His Personal Letters, 1928–1945*, 2 vols. (New York: Duell, Sloan and Pearce, 1950), p. 1241.

8. *New York Times*, May 23, 1940, pp. 1, 17, June 17, 1940, p. 5, August 6, 1940, pp. 1, 6, October 17, 1940, p. 10; undated memorandum for Mr. Early, and enclosed undated shorthand memo on White House letterhead, Stephen T. Early Papers, Roosevelt Library; telegram G. W. Johnstone to Key Pittman, June 16, 1940, Key Pittman Papers, Library of Congress, Washington, D.C.; W. D. H. [Hassett] to Early, October 12, 1940, Early Papers; Beatrice Bishop Berle and Travis Beal Jacobs (eds.), *Navigating the Rapids, 1918–1971: From the Papers of Adolf A. Berle* (New York: Harcourt Brace Jovanovich, Inc., 1973), pp. 343–44.

9. *The Secret Diary of Harold L. Ickes: The Lowering Clouds, 1939–1941* (New York: Simon and Schuster, 1954), pp. 289, 368, 373, 381, 395–96, 403; Henry L. Stimson Diary, December 19, 1940, Stimson Papers.

10. *New York Times*, December 18, 1940, p. 30; *Chicago Tribune*, April 14, 1941, p. 11.

11. John F. Carter to Miss Le Hand, April 22, 1941, and enclosed "Memorandum on the 'Copperhead' Government," PPF 1820, Roosevelt Papers; Microfilm of Roosevelt's Press Conferences,

April 25, 1941, roll 9, pp. 293–94; *Chicago Tribune*, April 26, 1941, p. 2.

12. Mimeographed statement of John T. Flynn, [April 25, 1941], America First Papers; telegram H. H. Wallace to Roosevelt, April 27, 1941, telegram Lincoln Fitzell, Jr., to Roosevelt, April 29, 1941, O.F. 4193, Roosevelt Papers.

13. Lindbergh to Roosevelt, April 28, 1941, O.F. 92, Roosevelt Papers; Lindbergh to Stimson, April 28, 1941, Lindbergh Papers; *Wartime Journals*, pp. 478–80.

14. Robert A. Taft to Lindbergh, April 30, 1941, mimeographed release by Oswald Garrison Villard, "Lindbergh to the Front," [1941], Lindbergh Papers; *Chicago Tribune*, June 5, 1941, p. 1.

15. Mimeographed address by Harold L. Ickes, "France Forever," given at Manhattan Center, New York City, July 14, 1941, Lindbergh Papers.

16. Lindbergh to Roosevelt, July 16, 1941, Early to Lindbergh, July 19, 1941, PPF 1080, Roosevelt Papers; *Wartime Journals*, p. 518.

17. *Secret Diary of Ickes: Lowering Clouds*, pp. 581–82; *Chicago Daily News*, July 25, 1941, p. 4.

18. *The Secret Diary of Harold L. Ickes: The Inside Struggle, 1936–1939* (New York: Simon and Schuster, 1954), p. 375; Roosevelt to Lowell Mellett, July 1, 1939, Ickes to Mellett, March 18, 1941, Ickes to Roosevelt, April 28, 1941, Mellett to Roosevelt, May 5, 1941, Lowell Mellett Papers, Franklin D. Roosevelt Library, Hyde Park, New York.

19. Harry L. Hopkins to Miss Tully, May 15, 1941, Roosevelt to Fiorello H. La Guardia, May 20, 1941, O.F. 4422, Roosevelt to Mellett, May 19, 1941, PPF 2409, Ickes to Roosevelt, September 17, 1941, PSF, Interior–Ickes, 1941 folder, Roosevelt Papers; C. D. Jackson to Mellett, July 3, 1941, Mellett Papers.

### 17/The Interventionists Organize

1. For a sympathetic history of the White Committee, see Walter Johnson, *The Battle Against Isolation* (Chicago: University of Chicago Press, 1944), *passim*.

2. *Washington Daily News*, December 23, 1940, p. 3; William Allen White to Roy W. Howard, December 24, 1941, telegram White to Clark Eichelberger, December 26, 1940, White Papers.

3. Statement by Lindbergh, December 23, 1940, Lindbergh Papers; *New York Times*, December 25, 1940, p. 14.

4. F. H. La Guardia to White, December 26, 1940, Roger S. Greene, Minutes of Executive Committee, January 2, 1941, Committee to Defend America Papers, Princeton University Library, Princeton, New Jersey; La Guardia to General Edwin M. Watson, December 27, 1940, PPF 1376, Thomas W. Lamont to Roosevelt, January 3, 1941, O.F. 4230, Roosevelt Papers; J. F. Stone to Cordell Hull, [December 28, 1940], Cordell Hull Papers, Library of Congress, Washington, D.C.; White to Lewis Douglas, December 28, 1940, White Papers.

5. For an excellent study of the "Century group" and Fight for Freedom, see Mark Lincoln Chadwin, *The Hawks of World War II* (Chapel Hill: University of North Carolina Press, 1968), *passim.*

6. This impression of the contrasting styles of the two organizations was obtained while researching the papers of both, which are deposited at the Princeton University Library, Princeton, New Jersey.

7. E. J. Kahn, Jr., "Democracy's Friend," *The New Yorker,* July 26, 1947, pp. 28–39, August 2, 1947, pp. 28–36, August 9, 1947, pp. 27–34; Friends of Democracy, Inc., *The America First Committee—The Nazi Transmission Belt* (New York, n.d.); *Chicago Tribune,* January 14, 1947, pp. 1, 6.

8. That organization originally had been named the Council Against Anti-Semitism. Telegram W. Warren Barbour, George Gordon Battle, and White to Mrs. Franklin D. Roosevelt, November 22, 1938, PPF 2, Roosevelt Papers.

## 18/ "Is Lindbergh a Nazi?"

1. *Facts in Review,* II (August 12, 1940), p. 378.

2. *Documents on German Foreign Policy, 1918–1945,* Series D (Washington: Government Printing Office, 1957–1964), IX, pp. 424–27, X, pp. 254–56, 413–15, XI, pp. 307–9, 949–50, 1230–31, XII, pp. 651–52.

3. William R. Castle to Lindbergh, August 9, 1940, Norman Thomas to Lindbergh, August 9, 1940, Lindbergh to Castle, August 16, 1940, Allen Valentine to Lindbergh, April 28, 1941, Lindbergh Papers.

4. Robert E. Wood to Lindbergh, June 2, 1941, Lindbergh to Wood, June 6, 1941, Wood to Lindbergh, August 12, 1941, Lindbergh Papers.

5. *The Wartime Journals of Charles A. Lindbergh* (New York:

Harcourt Brace Jovanovich, Inc., 1970), p. 452; interview with General Lindbergh, June 7, 1972.

6. *New York Times,* May 20, 1940, p. 16, May 23, 1940, pp. 1, 17, June 17, 1940, p. 5, August 6, 1940, pp. 1, 6, August 8, 1940, p. 3, October 17, 1940, p. 10, December 12, 1940, p. 18; *New York Herald Tribune,* January 26, 1941; unsigned letter to "Dear Nazi Lindbergh," August 15, 1940, Lindbergh Papers.

7. *New York Times,* April 23, 1941, p. 9, April 24, 1941, pp. 1, 12.

8. *PM,* April 24, 1941; *Chicago Herald-American,* April 25, 1941; *New York World-Telegram,* April 25, 1941; *Philadelphia Bulletin,* April 25, 1941; *Cincinnati Post,* May 3, 1941.

9. *New York Daily News,* May 23, 1941, p. 28; *Chicago Tribune,* May 24, 1941, pp. 1, 6; *Time,* XXXVII (June 2, 1941), p. 15; *Life,* X (June 9, 1941), p. 56.

10. John Roy Carlson, *Under Cover* (Cleveland and New York: World Publishing Co., 1943), pp. 249–52; *PM,* May 25, 1941; E. S. Webster, Jr., to R. Douglas Stuart, Jr., June 18, 1941, America First Papers; Lindbergh to author, February 17, 1972.

11. *PM,* June 12, 1941, pp. 20–21; *Chicago Sunday Times,* June 15, 1941, p. 15M; *Chicago Tribune,* June 14, 1941, p. 1; Alfred N. Phillips, Jr., to Gregory Mason, undated, O.F. 4461, Roosevelt Papers.

12. Darryl Zanuck to "All Department Heads," July 22, 1941, Fight for Freedom Committee Papers, Princeton University Library, Princeton, New Jersey.

13. *New Masses,* XXXVIII (January 7, 1941), p. 3; *Daily Worker,* April 25, 1941, p. 6; *Chicago Tribune,* August 20, 1941, p. 3.

14. L. M. Birkhead to Ulric Bell, August 15, 1941, Bell to Birkhead, August 20, 1941, Birkhead to Bell, October 23, 1941, Fight for Freedom Papers; *New York Times,* October 31, 1941.

15. Friends of Democracy, Inc., *Is Lindbergh a Nazi?* (New York, n.d.), *passim,* but see especially pp. 2–3, 8, 10, 16–17, 22.

### 19/"Who Are the War Agitators?"

1. Lindbergh, "The Air Defense of America," speech read at Columbia studio, Washington, D.C., May 19, 1940, Lindbergh Papers.

2. Lindbergh, "Our Drift Toward War," speech read over NBC, June 15, 1940, Lindbergh, "Our Relationship with Europe," address read in Chicago, August 4, 1940, final draft of Lind-

bergh address in Chicago, April 17, 1941, and final draft of Lindbergh address in New York, April 23, 1941, Lindbergh Papers.

3. Thomas W. Lamont to Lindbergh, May 29, 1940, Lindbergh to Lamont, June 7, 1940, Lindbergh Papers.

4. Several handwritten drafts of Lindbergh's "A Letter to Americans" are in the Lindbergh Papers, including those dated August 18, 1940, August 20, 1940, August 21, 1940, and September 22, 1940.

5. Lindbergh to author, February 17, 1972, and March 19, 1973.

6. Janet Ayer Fairbank to Lindbergh, June 24, 1941, Robert E. Wood to Lindbergh, July 17, 1941, August 12, 1941, Lindbergh Papers; office memorandum by R. Douglas Stuart, Jr., August 15, 1941, America First Papers.

7. *Des Moines Register,* September 1, 1941, p. 6, September 2, 1941, p. 4, September 11, 1941, p. 7; *Des Moines Sunday Register,* September 7, 1941, "Iowa News," p. 3; Page Hufty to L. E. King, October 1, 1941, R. F. Starzl to Chicago America First, September 16, 1941, John Carl Mundt to Stuart, September 27, 1941, America First Papers.

8. *Des Moines Sunday Register,* September 7, 1941, "Iowa News," p. 3; telegram Lindbergh to Stuart, September 9, 1941, America First Papers; *Des Moines Register,* September 10, 1941, p. 4; interview with Harry Schnibbe, Denver, Colorado, June 21, 1949.

9. *The Wartime Journals of Charles A. Lindbergh* (New York: Harcourt Brace Jovanovich, Inc., 1970), pp. 536–38; *Des Moines Register,* September 12, 1941, p. 1.

10. Lindbergh, "Who Are the War Agitators?," final typed draft, September 11, 1941, Lindbergh Papers. The full text of the address was also printed in both the *Des Moines Register* and the *Chicago Tribune* on September 12, 1941.

11. *Des Moines Register,* September 13, 1941, p. 4; Wayne S. Cole, *America First: The Battle Against Intervention, 1940–1941* (Madison: University of Wisconsin Press, 1953), pp. 145–54.

#### 20/ Capitalists, Intellectuals, and the British

1. Bruce L. Larson, *Lindbergh of Minnesota: A Political Biography* (New York: Harcourt Brace Jovanovich, Inc., 1973), *passim;* Wayne S. Cole, *Senator Gerald P. Nye and American Foreign*

*Relations* (Minneapolis: University of Minnesota Press, 1962), *passim.*

2. Final drafts of Lindbergh's broadcasts on October 13, 1939, and June 15, 1940, Lindbergh Papers; Charles A. Lindbergh, "Aviation, Geography, and Race," *Reader's Digest,* XXXV (November, 1939), pp. 64–67.

3. Charles A. Lindbergh, "A Letter to Americans," *Collier's* (March 29, 1941), pp. 14, 76; final drafts of Lindbergh speeches in St. Louis, May 3, 1941, in Minneapolis, May 10, 1941, and in San Francisco, July 1, 1941, Lindbergh Papers.

4. Final draft of Lindbergh speech in Des Moines, September 11, 1941, Lindbergh Papers.

5. Lindbergh, "Letter to Americans," *Collier's,* pp. 14, 76.

6. For examples, see Sir R. Lindsay to Mr. Eden, March 22, 1937, Foreign Office 414/274, pp. 172–78, Sir G. Schuster to Viscount Halifax, July 11, 1938, Foreign Office 800/324, pp. 9–11, Sir R. Lindsay to British Foreign Office, March 16, 1938, Foreign Office 371/22526, pp. 8–9, Marquess of Lothian to Viscount Halifax, December 14, 1939, Foreign Office 414/276, pp. 200–2, V. A. L. Mallet, "American Opinion on the War," received December 14, 1939, Foreign Office 371/22830, pp. 220–31, Lothian to Viscount Halifax, February 1, 1940, Halifax Papers, Foreign Office 800/324, pp. 141–63, British Foreign Office Records, Public Record Office, London, England.

7. Lothian to Foreign Office, June 6, 1940, Foreign Office 371/24239, p. 374, Winston Churchill to Lothian, June 9, 1940, Foreign Office 371/24239, pp. 362–63, British Office Records.

8. T. North Whitehead, "Policy for Publicity in the United States," November 29, 1940, Foreign Office 414/277, pp. 107–16, British Foreign Office Records.

9. *New York Times,* October 22, 1939, p. 29.

10. Mark Lincoln Chadwin, *The Hawks of World War II* (Chapel Hill: University of North Carolina Press, 1968), pp. 138–39, 186–87, 245.

11. H. Montgomery Hyde, *Room 3603: The Story of the British Intelligence Center in New York during World War II* (New York: Farrar, Straus and Company, 1962), pp. 2–5, 72–74.

### 21/The Jewish Interventionists

1. Lindbergh, "Who Are the War Agitators?," final draft read at the meeting in Des Moines, September 11, 1941, Lindbergh

Papers. The speech was also printed in the *Des Moines Register,* September 12, 1941, and *Chicago Tribune,* September 12, 1941.

2. *The Wartime Journals of Charles A. Lindbergh* (New York: Harcourt Brace Jovanovich, Inc., 1970), pp. 115, 218, 245, 481.
3. Handwritten draft by Lindbergh, undated, Lindbergh Papers.
4. *Des Moines Register,* September 13, 1941, p. 4, September 14, 1941, "Iowa News," p. 4; telegram John P. Lewis to William H. Regnery, September 15, 1941, America First Papers; telegram R. Douglas Stuart, Jr., to John T. Flynn, September 15, 1941, John T. Flynn Papers, University of Oregon Library, Eugene, Oregon.
5. Telegram Reinhold Niebuhr to Flynn, September 13, 1941, Flynn Papers; *Commonweal,* XXXIV (1941), p. 532.
6. Telegram Henry W. Hobson to Robert E. Wood, September 16, 1941, telegram Hugh Moore to Wood, September 22, 1941, America First Papers; *America's Answer to Lindbergh* (n.p., n.d.). The printed pamphlet does not provide any author, publisher, or date. But copies both in the America First Papers and in the Fight for Freedom Papers carry the stamp of Fight for Freedom, Inc. See also *New York Times,* September 13, 1941, p. 3.
7. *Daily Worker* (New York), September 13, 1941, p. 6, September 16, 1941, p. 5; *New Masses,* XL (September 30, 1941), p. 4.
8. *New York Times,* September 13, 1941, pp. 1, 3, September 15, 1941, p. 2; *Newsweek,* XVIII (September 22, 1941), pp. 16–17; *Washington Post,* October 7, 1941, p. 7.
9. *Chicago Tribune,* September 16, 1941, p. 12, October 17, 1941, p. 14, September 19, 1941, p. 6; *Life,* XI (September 29, 1941), p. 43.
10. For examples, see J. B. Bingham and J. R. Bingham to America First, September 14, 1941, Jules Sien to New York America First, September 15, 1941, Jean Bevan to New York America First, September 15, 1941, and Patricia MacManus to New York America First, September 23, 1941, America First Papers.
11. Catherine Landl to Lindbergh, September 12, 1941, and many other letters in both the America First and the Lindbergh Papers.
12. These and many similar letters are in the America First Papers.

13. Merwin K. Hart to Lindbergh, September 15, 1941, Gerald L. K. Smith to Lindbergh, October 9, 1941, Lindbergh Papers; *Social Justice,* October 6, 1941, p. 6; *Scribner's Commentator,* XI (1941), p. 3.
14. Telegram Frank E. Gannett to Wood, September 12, 1941, Norman Thomas to Stuart, September 23, 1941, W. S. Foulis to Stuart, October 23, 1941, America First Papers; *Milwaukee Sentinel,* September 17, 1941; *Chicago Tribune,* September 12, 1941, p. 1, September 13, 1941, p. 10, September 20, 1941, p. 10; and unidentified clipping, September 19, 1941, America First Papers.
15. Norman Thomas and Bertram D. Wolfe, *Keep America Out of War* (New York, 1939), pp. 153–54; Thomas to Stuart, September 10, 1941, Thomas to Wood, September 17, 1941, America First Papers; Thomas to Lindbergh, September 24, 1941, Lindbergh Papers; *Commonweal,* XXXIV (1941), p. 590; *New York Times,* September 23, 1941, p. 6.
16. Mary W. Hillyer to Stuart, September 17, 1941, Frederick J. Libby to Stuart, September 22, 1941, America First Papers; mimeographed press release of Keep America Out of War Congress, September 21, 1941, Villard Papers; *Washington Post,* September 21, 1941, p. 5.
17. Telegram George Gordon Battle to Oswald Garrison Villard, September 17, 1941, Battle to "Dear Friend," October, 1941, Villard to Battle, September 23, 1941, October 30, 1941, November 6, 1941, Villard Papers.
18. Robert M. Hutchins to Battle, November 14, 1941, Bennett Champ Clark to Villard, November 15, 1941, Villard Papers; Alf M. Landon to Battle, September 23, 1941, Lindbergh Papers.
19. Carbon of undated article reporting interview of Gerald P. Nye for the *American Israelite,* Nye Papers; *Des Moines Register,* September 21, 1941, p. 3; *Washington Post,* September 21, 1941, p. 5; mimeographed news release of excerpts from address by Senator Nye, Brooklyn, New York, September 22, 1941, America First Papers; Robert Taft to Edward S. Thurston, undated, Robert A. Taft Papers, Library of Congress, Washington, D.C. Taft's letter was signed but may not have been mailed.
20. *Chicago Tribune,* September 17, 1941, p. 2; Merle H. Miller to

Stuart, September 16, 1941, America First Papers; undated teletype exchange between Flynn and Stuart, Flynn to Mort Lewis, September 17, 1941, Flynn Papers.

21. Flynn to Lindbergh, September 15, 1941, Lindbergh Papers.
22. *Wartime Journals,* p. 541.
23. America First Committee Bulletin, #574, September 22, 1941, K. E. Nordine to D. H. Carrick, October 8, 1941, Dorothy Thum to Clay Pugh, September 24, 1941, and F. A. Chase to J. L. Wheeler, September 16, 1941, America First Papers; *Time,* XXXVIII (October 6, 1941), pp. 18–20.
24. Gregory Mason to T. C. Chubb, September 18, 1941, America First Papers.
25. Telegram Stuart to Flynn, September 15, 1941, Flynn Papers; America First Committee Bulletin, #553, September 15, 1941, book wire Stuart to local chapters, September 15, 1941, America First Papers; *Wartime Journals,* pp. 540–41.
26. *Wartime Journals,* pp. 540–42; Minutes of America First National Committee Meeting, September 18, 1941, America First Papers; interview with General Robert E. Wood, Chicago, Illinois, December 23, 1947; "Two Views on Lindbergh," *Catholic World,* 154 (November, 1941), pp. 206–9. National committee members present at the meeting were General Wood, A. J. Carlson, Miriam Clark, Janet Ayer Fairbank, John T. Flynn, Clay Judson, Alice Roosevelt Longworth, George N. Peek, Amos R. E. Pinchot, Stuart, and later Lindbergh. Present by invitation were Page Hufty, Richard A. Moore, Isaac Pennypacker, Samuel B. Pettengill, and Edwin Webster.
27. Chester Bowles to Stuart, September 19, 1941, William R. Castle to Stuart, September 15, 1941, September 21, 1941, Appendix to Minutes of National Committee Meeting, September 18, 1941, America First Papers.
28. *Chicago Tribune,* September 25, 1941, p. 2; *Washington Post,* September 25, 1941, p. 7; Stuart to all chapter chairmen, September 23, 1941, America First Papers.
29. Hyman Lischner to Wood, September 21, 1941, John L. Wheeler to Stuart, undated, America First Papers; *Washington Post,* September 30, 1941, p. 9; *Catholic World,* 154 (November, 1941), pp. 209–10.
30. Lindbergh, "A Heritage at Stake," final draft read at meeting in Fort Wayne, Indiana, October 3, 1941, Lindbergh Papers.
31. Interview with General Lindbergh, June 7, 1972.

32. Harry C. Schnibbe to K. D. Magruder, August 16, 1941, telegram Hufty to Ruth Sarles, September 13, 1941, America First Papers.
33. Joseph Boldt to Schnibbe, September 23, 1941, Schnibbe to Boldt, September 25, 1941, Boldt to Schnibbe, September 30, 1941, America First Papers.

### 22/"Government by Subterfuge"

1. Lindbergh's handwritten draft for "A Letter to Americans," August 18, 1940, Lindbergh, "Who Are the War Agitators?," final draft read in Des Moines, Iowa, September 11, 1941, Lindbergh Papers.
2. *Public Opinion Quarterly,* V (1941), pp. 323–25, 481, 485, VI (1942), pp. 151, 161–62; Hadley Cantril, "Opinion Trends in World War II: Some Guides to Interpretation," *Public Opinion Quarterly,* XII (1948), p. 37; Hadley Cantril (ed.), and Mildred Strunk, *Public Opinion, 1935–1946* (Princeton: Princeton University Press, 1951), pp. 968–77.
3. Wayne S. Cole, *America First: The Battle Against Intervention, 1940–1941* (Madison: University of Wisconsin Press, 1953), pp. 51–61.
4. *Ibid.,* pp. 61–64; Henry L. Stimson and McGeorge Bundy, *On Active Service in Peace and War* (New York: Harper & Brothers, 1948), pp. 368, 370–73, 376; Robert E. Sherwood, *Roosevelt and Hopkins: An Intimate History* (New York: Harper & Brothers, 1948), p. 382; Robert E. Wood to Franklin D. Roosevelt, October 22, 1941, Roosevelt Papers.
5. Final drafts of addresses Lindbergh read at America First rallies in Minneapolis, Minnesota, May 10, 1941, and in New York City, May 23, 1941, Lindbergh Papers.
6. Final draft of address Lindbergh read at America First rally in Philadelphia, Pennsylvania, May 29, 1941, Lindbergh Papers.
7. Telegram Lindbergh to *Baltimore Sun,* undated, Lindbergh Papers; *America First Bulletin,* June 14, 1941, pp. 1, 3, America First Papers.
8. Lindbergh, "Government by Representation or by Subterfuge?," final draft read at meeting in Cleveland, August 9, 1941, Lindbergh Papers.
9. Lindbergh, "A Heritage at Stake," final draft read at meeting in Fort Wayne, Indiana, October 3, 1941, Lindbergh Papers.
10. Lindbergh, "Facing the Record and the Facts," final draft read

at meeting in Madison Square Garden, New York, October 30, 1941, Lindbergh Papers.

11. Lindbergh, "What Do We Mean by Democracy and Freedom?," preliminary draft of speech that Lindbergh was to have read at Boston America First rally, December 12, 1941, Lindbergh Papers. The meeting was canceled after the Pearl Harbor attack.

12. Cole, *America First,* pp. 178–87.

13. *New York Times,* February 8, 1941, p. 4; *Newsweek,* XVII (February 10, 1941), p. 9; Chester Bowles to R. Douglas Stuart, Jr., July 15, 1941, America First Papers; *Newsweek,* XVIII (September 15, 1941), pp. 15–16; Lindbergh to Henrik Shipstead, April 20, 1942, Lindbergh Papers; *The Wartime Journals of Charles A. Lindbergh* (New York: Harcourt Brace Jovanovich, Inc., 1970), pp. 274, 576–77.

14. *Wartime Journals,* pp. 274–75, 487, 491–92, 546–47, 576–77; interview with General Lindbergh, June 7, 1972.

15. Cole, *America First,* pp. 187–88; *Washington Post,* September 21, 1941, II, p. 5.

### 23/The End Is Near

1. Wayne S. Cole, *America First: The Battle Against Intervention, 1940–1941* (Madison: University of Wisconsin Press, 1953), pp. 162–66.

2. R. Douglas Stuart, Jr., to Lindbergh, August 15, 1941, William Benton to Stuart, September 4, 1941, Stuart to Benton, September 16, 1941, America First Papers.

3. Hanford MacNider to Robert E. Wood, September 20, 1941, Lindbergh Papers.

4. *The Wartime Journals of Charles A. Lindbergh* (New York: Harcourt Brace Jovanovich, Inc., 1970), p. 540; Page Hufty to Mrs. E. S. Welch, August 29, 1941, Hufty to Henry Mooberry, October 6, 1941, America First Papers; Wood to Lindbergh, September 22, 1941, Lindbergh Papers; Wood to MacNider, September 22, 1941, Hanford MacNider Papers, Herbert Hoover Presidential Library, West Branch, Iowa; Wood to John T. Flynn, September 22, 1941, Flynn Papers.

5. *Wartime Journals,* p. 540; Wood to MacNider, September 22, 1941, MacNider Papers; Stuart to Wood, September 20, 1941, America First Papers.

6. Lindbergh to Wood, September 24, 1941, Lindbergh Papers.

7. *Wartime Journals,* pp. 544–45.

8. Hufty to Isaac A. Pennypacker, October 23, 1941, Stuart to Robert M. Hutchins, October 29, 1941, Stuart to Robert R. McCormick, October 30, 1941, America First Papers.
9. *Wartime Journals,* pp. 545–46.
10. Lindbergh to Wood, October 27, 1941, Lindbergh Papers.
11. *Ibid.*
12. *Ibid.*
13. Lindbergh, "A Heritage at Stake," final draft read at America First meeting, Fort Wayne, Indiana, October 3, 1941, Lindbergh Papers.
14. Lindbergh, "Facing the Record and the Facts," final draft read at America First meeting in Madison Square Garden, New York, October 30, 1941, Lindbergh Papers.

### 24/Pearl Harbor

1. *The Wartime Journals of Charles A. Lindbergh* (New York: Harcourt Brace Jovanovich, Inc., 1970), pp. 560–61.
2. Wayne S. Cole, *America First: The Battle Against Intervention, 1940–1941* (Madison: University of Wisconsin Press, 1953), pp. 189–93.
3. Charles A. Lindbergh, "What Substitute for War?," *Atlantic Monthly* (March, 1940), pp. 307–8; final draft of Lindbergh's address at Yale University, October 30, 1940, William R. Castle to Lindbergh, April 14, 1941, Lindbergh Papers.
4. Cole, *America First,* pp. 193–94.
5. *Wartime Journals,* p. 561; telegram Lindbergh to R. Douglas Stuart, Jr., December 8, 1941, Lindbergh Papers; *New York Times,* December 9, 1941, p. 44.
6. *Wartime Journals,* p. 561.
7. *Ibid.,* pp. 565–66.
8. *Ibid.,* p. 598; Cole, *America First,* pp. 194–95; Lindbergh to Robert E. Wood, December 26, 1941, Lindbergh Papers.
9. Cole, *America First,* p. 195.
10. Wood to Lindbergh, December 12, 1941, Lindbergh Papers.
11. Lindbergh to Members of America First Committee, December 14, 1941, Lindbergh Papers.

### 25/Rebuffed by FDR

1. *The Wartime Journals of Charles A. Lindbergh* (New York: Harcourt Brace Jovanovich, Inc., 1970), pp. 566–67.

2. *Ibid.,* pp. 569–72; Lindbergh to Philip R. Love, January 30, 1942, Lindbergh Papers; Lindbergh to H. H. Arnold, December 20, 1941, Arnold, "Memorandum of Record," December 30, 1941, H. H. Arnold Papers, Library of Congress, Washington, D.C.

3. These and other similar quotations are from letters in Lindbergh folder, Arnold Papers. O.F. 92 in the Roosevelt Papers contains many letters pro and con on the issue. See also *Newsweek,* XIX (January 12, 1942), p. 24.

4. Harold L. Ickes to Franklin D. Roosevelt, December 30, 1941, Roosevelt to Ickes, December 30, 1941, PSF: Interior: Harold Ickes, 1941, Roosevelt Papers; Stephen Early to Frank Knox, December 31, 1941, and enclosure, Early Papers; Early to Henry L. Stimson, December 31, 1941, and enclosure, Stimson Papers.

5. Knox to Roosevelt, January 1, 1942, Roosevelt to Stimson, January 12, 1942, PSF: War Department–Henry L. Stimson, Roosevelt Papers.

6. J. P. Warburg to John J. McCloy, January 9, 1942, and attached "Report on two meetings of the nucleus of America First, one of which was attended by Charles Lindbergh," December 19, 1941, memorandum by McCloy, January 12, 1942, Stimson Papers.

7. Rosalie M. Gordon to Lindbergh, January 22, 1942, and clippings from *New York World-Telegram,* January 9, 1942, *PM,* January 9, 1942, *New York Post,* January 9, 1942, Lindbergh Papers; telegram Mrs. Frank R. Fuller to Roosevelt, January 12, 1942, Laura Hayes Fuller to Mrs. Roosevelt, January 12, 1942, Roosevelt to Secretary of War and General Arnold, January 20, 1942, John W. Martyn to General Watson, January 26, 1942, O.F. 92, Roosevelt Papers.

8. *Wartime Journals,* pp. 568, 597–600.

9. *Ibid.,* pp. 573–74.

10. *Ibid.,* pp. 576–81; Stimson Diary, January 12, 1942, Stimson to Roosevelt, January 13, 1942, Stimson Papers; Lindbergh to Love, January 30, 1942, Lindbergh Papers.

11. Stimson to Roosevelt, January 13, 1942, Stimson Papers; Lindbergh to Love, January 30, 1942, Lindbergh Papers; *Wartime Journals,* pp. 581–84.

12. *Wartime Journals,* pp. 584–600; Lindbergh to Love, January 30, 1942, Lindbergh Papers.

13. *Wartime Journals,* p. 597. See also Lindbergh to Love, March 7, 1942, Lindbergh Papers.

### 26/A War to Fight

1. *The Wartime Journals of Charles A. Lindbergh* (New York: Harcourt Brace Jovanovich, Inc., 1970), pp. 300, 362–65, 375–77, 534, 608, 629. See also Reynold M. Wik, *Henry Ford and Grass-Roots America* (Ann Arbor: University of Michigan Press, 1972), *passim.*
2. *New York Times,* May 29, 1940, p. 9; Henry L. Stimson to Franklin D. Roosevelt, March 4, 1942, PSF: War Department–Henry L. Stimson, Roosevelt Papers; *Wartime Journals,* pp. 553n, 732–33.
3. *Wartime Journals,* pp. 603, 607–10, 621; Russell Gnau to Lindbergh, March 27, 1942, Lindbergh Papers.
4. Lindbergh to John A. O'Brien, October 29, 1942, Lindbergh to Amos R. E. Pinchot, December 5, 1942, Lindbergh Papers; *Wartime Journals,* pp. 675–76, 716–17.
5. *Wartime Journals,* pp. 699, 735–36, 750–54; Lindbergh memorandum, August 1–11, 1968, p. 55, Lindbergh Papers. For a thrilling account of an episode on one of his high-altitude flights, see Charles A. Lindbergh, *Of Flight and Life* (New York: Charles Scribner's Sons, 1948), pp. 3–8.
6. Forrest C. Pogue, *George C. Marshall: Organizer of Victory, 1943–1945* (New York: The Viking Press, 1973), pp. 119–20; H. H. Arnold, *Global Mission* (New York: Harper & Brothers, 1949), pp. 189, 359; Clay Judson to Lindbergh, January 26, 1942, Robert E. Wood to Lindbergh, September 26, 1944, Lindbergh Papers; interviews with General Wood, Chicago, Illinois, December 23, 1947, R. Douglas Stuart, Jr., San Francisco, California, April 6, 1949, Harry Schnibbe, Denver, Colorado, June 21, 1949; *Who's Who in America, 1948–1949,* pp. 1204, 1483, 1556, 2735.
7. Interview with General Lindbergh, Darien, Connecticut, June 13, 1972; *Wartime Journals,* pp. 769–924, but see especially pp. 887–89, 912.
8. *Wartime Journals,* pp. 864–65, 872–76, 911; interview with General Lindbergh, Washington, D.C., May 17, 1973.
9. Interview with General Lindbergh, May 17, 1973; *Wartime Journals,* pp. 916–22.

10. *Wartime Journals,* pp. 822, 834.
11. *Ibid.,* p. 819.
12. *Ibid.,* pp. 853–54, 856–57, 859–60, 875, 879–80, 882–84, 902–3, 919.
13. *Ibid.,* pp. 907, 919.
14. *Ibid.,* pp. 818, 870–74, 884, 904–13, 916–27.
15. *Ibid.,* pp. 930–41.
16. *Ibid.,* pp. 942–98, but see especially pp. 942–46, 998.
17. *Ibid.,* pp. 955–59, 969–71, 975–76, 983–89.
18. *Ibid.,* pp. 991–98; copy of final draft turned over to *Chicago Tribune,* July 25, 1945, Lindbergh Papers.

### 27/New Horizons

1. For examples, see Wayne S. Cole, *Senator Gerald P. Nye and American Foreign Relations* (Minneapolis: University of Minnesota Press, 1962), pp. 211–16; Burton K. Wheeler with Paul F. Healy, *Yankee from the West: The Candid, Turbulent Life Story of the Yankee-Born U.S. Senator from Montana* (Garden City: Doubleday & Company, Inc., 1962), pp. 400–13.
2. Press release, Indianapolis, Indiana, August 4, 1942, Lindbergh Papers; *The Wartime Journals of Charles A. Lindbergh* (New York: Harcourt Brace Jovanovich, Inc., 1970), pp. 683–89.
3. John Roy Carlson, *Under Cover: My Four Years in the Nazi Underworld of America—The Amazing Revelation of How Axis Agents and Our Enemies Within Are Now Plotting to Destroy the United States* (Cleveland and New York: World Publishing Company, 1943).
4. Based on reactions of many individuals when informed of the author's project on Lindbergh.
5. Robert E. Wood to Lindbergh, January 21, 1944, Lindbergh to Harry Elmer Barnes, November 30, 1944, December 30, 1944, April 7, 1945, Lindbergh Papers.
6. Interviews with General Lindbergh, June 13, 1972, and May 17, 1973.
7. *Wartime Journals,* p. xiv; memorandum on Lindbergh by Lt. Col. (ret.) Raymond H. Fredette, July 11, 1973, Lindbergh Papers.
8. Charles A. Lindbergh, "Our Best Chance to Survive," *Saturday Evening Post,* 227 (July 17, 1954), p. 25; interviews with General Lindbergh, June 13, 1972, and May 17, 1973.

9. "Letter from Lindbergh," *Life,* 67 (July 4, 1969), p. 60B; interview with General Lindbergh, May 17, 1973.

10. Charles A. Lindbergh, *Of Flight and Life* (New York: Charles Scribner's Sons, 1948), *passim,* but see especially p. 56.

11. Charles A. Lindbergh, *The Spirit of St. Louis* (New York: Charles Scribner's Sons, 1953), *passim,* but see especially pp. ix, 547.

12. *Wartime Journals, passim; Bring Me a Unicorn: Diaries and Letters of Anne Morrow Lindbergh, 1922–1928* (New York: Harcourt Brace Jovanovich, Inc., 1972), p. x; *Hour of Gold, Hour of Lead: Diaries and Letters of Anne Morrow Lindbergh, 1929–1932* (New York: Harcourt Brace Jovanovich, 1973).

13. Charles A. Lindbergh, "The Wisdom of Wildness," *Life,* 63 (December 22, 1967), pp. 8–10; Charles A. Lindbergh, "Feel the Earth," *Reader's Digest,* 101 (July, 1972), pp. 62–65; Charles A. Lindbergh, "Lessons from the Primitive," *Reader's Digest,* 101 (November, 1972), pp. 147–51; Charles A. Lindbergh, "The Way of Wildness," *Reader's Digest,* 99 (November, 1971), pp. 90–93; Charles A. Lindbergh, "Is Civilization Progress?," *Reader's Digest,* 85 (July, 1964), pp. 67–74; telephone conversation with General Lindbergh, July 4, 1973; interview with John Owen, Washington, D.C., June 12, 1973.

14. Interview with General Lindbergh, May 17, 1973.

15. Lindbergh to author, May 19, 1973.

16. Copy of final draft turned over to *Chicago Tribune,* July 25, 1945, Lindbergh Papers.

17. Final draft of address by Lindbergh at dinner of Aero Club of Washington, December 17, 1945, Lindbergh Papers.

18. Copy of speech or statement, Engineers Club, April 11, 1947, Lindbergh Papers.

19. Interview with General Lindbergh, May 17, 1973.

20. *Ibid.,* June 7, 1972, May 17, 1973; Lindbergh to author, May 19, 1973.

21. *Wartime Journals,* p. xv.

# Selected Bibliography

# Selected Bibliography

This book is based almost completely on research in original primary sources—oral, manuscript, and printed. The most valuable sources of information were the Charles A. Lindbergh Papers, Sterling Memorial Library, Yale University; the America First Committee Papers, Hoover Library on War, Revolution and Peace, Stanford, California; Lindbergh's published *Wartime Journals;* and personal conversations and correspondence with General Lindbergh. A few scholarly secondary accounts were helpful, and those have been cited in the notes. The selected bibliography that follows lists only the primary sources helpful for this study.

## Manuscripts

Carl W. Ackerman Papers, Library of Congress, Washington, D.C.

America First Committee Papers, Hoover Library on War, Revolution and Peace, Stanford, California.

Henry H. Arnold Papers, Library of Congress, Washington, D.C.

Harold M. Bixby Papers, Library of Congress, Washington, D.C.

William E. Borah Papers, Library of Congress, Washington, D.C.

British Foreign Office Records, Public Record Office, London, England.

Arthur Capper Papers, Kansas State Historical Society, Topeka, Kansas.

William R. Castle Papers, Herbert Hoover Presidential Library, West Branch, Iowa.

Committee to Defend America Papers, Princeton University Library, Princeton, New Jersey.

William E. Dodd Papers, Library of Congress, Washington, D.C.

## Selected Bibliography

Stephen T. Early Papers, Franklin D. Roosevelt Library, Hyde Park, New York.

Fight for Freedom Committee Papers, Princeton University Library, Princeton, New Jersey.

John T. Flynn Papers, Library, University of Oregon, Eugene, Oregon.

Carter Glass Papers, University of Virginia Library, University of Virginia, Charlottesville, Virginia.

Herbert Hoover Papers, Herbert Hoover Presidential Library, West Branch, Iowa.

Harry Hopkins Papers, Franklin D. Roosevelt Library, Hyde Park, New York.

Cordell Hull Papers, Library of Congress, Washington, D.C.

Hiram Johnson Papers, Bancroft Library, University of California, Berkeley, California.

Frank Knox Papers, Library of Congress, Washington, D.C.

LaFollette Family Papers, Library of Congress, Washington, D.C.

Fiorello H. La Guardia Papers, Municipal Archives and Records Center, New York Public Library, New York, New York.

Alf M. Landon Papers, Kansas State Historical Society, Topeka, Kansas.

Charles A. Lindbergh Papers, Sterling Memorial Library, Yale University, New Haven, Connecticut.

Hanford MacNider Papers, Herbert Hoover Presidential Library, West Branch, Iowa.

Verne Marshall Papers, Herbert Hoover Presidential Library, West Branch, Iowa.

Lowell Mellett Papers, Franklin D. Roosevelt Library, Hyde Park, New York.

Henry Morgenthau, Jr., Diaries and Presidential Diaries, Franklin D. Roosevelt Library, Hyde Park, New York.

George W. Norris Papers, Library of Congress, Washington, D.C.

Gerald P. Nye Papers, Chevy Chase, Maryland, and Herbert Hoover Presidential Library, West Branch, Iowa.

Amos R. E. Pinchot Papers, Library of Congress, Washington, D.C.

Key Pittman Papers, Library of Congress, Washington, D.C.

Franklin D. Roosevelt Papers, Franklin D. Roosevelt Library, Hyde Park, New York.

Henrik Shipstead Papers, Minnesota Historical Society, St. Paul, Minnesota.

# Selected Bibliography

Truman Smith, "Air Intelligence Activities: Office of the Military Attache, American Embassy, Berlin, Germany, August 1935–April 1939 With Special Reference to the Services of Colonel Charles A. Lindbergh, Air Corps (Res.)," Sterling Memorial Library, Yale University, New Haven, Connecticut.

Henry L. Stimson Diaries and Papers, Sterling Memorial Library, Yale University, New Haven, Connecticut.

Robert A. Taft Papers, Library of Congress, Washington, D.C.

United States Department of State Records, National Archives, Washington, D.C.

United States Senate Committee on Foreign Relations Papers, National Archives, Washington, D.C.

Arthur H. Vandenberg Papers, William L. Clements Library, University of Michigan, Ann Arbor, Michigan.

Oswald Garrison Villard Papers, Houghton Library, Harvard University, Cambridge, Massachusetts.

William Allen White Papers, Library of Congress, Washington, D.C.

Hugh R. Wilson Papers, Herbert Hoover Presidential Library, West Branch, Iowa.

Robert E. Wood Papers, Chicago, Illinois.

## Personal Interviews

Robert J. Bannister, Des Moines, Iowa, September 15, 1947.

Avery Brundage, Chicago, Illinois, December 18, 1948.

Philip LaFollette, Madison, Wisconsin, January 16, 1948.

Charles A. Lindbergh, Washington, D.C., and Darien, Connecticut, several personal conversations and telephone conversations in 1972 and 1973.

Verne Marshall, Cedar Rapids, Iowa, December 19, 1948.

Gerald P. Nye, Washington, D.C., and Chevy Chase, Maryland, many conversations and interviews between 1956 and 1971.

John S. Owen, Washington, D.C. April 7, 1973.

Hugh R. Parkinson, San Francisco, California, May 13, 1949.

Harry C. Schnibbe, Denver, Colorado, June 21, 1949.

R. Douglas Stuart, Jr., San Francisco, California, April 6, 1949, May 6, 1949, and June 17, 1949.

Mrs. Lyrl Clark Van Hyning, Chicago, Illinois, December 18, 1948.

Burton K. Wheeler, Washington, D.C., October 23, 1969.

Robert E. Wood, Chicago, Illinois, December 23, 1947, and August 11, 1949.

# Selected Bibliography

## Government Documents

GERMANY:
*Documents on German Foreign Policy, 1918–1945*. Series D. 13 vols. Washington: Government Printing Office, 1957–1964.

UNITED KINGDOM:
Woodward, E. L., and Butler, Rohan (eds.). *Documents on British Foreign Policy, 1919–1939*. Third Series. 10 vols. London: Her Majesty's Stationery Office, 1949–1961.

UNITED STATES:
*Hearings before the Committee on Foreign Affairs, House of Representatives*. 77th Congress, 1st session, 1941.
*Hearings before the Committee on Foreign Relations, United States Senate*. 77th Congress, 1st session, 1941.
United States Department of State. *Foreign Relations of the United States: Diplomatic Papers, 1938*. Vol. I: *General*. Washington: Government Printing Office, 1955.

## Letters, Journals, and Memoirs

Arnold, H. H. *Global Mission*. New York: Harper & Brothers, 1949.
Berle, Beatrice Bishop, and Jacobs, Travis Beal (eds.). *Navigating the Rapids, 1918–1971: From the Papers of Adolf A. Berle*. New York: Harcourt Brace Jovanovich, Inc., 1973.
Bullitt, Orville H. (ed.). *For the President, Personal and Secret: Correspondence Between Franklin D. Roosevelt and William C. Bullitt*. Boston: Houghton Mifflin Company, 1972.
Carlson, John Roy. *Under Cover: My Four Years in the Nazi Underworld of America—The Amazing Revelation of How Axis Agents and Our Enemies Within Are Now Plotting to Destroy the United States*. Cleveland and New York: World Publishing Company, 1943.
Hull, Cordell. *The Memoirs of Cordell Hull*. 2 vols. New York: Macmillan Company, 1948.
Ickes, Harold L. *The Secret Diary of Harold L. Ickes*. 3 vols. New York: Simon and Schuster, 1953–1954.
Keyhoe, Donald E. *Flying with Lindbergh*. New York: Grosset & Dunlap, 1928.
Lindbergh, Anne Morrow. *Bring Me a Unicorn: Diaries and Letters of Anne Morrow Lindbergh, 1922–1928*. New York: Harcourt Brace Jovanovich, Inc., 1972.

# Selected Bibliography

————. *Hour of Gold, Hour of Lead: Diaries and Letters of Anne Morrow Lindbergh, 1929–1932.* New York: Harcourt Brace Jovanovich, 1973.

————. *Listen! the Wind.* New York: Harcourt, Brace and Company, 1938.

————. *North to the Orient.* New York: Harcourt, Brace and Company, 1935.

————. *The Wave of the Future: A Confession of Faith.* New York: Harcourt, Brace and Company, 1940.

Lindbergh, Charles A. *Boyhood on the Upper Mississippi: A Reminiscent Letter.* St. Paul: Minnesota Historical Society, 1972.

————. *Of Flight and Life.* New York: Charles Scribner's Sons, 1948.

————. *The Spirit of St. Louis.* New York: Charles Scribner's Sons, 1953.

————. *The Wartime Journals of Charles A. Lindbergh.* New York: Harcourt Brace Jovanovich, Inc., 1970.

————. *We.* New York and London: G. P. Putnam's Sons, 1927.

Nicolson, Nigel (ed.). *Harold Nicolson: Diaries and Letters, 1930–1939.* New York: Atheneum, 1966.

Nixon, Edgar B. (ed.). *Franklin D. Roosevelt and Foreign Affairs.* 3 vols. Cambridge: Belknap Press of Harvard University Press, 1969.

Roosevelt, Elliott (ed.), assisted by Joseph P. Lash. *F. D. R.: His Personal Letters, 1928–1945.* 2 vols. New York: Duell, Sloan and Pearce, 1950.

Roosevelt, James, and Shalett, Sidney. *Affectionately, F. D. R.* New York: Avon Book Division, 1959.

Rosenman, Samuel I. (ed.). *The Public Papers and Addresses of Franklin D. Roosevelt.* 13 vols. New York: Random House, 1938–1950.

Sherwood, Robert E. *Roosevelt and Hopkins: An Intimate History.* New York: Harper & Brothers, 1948.

Slessor, John. *The Central Blue: Recollections and Reflections.* London: Cassell and Company, Ltd., 1957.

Stimson, Henry L., and Bundy, McGeorge. *On Active Service in Peace and War.* New York: Harper & Brothers, 1948.

Twining, Nathan F. *Neither Liberty nor Safety: A Hard Look at U.S. Military Policy and Strategy.* New York: Holt, Rinehart and Winston, 1966.

**283**

# Selected Bibliography

Vandenberg, Arthur H., Jr. (ed.), with the collaboration of Joe Alex Morris. *The Private Papers of Senator Vandenberg.* Boston: Houghton Mifflin Company, 1952.

Wheeler, Burton K., with Paul F. Healy. *Yankee from the West: The Candid, Turbulent Life Story of the Yankee-Born U.S. Senator from Montana.* Garden City: Doubleday & Company, Inc., 1962.

Young, Donald (ed.). *Adventure in Politics: The Memoirs of Philip LaFollette.* New York: Holt, Rinehart and Winston, 1970.

# Index

# Index

# Index

# Index

# Index

# Index

**291**

# Index

# Index

**293**

# Index

# Index

**295**

# Index

# Index

**297**

# Index